ENTREPRENEURIAL VOCATIONS

SCHOLARS PRESS
Studies in the Humanities

John Donne: Suicide	William A. Clebsch, editor
Tragedy as a Critique of Virtue: The Novel and Ethical Reflection	John D. Barbour
Lyric Apocalypse: Reconstruction in Ancient and Modern Poetry	John W. Erwin
The Unusable Past: America's Puritan Tradition, 1830 to 1930	Jan C. Dawson
The Visual Arts and Christianity in America: The Colonial Period through the Nineteenth Century	John Dillenberger
Chaos to Cosmos: Studies in Biblical Patterns of Creation	Susan Niditch
Melville and the Gods	William Hamilton
The Character of the Euripidean Hippolytos: An Ethno-Psychoanalytical Study	George Devereux
To See Ourselves As Others See Us: Christians, Jews, "Others" in Late Antiquity	Jacob Neusner, Ernest S. Frerichs, editors
Civitas: Religious Interpretations of the City	Peter S. Hawkins, editor
The Riddle of Liberty: Emerson on Alienation, Freedom, and Obedience	Lou Ann Lange
Why Persimmons and Other Poems	Stanley Romaine Hopper
Gregor Sebba: Lectures on Creativity	Helen Sebba, Hendrikus Boers, editors
Beyond the Classics? Essays in Religious Studies and Liberal Education	Frank E. Reynolds, Sheryl L. Burkhalter, editors
Teaching the Introductory Course in Religious Studies: A Sourcebook	Mark Juergensmeyer, editor
Tracing Common Themes: Comparative Courses in the Study of Religion	John B. Carman Steven P. Hopkins
The Ways of Philosophy: Searching for a Worthwhile Life	A. L. Herman
Collecting Myself: A Writer's Retrospective	A. Roy Eckardt
Conscience and Command: A Motive Theory of Law	Dale Segrest
The Becoming of Time: Integrating Physical and Religious Time	Lawrence W. Fagg
Entrepreneurial Vocations	Martin H. Krieger

Entrepreneurial Vocations

Learning from the Callings of Augustine, Moses, Mothers, Antigone, Oedipus, and Prospero

by

Martin H. Krieger

Scholars Press
Atlanta, Georgia

ENTREPRENEURIAL VOCATIONS
Learning from the Callings of Augustine, Moses, Mothers, Antigone, Oedipus, and Prospero

by

Martin H. Krieger

Scholars Press

Portions of this book, reprinted herein with permission of the publishers, appeared in somewhat different form in : "Contingency in planning: Statistics, fortune, and history," *Journal of Planning Education and Research* 10 (1991): 157–161; "Courage and character in planning," *Journal of Planning Education and Research* 7 (1988): 191–194; "Temptations of Design: A Meditation on Practice," *Research in Philosophy and Technology* 10 (1990): 217–230. The *Journal of Planning Education and Research* is copyrighted and published by the Association of Collegiate Schools of Planning. Portions of chapter 3 appear in R. Zemke and F. Clark, eds., *Occupational Science* (Philadelphia: F.A. Davis, 1996).

Library of Congress Cataloging in Publication Data
Krieger, Martin H.
Entrepreneurial vocations : learning from the callings of Augustine, Moses, mothers, Antigone, Oedipus, and Prospero / by Martin H. Krieger.
p. cm. — (Scholars Press studies in the humanities series ; no. 21)
Includes bibliographical references.
ISBN 0-7885-0252-2 (cloth : alk. paper). — ISBN 0-7885-0253-0 (paper : alk. paper)
1. Business—Religious aspects—Christianity.
2. Entrepreneurship—Philosophy. 3. Management—Philosophy.
4. Vocation. I. Title. II. Series.
BR115.E3K66 1996
338'.04'01—dc20 96-12283
CIP

Printed in the United States of America
on acid-free paper

For Abraham and Bob, and John, Joan, and Mirta

About the Author

Martin H. Krieger is professor of planning at the School of Urban Planning and Development of the University of Southern California. He has taught at Berkeley, Minnesota, MIT, and Michigan, and has been a Fellow at the Center for Advanced Study in the Behavioral Sciences and at the National Humanities Center.

By the same author:

Advice and Planning (Temple University Press, 1981)

Marginalism and Discontinuity: Tools for the Crafts of Knowledge and Decision (Russell Sage Foundation, 1989)

Doing Physics: How Physicists Take Hold of the World (Indiana University Press, 1992)

The Constitutions of Matter: Mathematically Modeling the Most Everyday of Physical Phenomena (University of Chicago Press, 1996)

Contents

Preface

Creation and Tragedy

Entrepreneurship. The Argument. Homily. Acknowledgments

What do entrepreneurs really do? That is the question I want to address, in a description that actual entrepreneurs—who in fact operate over a very wide range of human activity—will recognize as possessing the ring of truth. ("That's it, just right, sure!") In so doing, I hope to provide those with less experience or who do not ordinarily think of themselves as entrepreneurs with a way of recognizing their future as they encounter it, paying attention to what really matters.

Entrepreneurship is about the development of institutions that are viable and lively out of what does not exist or is perhaps shaky and moribund.[1] How does something begin, or arise from disorder or even nothing?[2] I take this to be an account of Creation, just what God did in Genesis (*B'reshit,* In the beginning) albeit carried out in our mundane world, whether it be in the sphere of commerce, government, religion, or the military or in good works. Since entrepreneurial endeavors may displace or literally destroy ongoing institutions, or fail dreadfully, the account of entrepreneurship is not only about creation; it is also about tragedy.

The proverbial small businesses I discuss here are sacred institutions, religious movements, and infants. And so I describe the establishment of the Christian church (Paul and Augustine), the formation of the Israelites (Moses), and the development and growth and eventual independence of children (and so their mothers). And I am concerned with matters of courage and character (Antigone), tragic errancy (Oedipus), and the redemption that provides closure for that sequence of creation and tragedy and so leads to more everyday, taken-for-granted institutions (Prospero of *The Tempest*). Along the way, I suggest that conventional commercial and governmental entrepreneurship is readily and perhaps best characterized in analogy to the development of these small businesses, and by terms such as creation, tragedy, heroism, virtue, covenant, character, errancy, mission, revelation, and redemption—sacred terms—because our notions of entrepreneurship are rooted in the religious and mythic realm and in the republican tradition of virtue and fortune.[3]

Plainly, I shall be preaching, bringing some of the greatest human stories to bear on what we might do every day. (This book is for ministers as well as for entrepreneurs.) So I have deliberately employed a mixed style, in which arcane and technical language is interwoven with the colloquial, much as transcendent purposes are interwoven with the mundane in entrepreneurship. I have placed the reader at the center of my attention, often referring to the reader as "you" or to author and reader as "we." And I have treated the figures I discuss as present to us now, as exemplars rather than as ancient and distant. At the same time I have tried to keep in mind their distinctive and diverse cultures and communities. Finally, I sometimes refer to the entrepreneur as "he" and sometimes as "she," to expose some of the implicit assumptions we make about entrepreneurship. Although I am quite sure that a man may mother quite well, it proved too jarring to refer to mothers as "he."

The appendix provides some suggestions for self-study or for teaching the material I discuss here. Throughout the text and the notes, I occasionally consider the problems of understanding one's entrepreneurial role in terms of the models that I employ.

The critical text concerning the relationship of religion to entrepreneurship within capitalism is Max Weber's *Protestant Ethic and the Spirit of Capitalism* (1904–1905, 1920). Weber argues that certain features of ascetic Protestantism (say, Calvinism as contrasted to Lutheranism) encourage entrepreneurial endeavor. Although unintended by the Reformation actors, eventually the notion of a religious calling (*Beruf*) became the devoted commitment to commercial endeavor, a commitment to the accumulation of wealth and the efficient use of time and effort.[4] It is worth noting that Weber is concerned with an entrepreneurship that is actually quite tame, compared to the swashbuckling image one finds in the economist Joseph Schumpeter (1883–1950), who spoke of "creative destruction." Weber is concerned with the bourgeois organization of labor rather than speculative promotions.

> To the English Puritans, the Jews of their time were representatives of that type of capitalism which was involved in war, Government contracts, State monopolies, speculative promotions, and the construction and financial projects of princes, which they themselves condemned. In fact the difference may, in general, with the necessary qualifications, be formulated: that Jewish capitalism was speculative pariah-capitalism, while the Puritan was bourgeois organization of labour.[5]

Weber's analysis of the motives of the entrepreneur has authorized scholars to more generally link sacred ideology to everyday culture and practice.[6] The features of modern commercial entrepreneurship that I shall describe in sacred terms might well be intrinsic to its history; in effect, they might be throwbacks. My point of view here is somewhat broader than Weber's, my claim somewhat less specific: notions central to the sacred, to religion, and to theology play crucial roles in everyday secular human practice. We might use religious notions to describe what would be taken to be mundane, everyday, commercial, entrepreneurial activity, notions understood with their full religious import, recalling their particular meaning and location in sacred stories. What entrepreneurs actually do is religious. And some of the best exemplars of entrepreneurship are within the religious realm.

Salvation and redemption might be achieved symbolically through the accumulation of wealth, as Weber suggests. But, I shall argue, entrepreneurship provides authentic redemption as it is understood theologically. In time one's speculation is shown to be the truth or not (as success or as failure), with all of the sacred implications of such a journey from lostness to salvation. Entrepreneurs are religious actors.[7]

As for my own religious beliefs, I think they are not critical to what I say here.[8] But I could not say what I do say, and think what I think, if I did not take God seriously.[9] Whatever authority we attribute to God, however, there is no reason to believe our interpretation of God will be right most of the time, or that God's providence will nicely fit our models or theories.

Entrepreneurship

There is a large and varied literature on entrepreneurship, public and private. Economists have been fascinated by the entrepreneur. They have for the most part shunted aside analytic descriptions of the entrepreneurial role in favor of systemic analysis of equilibrium in which the entrepreneur hardly appears at all.[10] The small-business and venture-management literature is rich with examples and cases, and filled with useful advice.[11] The literature on leadership is suggestive, with the product or the substance of the entrepreneurial endeavor often in the background.[12] Historians shuttle between telling stories of great men and women and stories of organizations and environments.[13] Development economists appreciate the importance of entrepreneurship for shaking economies out of low-equilibrium sinks.[14] And there is a great deal of empirical work on the entrepreneur.[15]

Following Schumpeter, I take entrepreneurs to be creative destroyers, incessantly revolutionizing the structure of society from within, destroying the old, creating the new. Such an entrepreneur sets forth a perennial gale of creative destruction, the new replacing the old, much like Hegel's "bacchanalian revel" of historical succession. The entrepreneur has a will to found a new kingdom, a will to conquer, and a joy in creating.[16]

Yet, while the entrepreneur may in the end wreak great havoc and change and even transformation, the actual entrepreneur in her everyday practice is almost always careful, incremental in her actions, figuring out ways to get around risk—by means of backups, strategic plans, and insurances of various sorts, and by possessing information and talent that makes what others take as a risky or uncertain situation seem to her manageable and more like a sure practical thing.[17] (And, in the matter of course, she does sometimes fail.) Moreover, the innovating entrepreneur is not only a strong contesting individualist; she must also be able to engender agreement and cooperation among the interested parties if a project is to come to fruition.[18] She must not only exhibit the liberal values of fairness and contractual reliability; she must also reflect the republican virtues and the capacity to covenant.[19]

The Argument

Chapter 1 takes Augustine's transformation of the African Christian church from a parochial to a catholic institution as an archetype for how an organization becomes entrepreneurial. Augustine is a very great actor, but his autonomy is defined by his destiny. He is seen to make big decisions, yet to find that rather than making choices he is elected by others to fulfill roles he then grows into. So, learning from Paul, he is driven into a mission, forced to become authoritative as the bishop of Hippo. At first he is a reluctant prophet, then an enthusiastic one. Here we see how an entrepreneur is made by the endeavors given to him.

Moses' task was not so much to grow an organization as to ensure its members' commitment to its mission and so to themselves. Their story tells of binding and resistance and backsliding, of sacrifice and scapegoat, all in the service of a covenant that must be made and remade through ritual repetitions. So a people is made resilient enough to march through the desert and reach the Promised Land, its leader not quite making it and for good reason. In this second chapter I describe how a people are educated in an entrepreneurial idea that is to be their story and their history.

I should note how illiberal and violent are the worlds of Augustine and Moses, how tragic their lives. Entrepreneurship, I think, demands such awfulness, such sacrifice and scapegoating. There is, however, no rationalizing therapeutic justification for such awfulness, although, as we shall see, there are redemptive moves we might make.

Mothers, too, want their infants to grow so that they might be able to march through the desert to a promised land. And so a mother, with the active leadership of her infant himself, must allow the binding her infant has with her to extend into a binding with the world so that the infant is committed to reality. Development is no straightforward path; it presents enormous challenges and tragic losses; it demands invention and sacrifice. But if we are fortunate, infant enterprises, which to be sure are going concerns from the very beginning, become on their own and no longer so dependent. And so mother and child can both eventually be on their own; good-enough mothers and good-enough infants learn to work with fortune. Chapter 3 is an account of how entrepreneurship becomes committed to marketing in the service of growth and pleasure, a strategy that also forces the entrepreneurial endeavor to face the facts of life.

It will perhaps seems strange to shift to motherhood after having discussed figures such as Augustine and Moses. I wanted to analyze how enterprises are launched. What attracted me to motherhood as a model was the sacred character of mothers and their infants, and the extraordinary descriptions provided by D. W. Winnicott and Selma Fraiberg of that relationship. There is perhaps one other source of incongruity in what follows, my discussion of finance and bankruptcy, here meant to contrast redemption in the sacred and the mundane realms.

Chapters 4 and 5 describe how entrepreneurship is justified, how its enormous disruptions are shown to be necessary and at the same time healed, so that we might go on together without unending retribution. To be Oedipus is to be that creative destroyer in whose pollutions and incests and tragedy lie innovation and sacrifice. To be his daughter and sister Antigone is to be that courageous figure who insists on devotion and loyalty to what is to be destroyed. To be within this Sophoclean world is to fully appreciate why redemption, an ending or at least a momentary closure to these sequences of overturnings, is so necessary if ordinary everyday life is to continue to be possible. Hence the appeal of biblical jubilee and commercial bankruptcy, memorializing philanthropy, and the veil of order provided by the magical devices of story and history. To be Prospero of *The Tempest* is to realize the deadening limits of such a veil, the ultimate fertility of disorder and surprise.

Put thematically, entrepreneurs prevail over a domain, their efforts being endowed with the meaningfulness of redemption. They reorganize the means of production and consumption, they make something out of nothing, they give reality to ideas. To describe what entrepreneurs actually do, we examine emblematic actors in their historically particular situations. So I describe Augustine, his success and methods unusual for their transcendent purpose, their organizational practicality, and their violent procedures. Choosing an inclusive and authoritative vision, what might be called ecumenical and episcopal, Augustine dispossessed those whose vision was puritan and self-defined. Moses' mission, on the other hand, was congregational: forming a people through a covenant, having them march as a people so they actually become a people, dealing with waywardness violently if need be. It is through vision and hope, understood transcendently, that Moses understands his work. Finally, when there is a hierarchized division of powers, as in a presbyterium, there will be formal conflicts among authorities, as in Antigone's opposition to Creon. There is unresolvable conflict among traditions and conventions, here between the particular and the universal. Latterly, markets have proven attractive to entrepreneurs since they allow for small incursions or niches that need not be seen as challenges to authority, or as denials of community (since there is a diversity of wants), or as creative destructions.

Family life exhibits the authority of the episcopal, the community of the congregational, and the conflicts of the presbyterial. But its ties are altogether more particular and poignant, driven by the enormous capacities of infants to remake the world in the service of their growing up. Entrepreneurial endeavors are driven more by their babies, their ideas and conceptions, than by the entrepreneur or the organization. The ideas inspire the entrepreneur and the world to act in the service of the realization of those ideas.

Once there is entrepreneurial dominion or success, redemption is necessary to justify that success. So a crucial task of entrepreneurship is design: a reconciliation of knowledge (moral and scientific), circumstance, and technology. Judgment is the mode in which we express design, and following Kant I take it that judgment is an objective claim, a form of leadership: if you could see as I do—and you ought to since you are a person like me, a member of my community, and I will show you how to see as I do—you will come to appreciate the cogency of my judgment and so follow in my vision. Of course, the other may make the same claim, and hence there is ongoing argument. Along the way, we must learn to prevail without perfection, so allowing for the leftovers and pollutions that lead to the subsequent generations of entrepreneurial endeavor. Judgment and design are reconciling, in that they put a disturbed house into a provisional order.

At the end of *The Tempest,* Prospero gives up his magic for real power. Much the same happens to Oedipus by the end of *Oedipus at Colonus*. He has come to realize how limited is his intelligence and technical skill, just what he used in solving the riddle of the Sphinx. Problem solving might lead to reconciliation; putting the world in an order that does not have so gaping a flank, one is done in by Oedipus's sort of blindness. One has to listen and hear, as do prophets and mothers, not just be adept. Oedipus can act, he can be so destructive and insensitive in his incests (and enjoy his role, for he did solve the riddle and this is his reward), he can be so sure, because he denies what we might well suspect is his almost sure knowledge of his situation.[20] In *Oedipus the King* he is forced to acknowledge a truth he already knows—somehow—before he meets Laius at the crossroad. Of course, this is just the fate of the entrepreneur, who if she knew what she was up to would put her money into a certificate of deposit—but she pretends not to know, and so perhaps she does more than she would have otherwise ever conceived possible.[21]

Homily

Again, I want to offer an account of entrepreneurs and their activities that will provide such actors with a recognizable description of what they do, making thematic what usually remains inchoate and tacit but what everyone knows, and so transform how entrepreneurs think of themselves.[22] This account is not so much a how-to, as a how-to-be: a moral description, an existential account of our situations. Throughout the text I am systematically concerned with how and what we might learn from these descriptions, how telling and retelling a story forms us as persons. So was Augustine concerned about learning from Paul, and were the Israelites formed by telling their own story.

Again, I shall be preaching. I tell stories that allow us an identity and that provide a new beginning and so a new meaning to our otherwise given stories, in effect an account of Creation.[23] And I talk about religious and humanistic texts, where specific details matter enormously and can bear the weight of interpretation. Here God is in the details. (Manifestly, chapter 3 on motherhood is exceptional, since it refers to common experience as much as it refers to texts describing that experience. Still, our concern is with concrete detail that can bear the weight of interpretation.) We want to concentrate on what entrepreneurs actually do, and so I offer accounts that would affect actual actors in just those places they find themselves.

Many if not most readers of this book may not have read Augustine's or Moses' or Oedipus's or Prospero's books. I have written with them in mind.

And I suggest some alternatives, such as films, in the appendix. Still, it matters to have read the books I discuss, for while their plots and structures might be summarized, their power as works and narratives depends on the details, the particulars of character, development, and tone. (And it matters to have been a mother.) These figures are not at all modern and liberal. They and their actions, violent and virtuous, do make sense in the context of the works in which they are presented and the cultures for which they were originally written. But for us they might well seem absurd were we to know them only in summary and structure. I maintain that actual entrepreneurs are as complex and contradictory as are these figures from other times and worlds. And to rationalize entrepreneurship, to get rid of these illiberal and contradictory elements, is to mistake what entrepreneurs do.

Of course, I am not recommending that one imitate these figures: kill your father, solve a riddle, and marry your mother, let us say. Rather, I believe that entrepreneurs in their own ways do imitate these figures, with all of the awful features one might imagine.

Such descriptive phenomenology demands that we borrow from a variety of fields, mixing lexicons that are ordinarily kept separate.[24] I have, as it were, assumed that in the service of realistic description students are willing to participate in a curriculum that reads some of what are called the Great Books, yet reads them in the context of the cultures and histories in which they were written. Those books do speak to us. But if we know how they were meant to speak to their contemporaries, we learn a great deal more about stuff we find unpalatable and not very modern, yet fundamental to actual entrepreneurial practice.

The versions of the stories I have chosen to tell are tragic as well as creative. For I am concerned with matters of overturning and disruption, with blindness and insight, with loss that is inevitable and redemptive. In each case I have told only one such version, provided just one interpretation of a canonical text, an interpretation that serves my theoretical concerns. (I have also aimed for scholarly authority, but not so much for balance and comprehensiveness.) Thus, a story might become a story for us, a homily, a sermon: a particular story with an ultimate meaning, part of a canonical set of stories we take to define who we are in the largest of senses.

One last proviso: I have assumed that my reader is more likely to have a social science-oriented education, such as in a professional business or planning or law curriculum, than to have studied the classics, theology, literature, or child development. That assumption has determined some of the implicit polemics I find myself engaged in, more than the actual descriptions I have provided. The methodological discussions early on in each of the chapters are meant to encourage entrepreneurial action by showing how disabling is this prudential tradition. One can always show it makes no rational sense to pursue any particular entrepreneurial endeavor.[25]

Acknowledgments
My immediate debt is to the Lilly Endowment and to Craig Dykstra for their support for the research and writing of this book. Craig and the Endowment were extraordinarily responsive and helpful, both materially and substantively. As important was my appointment as the Zell-Lurie Fellow in the Teaching of Entrepreneurship (1990–1991) at the School of Business Administration at the University of Michigan, Ann Arbor. Twenty years of disparate teaching experience came together in my year in Ann Arbor. I am grateful to Dean B. Joseph White and Professor C. Merle Crawford for their hospitality, and to my extraordinarily fine students, undergraduate and graduate, that year. Behind all of this lies the encouragement and advice of Robert Payton, as well as an earlier grant on professional education from the Exxon Education Foundation. And I am grateful to my colleagues for accommodating my leaves with good cheer and openness. My students at the University of Southern California have been active contributors in formulating these ideas.

Arpad Szabo pointed me to *Oedipus at Colonus* and *The Tempest* in one of his passionate conversations twenty years ago. I owe to Columbia College an education that permitted me to appreciate such advice. More recently, what I have learned from Rabbi Danny Landes and John Bennett, Jr., shows directly in the text. Dolores Hayden and Peter Marris helped make clear to me what I needed to do. And to Abraham Polonsky, the Honeymans, and the Dewar-Nelsons, I owe the lovely debt of friendship; for the Cheerful Helpers mothers my love and gratitude are enormous. My son, David, is my homeroom teacher in all of these matters.

1

Building and Growing
Augustine and Paul on Dominion and Redemption

A Life, Big Decisions, Election. Entrepreneurship as Story. Creating an Organization, Apocalyptic Sectarianism, Dominion and Redemption as Entrepreneurial Rewards. Paul. Prophecy and Creation. An Apologetics for Hierarchical Authority?

Entrepreneurs perform virtual miracles by rather more mundane devices, making something out of what appears, at least to others, to be nothing. In that hiatus between what we might predict can be done, given the available resources and potential constraints, and what is actually achieved (or often what fails)—they act.

Entrepreneurs take what others view as contingent and proceed to institutionalize it and so make it necessary. They manufacture just what is then taken as transcendent and beyond ordinary device. Those who are most expert at doing this, both in their actions and in their conceptualizations, have traditionally worked within the realm of religion and theology. Perhaps the greatest such thinker and one of the greatest such actors is Augustine (354–430 CE). And much of what he knew he learned from Paul (d. ca. 67 CE). Both Augustine and Paul created what we might call the prototype of the modern church: ecumenical, growing, and open to the needs of its members, yet authoritative and institutionalized within the umbrella of a powerful state (Rome). They created "a new combination of the means of production," to follow Joseph Schumpeter, which then thrived and in so doing displaced a variety of alternatives.

A Life

One of the great archetypal male life stories goes something like this: The hero is born in a backward area and early on shows very great promise. Not only is he technically skillful and ambitious, he is a seeker for the truth as well, willing to explore various alternatives deeply and critically. Many of the common answers turn out to be unsatisfying for him. Still, his talent brings him some renown, and in his early adulthood he literally moves to the center of society. He makes this move clandestinely, for his mother is worried that he will abandon himself to worldly technical success, leaving behind a search for the real truth. So he sneaks off in the night; she is left behind and bereft.

At the center of the society, he is recognized for his skill and is rapidly promoted, makes influential friends, and is fascinated and perhaps at times repulsed by the excesses of city and civilization. He continues to try out new ideas (his mother was wrong about her son's ultimate corruptibility), and because of his charisma and learning, a group of followers and students develops around him

Almost at the pinnacle of worldly success, the hero has an inspired vision of the truth and of his true purpose, abandons his conventional technical success, forms a small, almost monastic study group, and returns home because the center cannot hold. It is now seen as degenerate rather than exciting. He vows to lead a quiet and devoted life, as he had promised his dying mother.

Back home the hero tries to avoid situations in which those who recognized his reputed technical skill or his charisma would end up recruiting him to more ordinary duties rather than a life of seeking and study. He does not want to become successful again, even if it involved the truth. His and his friends' lives are to be sacred, purified of the contingencies and temptations of ordinary life.[1]

The hero visits some acquaintances, in their own way seekers, who are part of a struggling enterprise led by a senior statesman. So the hero feels safe and comfortable, sure they do not need another leader. In the middle of a meeting, the acquaintances raise their voices, call him to be their leader, and press-gang him into a service that is intrinsic to his role as a seeker but surely not a role he would choose for himself. He is elected, so to speak, and at that point he literally weeps for his once having disdained being a practical leader and perhaps for the loss of his quiet life. The acquaintances believe that their enterprise is rather modest, and that his tears are of grand hopes disappointed rather than of shame and awe. His technical skill and his mastery of the truth make him an inspired choice, so to speak, and in a short time the senior statesman arranges to step aside, thereby putting the hero even farther from his chosen life. Yet the hero turns out to be a very great leader, his passion and intellect, his charisma and policy, his presence and judgment, recognizable to others and to himself as gifts that have found their true purpose.

Now heading an even larger organization, he develops a strategy and doctrine that allows that organization to grow, extend its reach, meet the needs of a wider society, and become even more relevant to the everyday lives of its members. Along the way he has to deal with other leaders and impostors, whom he feels are not merely competition but rather represent disastrous alternatives for members and nonmembers alike. His practical, strategic, and leadership skills show themselves in dramatic ways. So he uses the power of the state to defeat, literally to torture, the impostors, although if they are willing to join his organization he will allow them in quite openly. His capacity to argue in courts of law and power, his dramatic persona, his intelligence, and his capacity for sheer device and deviousness make his triumphs very great and influential.

A person of great passion and reflectiveness becomes one of action and judgment. His technical skill now serves a higher interest. He develops products, processes, and markets that enable the organization to grow for a millennium. Along the way he writes a best-selling autobiography that concentrates as much on his mistaken earlier life as on his later successes. Even Nobel Prize scientists quote from it and so accept its authority.[2]

I live in Los Angeles and there must be several dozen recognizably similar screenplay treatments of this sort floating around town at any one time. Perhaps the hero comes out of politics or Wall Street. And the synopsis above applies to many a film that is already made, with minor changes of tone or detail.

But, of course, this is the story of Augustine of Hippo, the great church father of the fifth century. The backward area is Thagaste in North Africa (Souk Ahras, Algeria), at the time the breadbasket of the Roman Empire; his technical skill is rhetoric, rather than politics or finance; his seeking involves not only Christianity but also Manichaeism and Neoplatonism; the center is Rome and Milan; and his mother is Monica. His truth is in the end Catholic Christianity; back home is Hippo (Annaba, Algeria), again in North Africa; and the competitors and impostors are the Donatist Church (vs. Augustine's Catholic one) and, later, the Pelagians. The time is late antiquity with the African Christian church rife and riven with dissent and purism. And the best-selling autobiography is his *Confessions* (401 CE), perhaps the first work of antiquity that we might read with modern eyes.

I tell this story in part as a parable, leading to exhortation and lessons and preaching. Moreover, a number of deep questions concerning decision making, institutionalization, and reward are exemplified here, both in story and in language. My claim, to put it baldly, is that Augustine and his action epitomize entrepreneurship and its dilemmas in detail. Significantly, those questions are even more poignant for moderns, who are often trained in the social sciences. Even more generally, what we shall discover as we explore other figures, such as Paul, Moses, mothers, Antigone, Oedipus, and Prospero, is that some of the deepest questions of modern society and entrepreneurial endeavor are presented in the narrative lives of these figures. The language that is characteristic of religion and the humanities provides us with ways of thinking about ourselves that give reality to modern dilemmas not readily addressed otherwise. Finally, what is most palpably of value is that these considerations allow actual actors to understand what they are doing so they might act with greater effect and meaning—as entrepreneurs in business, government, and the voluntary sectors.

Big Decisions[3]

In book 8 of the *Confessions,* having earlier entertained us with an extensive account of his wayward life until then, Augustine says: "I supposed that the reason for my postponing from day to day the moment when I would despise worldly ambition and follow you [God, the audience for these confessions] was that I had not seen any certainty by which to direct my course" (§18). Augustine was seeking a decision procedure, one that would be well grounded in evidence and argument, one that would be objective and systematic. His talents as a rhetorician, his philosophic acuteness, demanded a form of guidance that would have a life of its own, a sureness that would be objectively warranted and certifiable.

I should note that these are confessions, written after the fact. They were written by a very great dramatist who appreciated the power of tension, a man driven by personal desires and drives of the most extreme and powerful sort. We, as readers, are being set up for the moment when this reasonable desire for objective judgment is shown to be the greatest of errors, at least in decisions of this sort.

The next several pages vividly describe our state when we are about to make a major commitment.

> Finally in the agony of hesitation I made many physical gestures of the kind men make when they want to achieve something and lack the strength, either because they lack the actual limbs or because their limbs are fettered with chains or weak with sickness or in some way hindered. If I tore my hair, if I struck my forehead, if I intertwined my fingers and clasped my

> knee, I did that because to do so was my will. But I could have willed this and then not done it if my limbs had not possessed the power to obey. So I did many actions in which the will to act was not equalled by the power. Yet I was not doing what with an incomparably greater longing I yearned to do [make the decision and act on it], and could have done the moment I so resolved. (§20)

Augustine then goes on to discuss in glorious and subtle detail the resistances to his decision making.

The tension is unbearable, the agony brings tears and distress. For argument had done as much work as it possibly could; what is now needed is that decision that allows one to enter into a venture. Augustine hears a voice, "a boy or a girl (I know not which)," saying, "Pick up and read, pick up and read."

> I seized it [the book of the apostle Paul], opened it and in silence read the first passage on which my eyes lit: "Not in riots and drunken parties, not in eroticism and indecencies, not in strife and rivalry [as Augustine had been living], but put on the Lord Jesus Christ and make no provision for the flesh in its lusts" (Romans 13:13–14).
>
> I neither wished nor needed to read further. At once, with the last words of this sentence, it was if a light of relief from all anxiety flooded into my heart [recall Paul on the road to Damascus]. All the shadows of doubt were dispelled. (§29)

Augustine is making the major decision of his life. He is a man in great turmoil and anguish. And that decision is driven by some sounds he hears in a garden in Milan, something like *tolle lege*, the Latin for "Pick up and read." It might have been a child, maybe leaves rustling. From Augustine's point of view he is receiving an authentic divine oracle, retrospectively attested to by his subsequent life.[4] Yet we know know from Augustine that he has heard what he took to be the truth before, but those had been other truths heard in other fashions.

We might argue that Augustine has presented in his writings a rather detailed supporting argument for the choice he makes. The decision merely awaited his being ready to hear his own arguments. That moment of conversion is an historical happenstance that would have occurred the next month or perhaps the next year. More generally, there are several inventors or scientists or entrepreneurs with roughly the same idea at the time of any single great discovery or enterprise.[5] The one that happens to become the revered individual is a matter of luck and marketing and promotion.

While Augustine might have appreciated such an observation about the ways of Providence, his experience tells him otherwise. He knows that without God's call he could have continued in his errant ways; for although he was dissatisfied, he was also engaged in a powerful internal argument that might never have been sufficiently resolved for him to act. Moreover, the divine voice presents itself in distinctive ways; God's call is not something to be so readily dismissed. While those who are engaged in less religious but equally sacred endeavors such as science or enterprise may not claim they hear God's call, they do hear guiding messages, they do find that nature and markets sometimes speak to them in directive voices. Those messages, perhaps presented in quite mundane and practical guises, are about the meaning of their endeavors, naming the path they might follow. And in their projects there are turning points, and they navigate through them with providential guidance. This is the only kind of guidance that will be monitory for them in these circumstances. Otherwise, they would not take these moments as turning points, and they would be willing to rely on more formulaic modes of decision. So they must hear the message that will call them to order.

None of this is mystical mumbo jumbo. Rather it is the way things are actually experienced when we are about to make a big decision.[6] Perhaps we have arrayed in front of us the choices that we might make, but we find ourselves lost in analysis and reflection. How are we to act? Surely the message we hear can lead us to tragedy rather than to triumph. But that is not because we have not been careful and methodical and even scientific. Rather, at this point prudential considerations prove indecisive and positively confusing.

What is called for is judgment, in which larger frameworks of analysis are evaluated and a suitable one is fashioned out of the particular details of the problem at hand. There is a hidden music playing in the story we experience, music that we finally hear. And sometimes we follow our speculative intuition or animal spirits (to use John Maynard Keynes's term).[7]

A confession is a story, told retrospectively, in which there is a crucial moment prepared for by delay and our procrastination, when we hear a voice or that music and follow its lead. What that story provides is justification, a proper ordering and place for our experience so that it is meaningful. As a history, the story insists on its diverse details, details that might otherwise be seen as irrelevant or diversionary rather than as a necessary part of a struggle or a destiny. What might have never occurred actually did, in this place, at this time, and it worked out this way. It is revelation. And the story shows how we fulfill the call we have heard.

Actual commercial entrepreneurs find this description straightforward and true to life. What they recognize as their own practical experience is thereby given a structure and form, what they know is crucial *is* crucial in this description—as I hope will be the case for all the descriptions I shall be providing. For novices the description is much more problematic. To hear voices or music might well be dangerous and diversionary. It is daunting to be told that it happens *this* way; and as you enact your role, you will find in the particulars of what you are doing that you will be reenacting this story. But it is encouraging as well, giving significance to what otherwise appears to be happenstance.

To tell stories of imprudent actors and crucial decisions is to give courage to those who must act, who find they must choose, who are driven by desires that cannot be readily satisfied. Their acts are then justified, located in time and place, in precedence and consequence and meaning, namely, in a story.[8] And the story is sometimes awful and tragic, as we shall see for Augustine. The great triumph of modern social science is to ban the tragic and emphasize the prudential. But here we have stories in which matters of fate and meaning, of history and fortune, of the crucial moments and the critical paths we elect, define what is necessary and what is contingent. Errancy is not something we might avoid, although there is no reason to be arbitrarily imprudent and even some reason to be foolish.[9] Rather, errancy, that we go awry in potentially tragic ways, is the fact that enables us to succeed or to fail.

Election: The Bishop of Hippo

As I have indicated in my schematic description of Augustine's life, he is press-ganged into becoming a priest and eventually becomes a bishop, a rather different life than the monastic and studious career he planned upon his conversion: "I feared the office of a bishop to such an extent that, as soon as my reputation came to matter among 'servants of God,' I would not go to any place where I knew there was no bishop."[10] But here is what happened, in Peter Brown's account:

> [I]n a sermon, the bishop, Valerius [so there is one there already], spoke pointedly of the urgent needs of his church; the congregation turned to find, as they expected, Augustine standing among them in the nave; with the persistent shouting required for such a procedure, they pushed him forward to the raised throne of the bishop and the benches of the priest, which ran

> around the curved apse at the far end of the basilica. The leading Catholic citizens of Hippo would have gathered around Augustine, as the bishop accepted his forced agreement to become a priest in the town. (p. 139)

Augustine is elected, chosen, forced into a role he would never have selected, one he had disdained.[11] So he begins to preach, is soon elevated by Valerius to be bishop, and is again forced, by the necessity of his role and his being called, to become a judge, evangelist, and an articulator of doctrine. For a bishop must respond to the demands of his congregations, to their everyday needs and concerns. And if you are Augustine you respond with passion and invention and devotion. Augustine became the Augustine we now know despite his plans, and through challenges he would never have thought to seek were they not thrust upon him.

Here choice is accepting and rising to occasions, opportunity is election, and virtue is the manner in which we take on our elections. You find yourself in a position, prepared despite your plans, and the biggest decisions are elected and made for you. That is, if you accept those elections and act with virtue and excellence. For I take it that entrepreneurial endeavors are in the end matters of character.

Moreover, you are transformed by enacting a role. Augustine becomes the very great and terrible figure we know by the tasks he encounters and takes on, the everyday judgments, the ecclesiastical battles, the demands for doctrinal syntheses, the politics and service inherent in his role. No ordinary person, he is presented with rather ordinary tasks for his society, and what he makes of them is his destiny. Entrepreneurs find that they are elected, that they must be virtuous, and that they are transformed by the tasks they find as much as by those they set for themselves.

Entrepreneurship as Story

The academic literature on entrepreneurship describes an autonomous actor, perhaps optimizing, perhaps judging, perhaps creating and destroying, perhaps risking, perhaps arranging and scheming.[12] The popular literature on entrepreneurship combines the image of the genius with that of the scrupulous manager-leader, with the great idea whose time might be now. But Augustine's story, and I think the actual stories of entrepreneurs, is better captured by notions of conversion, election, virtue, and transformation. And while we might secularize these notions, they are here and elsewhere intrinsically part of the sacred and religious realm, unavoidably laden with that legacy that makes what is contingent necessary, what is planned transcended. Moreover, the experience of the entrepreneur feels just this sacred way. The consequences of your actions are deeper and more profound than could be expected. They are recognizably miraculous and tragic. Entrepreneurship is in the realm of myth and story and the sacred. Actions do more and mean more coherently, and in more roundabout ways, than we might ever expect or hope or fear, even from a story.

The task here is to provide a phenomenology that allows entrepreneurs to act with greater effectiveness and authority and sensible confidence. While the theme of science is to demythologize or disenchant the world, our task is to take those myths and enchantments and give ourselves command over them by identifying both the sources of their power and their modes of appearance in our lives as we enact sacred roles.[13]

Entrepreneurship is a mode of judgment, insisting on the meaningfulness of the world. Much as in the kindred endeavors of storytelling and history, it is disciplined by the practice of what will work in actual situations, and it is justified by the adoption of those meanings by others.[14] Entrepreneurship, as judgment, revalues the world. Insofar as that judgment is widely adopted, the entrepreneur is proven right and receives the rewards of *dominion* and *redemption*.[15] So entrepreneurship makes sense only retrospectively, when the meaning of what is being done has been worked out. That meaning is as much about the nature of dominion and redemption (and their failure). But, in fact, for the entrepreneur at least, such rational prudence does not displace the uniqueness and sacredness of the endeavor one is engaged in. Put differently, here error is fully meaningful, never to be compensated for. Errancy is necessary, vital to growth and transformation. Surely we would not want to be much too foolish and imprudent, but our mission is defined by tragedy and triumph.[16]

In speaking this way about entrepreneurship and about Augustine to students in business school, whose graduate programs are deeply influenced by the social sciences, a number of questions recur. These questions reflect both the students' canonical training and their experience outside of school within the world of enterprise and government and public service. And these questions are asked as much in personal anguish as in intellectual curiosity. Students say, I sense that what you say is poignantly true. What does that mean for my analytical coursework?

Entrepreneurship is a matter more of action and election than of rational planning and analysis. The languages of economics, psychology, or statistics, at least in their canonical forms, will paralyze the entrepreneur if they are taken as more than a source of prudential advice. Their irony and skepticism, their groundedness in distinguishing confounding cases and a concern for eliminating exceptions, is bound to demoralize the entrepreneur.

The entrepreneur's realm is just that in which predictability would counsel inaction, in which scientific authority has little to offer but doubt, in which the confounding and the exceptional are the sources for growth. Otherwise, investors and corporate managers could take over the entrepreneurial role.

Entrepreneurs defy odds and payoffs as rational accounts of their situations. They are not simply risk takers, buying options to balance out their portfolios. They take on situations insufficiently disciplined by prudential considerations to be rational in the economic sense.

The second question that is often asked is, How am I to find "it"? "It" is the secret, the new combination of the means of production, the widget that takes over the market, the ideology that catches on like wildfire. Let us call it the entrepreneurial idea. The presumption here, one that is often wrong, is that the secret lies in the idea, rather than in marketing, strategy, or a fortunate external situation. The entrepreneur is best understood as someone who is ready to hear the call of opportunities as they are presented. Recognizing an opportunity is a matter of matching the idea to one's capacities, not of the idea's intrinsic features. The task is to eliminate really foolish choices (for which prudential considerations are often the best means), and to adopt a reasonably good opportunity and meet its challenge. The idea is recognized and adopted and grown. The task is one of prudence, to eliminate obvious mistakes, and of stewardship, taking on what you are given, realizing it for your society.

A third question is, How is what you have been saying to be applied to actual practice? There is no actual practice and action without a description that highlights what is important and how it is connected with other such important features, one that an entrepreneur would find poignant and congenial and encouraging. Such a description provides a moral world in which notions of courage or virtue make sense. It provides a way of thinking of the course of action, a schema or plot that makes it possible to see what we do as coherent and meaningful. Such a theoretical structure is not so much applied as adopted, not so much tested as used, not so much true as encouraging.

Creating an Organization

Augustine defines himself by his big decisions, matters of conversion and election. He finds himself with an opportunity, and in taking on that opportunity he becomes committed to its fulfillment. He is transformed by being chosen and then enacting that election. Such election is not passive, for it is how he responds to a call that is of ultimate significance. He then tells a story, providing a testimonial, of how he was tested and he triumphed (or failed). Such a story is particular and contingent, yet necessary. Its details matter enormously, as he has come to understand those details and that story. What haunts the story is that possibility of tragedy, errancy, misplacedness: sin, the source of interestingness and the evidence that we are separated from God and so might receive credit for our actions. Augustine is being tested, and he proves himself in how he meets those tests and trials. But his errancy has meaning only in a story or in a testimonial. Otherwise it is just one more event or choice. Augustine senses that things could have turned out otherwise. But in his actual life he comes to know that it could not have happened otherwise, and the outcome is neither inevitable nor fair.

Apocalyptic Sectarianism

Entrepreneurship is both invention and the dominion of that invention, so that what was once a curiosity is now widely taken as the prevailing practice. Augustine's greatest achievement, outside of his literary and theological works, is surely the development and enormous growth of an institution, the restoration and redemption of the African Christian church to Catholicism, so it became an established institution.[17] That achievement is archetypal, mirroring Paul's actions three hundred years earlier and Moses' more than a thousand years earlier still; prefiguring the greatest achievements of entrepreneurial and consumerist capitalism fifteen hundred years later. For, again, ideas or inventions or doctrines are of only antiquarian interest if they are not adopted and enhanced, defining and meeting the needs of a society. Put theologically, how should our ecclesia be ecumenical? How should we evangelize?[18] (We shall get to the definition of these terms shortly.) Which forms of institutional enhancement are enlarging, which are corrupting? And how does it make sense to speak of the corruption of an idea or a product or an institution?

Augustine's great entrepreneurial achievement was the development and growth of a form of ecclesia that was ecumenical and evangelical, in a community rife with apocalyptic sectarianism. *Ecclesia*, as in ecclesiastical, is concerned with the institution of the church or of an assembly of members. *Ecumenical* refers to the universality of such a church or a movement, literally the capacity to inhabit the earth. *Evangelical* refers to an original (Christian) message, and secondarily to a reforming and missionary impulse. *Apocalyptic* (from the Greek) is revelation, the uncovering of the truth. And *sectarianism* is the division of a movement into organized ecclesiastical bodies each of which is in opposition to or differentiation from other such bodies (in contrast to ecumenical institutions).

Augustine shows how an institution could grow, absorb and delegitimate its competitors, appeal to a much wider audience, become authoritative, and employ the powers of the state to further those goals. Moreover, in claiming such universality and preeminence, he shows that one need not—in fact, ought not—claim a standard of perfectibility. Rather, the institution allows ordinary folks to "buy in" at their own level, and under its tutelage they might grow in stature. This is his very great entrepreneurial secret.

So far what I have been saying has been abstract and schematic. Let us return to the Roman Empire and the late fourth century.

To be the bishop of Hippo is surely a curious honor for Augustine. In Hippo and in much of North Africa (but not in Thagaste, where Augustine and Monica come from) the dominant Christian church is not Catholic but Donatist (after Donatus, fourth-century bishop of Carthage).[19] At this time the church is divided between Donatist and Catholic bishops, neither recognizing the other, reflecting a sectarian split earlier in the century. The Donatists had seen the Catholic bishops hand over the Holy Scriptures to be burned by pagan magistrates, an unforgivable act of treason, of collaboration with secular impurity. Each sect claims to be the authentic one, each reflects the unique personal and purist African tradition,[20] yet they have come to differ from each other dramatically. The Donatist Church, by its origin, is purist and perfectibilist and evangelical, aiming to preserve the truth and the tradition. What is impure and sinful is to be excluded, and the church will have no traffic with such. For this church can be polluted, made ritually unclean, by such contact. Hence it is an exclusionary purist personal institution.[21] On the other hand, the Catholic Church is more worldly, it has trafficked with Roman power, and it continues to do so.

Augustine's great invention is to take the impurity of the African Catholic Church and make it into a virtue. For, it is argued, it is God's will that the church gain dominion over all (its ecumenism); demanding that the church is to be pure is putting human frailties in the way of God's will. The church will become an inclusive church, the sinfulness of its members a sign of their ties to the church, the church being necessary to provide pastoral guidance and authority in their lives. Moreover, pagans are not to be excluded but to be included, their pasts (like Augustine's) being the occasion for their growth, their pagan rituals now treated as of little religious significance to Catholics. (Here think of modern missionaries allowing for such native rituals within orthodox observances.[22]) Ecclesia is to be ecumenical, evangelical, and antisectarian.

To be a member, to be under the church's umbrella, is to be subject to the church's authority and discipline. If the Donatists emphasize personal choice, the Catholics emphasize obedience and authority. That authority is rational, grounded in doctrine and law and pastoral judgment that is perceived as fair. Not only will the church traffic with the worldly and the sinful, it will gain dominion over them. Sin is natural and necessary in this world, and the church is as much in this world as in another one. Such a church cannot be polluted because it is already touched by the sinful, and it thrives. To be a member is to be under pastoral authority; doctrinal assent, getting the articles of faith right and being pure, is something that comes later, and perhaps not in this world.[23]

The church in this conception is eschatological, oriented toward its ultimate destinty. In the present, in this time and in this world, it shares in this world's ultimate future.[24] The church is not to be sharply separate from the ordinary polluted world, and so it must be subject to the world's desecrations. The church is an institution neither solely of this world nor solely of another. For the Gnostics and Donatists it is possible to have a bit of the Kingdom of Heaven here on earth, within their purified sphere. To Augustine, theirs is a false home, and by being freed from such an error one can be fully involved in this world without giving up the other.

Here the apocalyptic is "on the way." The church's authority comes from its ultimate being, now expressed through mundane means of rhetoric and discipline, of sermon and even state violence, yet it is not reducible as such to those means.[25]

Such an eschatological conception is a very great invention, a powerful device that theologically places the institution within its everyday, mundane, imperfect context, forcing it to be developing and dynamic, necessarily in need of a strategy. Practically, it forces the institution to deal with its actual world or its market. Of course, what will prove interesting is when such an eschatological conception proves inappropriate, when the world is so hostile that the church must husband its capacities rather more carefully.

While the Donatists might make a claim to purity and truth, Augustine, rhetorician that he is, makes a claim to an audience and its conviction. Augustine then uses state power (or state power allows itself to be employed) to disenfranchise the Donatist bishops, to force conversion of Donatist Christians by both argument and in the end torture and state discipline. Such discipline leads a person to an evangelical vision, and it is the task of the church to encourage, by force if necessary, one's willful assent to its authority. Augustine, now far from the monastery, has come to see his role in terms of dreadful responsibility (what else is the use of state power here?) and stringent authority. He has been transformed by the demands of a church and a role, so that he is deeply involved with everyday pastoral activities and with great and sometimes violent campaigns to bring the world to the church.[26]

There is much that is not at all attractive about Augustine at this time. Whatever draws us sympathetically to the Augustine of the *Confessions* now repulses us as we watch his ruthless behavior in the name of authority. Yet it is absolutely fascinating, and in the end strangely attractive. For moderns, Augustine is simply illiberal. There is no commitment to the individual (the Donatists are somewhat more appealing here), or to liberty, or to conventional institutions (a Burkean conservatism).[27] Notions of due process, of fairness, or even of balanced argument have no place here. Augustine's rhetoric aims to win, and to win resoundingly, for that is his mission, his election, his authority.

Augustine is strangely attractive because his exercises of authority and discipline, and his intolerance of difference, may well reflect some of our own experiences. He sees himself as acting as the father and the mother in bringing his children to their senses.[28] Moreover, Augustine here mirrors the unmentionable horrors of the building of many institutions, the horrors of entrepreneurship as it is actually carried out. So we are fascinated by an obscene revelation. None of this need be taken to justify violence, forced confession and conversion, or intolerance. That such illiberal and authoritarian actions and beliefs may almost always go along with entrepreneurial endeavors is what concerns me here, and it one of the main reasons why I tell the story of Augustine as bishop.[29]

What do we learn from Augustine about building an institution that will grow to inhabit the earth? Most crucially, one's ecclesia must be ecumenical: the institution becomes universal by its willingness to be inclusive. That inclusiveness does not preclude but in fact encourages the authority of the institution: membership is a matter of obedience to authority, an authority that allows, as it must, for errancy and impurity. Doctrinal conformity comes well after membership. Coordinately, that authority must act as pastor to its subjects; it must provide a world that meets their needs and incorporates their complex diversity. Its rhetoric is crucial, for that is its mode of gaining the conviction that leads to authentic redemptive action. Perfectibilist and individualist policies, rival claimants for authority, and tolerance of differences that deny central authority are destructive of the institution. And violence and state power may well be employed for the ultimate good of society.

Entrepreneurial endeavors grow if they are inclusive in their marketing, if they are clear about their goals and purposes yet tolerant of argument within the institution (for otherwise the institution would fall apart from within), and if they actually provide what people need. Yet they must also be willing to use all the tools of argument to educate people to their needs; they might well employ modes of coercion to deal with competitors; and they must be sure to isolate and remove those purists who would give up the institution's viability for their own ideas of what the institution should be. Entrepreneurship is not at all nice and sweet; accompanying it is a powerful rhetoric, violence, and sacrifice. Entrepreneurs are not simply leaders or managers; they are sources of authority who may well act authoritarianly. If they did not need to do so, they would be subject, again, to those regimes of prudential and rational consideration characteristic of a management science. We would be in an ordinary marginalist corporate world. That is not the world of the entrepreneur, a world in which the horror and the sacrifice and the violence are intrinsic to the story. And this is a story that is perhaps always tragic, no matter the triumphs and the inventions and the successes.

None of this should make us feel better about violence or coercion. But that they accompany our most celebrated heroic stories is no mere curiosity. Correspondingly, Schumpeter understood most poignantly that the triumph of modern liberalism might well be the death of capitalism, the ending of the bacchanalian revel of creative destruction that characterizes capitalism at its most vigorous. But insofar as we do participate in entrepreneurship, that tragic dimension, that temptation to authoritarianism, is fully present. The growth of an inclusive institution brings along with it authoritarian, disciplining, sacrificial acts. Technically, Augustine creates a church that is *epis-*

copal, one in which the authority of the bishop is crucial. We might well ask, as we shall in later chapters, whether we might have congregational and presbyterial forms of entrepreneurship. The answer is yes, but we shall not be able to avoid the problems of authority and sacrifice.

Again, my purpose here is to provide a richer way of describing and so understanding entrepreneurial endeavors, one in which what are ordinarily seen as atavistic and dreadful features are shown to be intrinsic to the institution. Tragedy and errancy are not only unavoidable; they are the sources, the engines, the germs of transformation. And rhetoric, preaching, and allegory are not irrational or unscientific as such; rather, they give us access to convictions we could not achieve by more prudential means. How Augustine created a more generous, inclusive institution provides us with one lesson. It is an institution that embraced pollutions and difference in a bear hug, and it is that inclusiveness as much as its resort to authority that allowed it to grow. That such efforts are dangerous is part of that same lesson. That entrepreneurship requires the assumption or usurpation of authority, and that such acts are often violent and sacrificial is the sobering fact in that lesson. A liberal management science, even with a Machiavellian tone, is what psychoanalysis calls a family romance—about another better family than the one we live in now, where the father and the mother love us unconditionally and simply. But actual entrepreneurial endeavors are rather more like real families, in which authority, discipline, and transgression are unavoidable (although they ought not be tyrannical). Children, in their fantasies, have a romance that their parents cannot entertain if they are to be good parents.

Dominion and Redemption as Entrepreneurial Rewards

In his old age, Augustine found himself engaged in activities, such as the common pagan rituals demanded by his flock, for which he once condemned the Donatists. While the Donatists had been forcibly controlled, Catholic bishops now presided over many who still retained Donatist sympathies. Moreover, the occupation of the Roman heartland of Africa by the Arian Vandals coincides with Augustine's death in 430 CE.[30] (The sack of Rome took place in 410.) The consequences of this invasion by the pagan world were enormous and ironic for that sacred world of the church: If at one time Augustinian Christianity was at the edge of the established Roman order, by the end of the next hundred and fifty years Christianity was at its center. However, the eschatological church that is perhaps Augustine's great invention was replaced in the seventh century by an ascetic one. A church that was once of the City and sin and variety was now of the Desert and its purity and solidarity. The sacred and the secular became rather more separated; a Donatist-like ideal came to dominate, yet with a mission to resacralize the world. A church that trafficked with classical culture became one in which the center was biblical and in which classical sources were unread.[31]

Triumph and success are ironic. What you once railed against becomes, dialectically, a legacy that you represent. What you defined yourself against now becomes you. The repressed not only returns, but in fact it never fully left. And triumph is contingent, for external events beyond your comprehension radically alter the meaning of your entrepreneurial endeavor. So an eschatological church is no defense against sheer external power.[32] What is perhaps needed is that ascetic Donatist/Gnostic ideal that preserves the church for another day. Only if the sacred is sharply separated from the profane and secular will the church and its mission survive.

The rewards of entrepreneurial endeavors are subject to confiscation. An act of creative destruction will succeed another such act, revising its meaning, overturning its triumph. What was once the scheme that allowed for growth now becomes dangerously vulnerable to destructive forces. Of course, we might argue that Augustine invented a church that is eventually the one that does grow and thrive. But in 430, and in the next century or two, that outcome was not clear at all.

The legacy of an entrepreneurial endeavor may be its denial. Hence the desire to normalize a flourishing entrepreneurial startup so that it becomes corporate and bureaucratic and managed. At the same time the temptation is to aim for controlled or continuous revolution from within. But that desire has to reckon not only with the self-consuming and possibly even demoralizing consequences of such a bacchanalian revel turned on itself, but also with the changing external circumstances, which may now militate against entrepreneurship in this arena. It is better at these times to be conservative and even withdraw than to be destroyed altogether.

Augustine wrote *The City of God* in the second and third decades of the fifth century in light of the sack of Rome (a symbolic end of the Roman Empire). Whatever else they do, such apparently external contingencies can destroy what once seemed inevitable and invincible. More generally, an entrepreneurial endeavor that once made necessary what was otherwise thought to be contingent might subsequently be overturned and so suffer catastrophe. The entrepreneur's problem, or perhaps it is a temptation, is to ensure the dominion of that entrepreneurial endeavor. The meaning of the endeavor must be shifted from the realm of pride, having creatively destroyed the predecessor, to that of redemption, a state of perspective and gratitude and generosity toward what comes next.

Augustine's solution, when his church is under siege as a consequence of its political success and so has to deal with a much more varied audience (in part from the neopagan Roman aristocrats coming to Africa as refugees from Italy), is to redefine dominion and redemption so they are more resilient and transcendent. The church's dominion must now be extended over all of history (and not be just a particular outgrowth of a Judaic sect in Roman times). And so he enlarges the presence of the church to an eschatological community present throughout history, always between this world and the next and, until the apocalyptic moment, inextricably linked to all of this world. We know this by our own apocalyptic experience, however modest: we long for something different in this world, we are "resident aliens" (*peregrini*),[33] otherworldly in this world. We yearn for more, we love the future. That yearning is represented by the conflict between two cities, Babylon and Jerusalem. We have always resided in liberated or redeemed Jerusalem even if we are enslaved in Babylon.[34] Christianity represents that yearning, that love, that alienation. The City of God that Christianity has made explicit has always been present. Its dominion is very great indeed, impossible to be leveled and demolished.

As for redemption, the pride of a church triumphant (in this world) is surely to be humbled. Second-best is good, good enough. Perspective and gratitude, rather than purity and pride, are not compromises but the way we must live. So the everyday bonds, even the demands of sexuality for example, cannot be denied. So Augustine must demand of himself what he once demanded of the Donatists, an even more inclusive, less prideful stance.

Now we might reasonably argue that the rewards of entrepreneurial endeavors, at least those in the realm of commerce, real estate, and manufacture, are rewards of pecuniary profit.[35] Presumably, profits can be retained and enhanced, whatever may happen to the entrepreneurial endeavor, even though, historically, we know how such wealth has been squandered and mismanaged, ruining many a fortune. My elegiac tone seems sadly misplaced. Disappointment and loss are not tragedy, but rather mistakes of policy and management.

However, the rewards of entrepreneurship are only incidentally pecuniary profit, taken as deserved reward for arbitrage and adventure. Pecuniary reward is an occasional fact about how some markets and states happen to work together. Rather, the entrepreneur almost always feels that success is a matter of grace and fortune, albeit given the entrepreneur's very great talent and skill. Whatever else, there is in such endeavors a gift to be received, freely given (by whom is left open), beyond obligation or desert or reasons we might anticipate or even appreciate. Entrepreneurship is a matter of something more than we could otherwise rationally justify. Conversely, if the entrepreneur did not respond fully and generously and sensitively to the opportunities presented, or if the entrepreneur and the endeavor did not stay fast on the treacherous path, the wayside of abandonment is as great and as deep as an ocean. Entrepreneurs do not do arbitrage or adventure or whatever. Entrepreneurs prevail or they vanish.

The rewards of entrepreneurship are exactly those of dominion and redemption. Can your endeavor prevail over a domain, perhaps along the way sacrificing incompatible endeavors? Can there be a meaningful story, a redeeming of history, about why you ought to have prevailed (as you have, let us say), one in which your prevalence is testimony to Providence and order and meaning. You are proven right not only by your bald success, but by justice itself. What was once contingent is now seen as rationally necessary. For Augustine, in *The City of God*, Christianity not only prevails but is inevitable, foreseen or prefigured eternally in the past.[36]

The entrepreneur as that courageous and virtuous protagonist is the particular means of realizing what is eventually taken as inevitable. The entrepreneur then incurs an obligation; the pecuniary gifts received are neither desert nor reward. Rather, these gifts come along with a debt that needs acknowledgment. The responsibilities of wealth are those of serial reciprocity (namely, passing that gift on) and stewardship (caring for what we have been given).[37]

This homily is directed to the entrepreneur. The experience of the entrepreneur and the logic of entrepreneurial endeavors are such that dominion and redemption are its rewards, and rewards of that sort incur subsequent obligations if they are to be authentic. Our prevailing, at least for now, might seem to us to be self-evident; yet think of how Augustine might have felt had he lived five more years. But the story we tell and the life we lead are redemptive only if they are testimony to a larger meaning and a greater good. To have been elected to our positions and to have risen to the occasion sets the stage for such a redemptive existence. Of course, we then have to deliver on what we have promised.

When we are an overweening success, we might well be tempted to take full credit for our entrepreneurial endeavor. But since such success surely builds tragedy within itself, at least in actual history, we might well find pride a temptation, a turning away from our true obligations, away from the gratitude and humility that would be revealed in a fairer, less triumphal history. We might note that historically the capitalist entrepreneur depended intimately on arrangements provided by the state (private property, bankruptcy laws), and to ignore those state provisions now is to be perilously and literally close to confiscation of our property and imprisonment for debt.

Moreover, entrepreneurial success demands an eschatological vision, that meeting of the sacred and the profane in this world, the sacred not to be polluted by profanity, its integrity untouchable. To be successful is to see, as did Augustine, how to realize a transcendent vision with the materials at hand, how to realize that vision again and again. If the logic of success is eschatological, then the rewards are just those of dominion and redemption.[38] For eschatology, the study of final things, refers to a universal dominion and a truth we finally understand clearly and unveiled.

A last feature of entrepreneurship I want to speak of is creativity. We shall understand creativity as craft and mastery and as prophecy and revelation. And we learn how to be prophets through predecessors we find ourselves imitating.

To understand Augustine, we must understand Paul both as a prefigurement of Augustine and as Augustine's self-consciously chosen model. We want to ask, What did Augustine learn from Paul? And what could it mean to "learn from"? Paul's Jewishness and his rabbinic background, what Paul cannot in the end forget, is just what Augustine must inherit. It is a model of how we are as entrepreneurs indebted to what we have supposedly rejected and superseded. The lesson here is terrifying yet ultimately comforting. For to reject all, to fly blind, must be disastrous. The repressed not only returns but it is the means through which we triumph and fail and so are redeemed. Such is not always the most happy of stories, but it is the story we find ourselves telling. Again, and again.

It may be useful at this point to allow the agnostic and nonbeliever to breathe, not to speak of confessors to other religions. My claims here are descriptive and phenomenological. They are tested by their adequacy in accounting for our own experience and our situations. Such a phenomenology could be claimed to have ontological and religious implications: if you think this way, surely you believe in God. As far as I can tell, this is an open implication.[39] Still, "God" is vital to our discourse. But for now, on to Paul.

Paul

By his own testimony and actions, we know that Augustine learned from Paul how to be the Catholic Christian and the bishop he became, sometimes learning literally, sometimes by inspiration, and sometimes by what we shall call typology (a formal repetition, as in a typeface). Augustine's sudden and sharp conversion is modeled after Paul's, in one case hearing children's voices and then turning to Paul and being flooded by light, in the other seeing a bright light and hearing a message from the Lord.[40] While it has been argued that Paul might also be seen as a prophet within Judaism, receiving a prophetic call as a typological repetition of Old Testament prophets, and so rather more smoothly moving between Judaism and what we now take to be Christianity, the abrupt conversion of Paul is central to his own and to Luke's account in *Acts*. Subsequently, he redoes his life, his theology, and his mission. What he once took as revelation, Jewish ritual law, is now seen as an in-effect temptation that leads us astray. He comes to see his previous life as just on the way to Christianity, and in that sense it is mistaken. The story of his conversion, like Augustine's, pries an ordinary moment out of the ordinary—falling off a proverbial donkey on the road to Damascus, or hearing rustling of leaves in a garden in Milan—and remakes it into a marked moment. The truth strikes one through otherwise mundane means.

Even though Augustine's story is a repetition of Paul's, and Paul's is a repetition of Old Testament prophets', we study Augustine's conversion in so much detail because of the legacy he provided in the *Confessions*, a theologically as well as narratively dramatic autobiography, just what concerns us here. What is of interest when we think of ourselves as entrepreneurs are those confessions, conversion stories told by the protagonist, rather than accounts by others of what happened. Confessions are not conventional histories. They are attempts to claim dominion and redemption.

From Paul, Augustine also learned that he must wield authority, that he has a mission to those who are impure. Here I quote from Peter Brown's biography.

> Immediately after his ordination as a priest, Augustine wrote a desperate letter to his bishop, Valerius, begging for some time to retire to study the Scriptures....The letter is all the more poignant, for having been written some short time after Augustine had thrown himself enthusiastically into his active life as a priest. The experience had come to him as a galling revelation of his own limitations....The [advice] which he drew from the Scriptures, will eventually crystallize into an ideal of ecclesiastical authority, that will dominate Augustine's life until his death. Plainly, what he absorbed at this time, were the lessons of the active life of St. Paul. He will identify himself passionately with the ideal of authority shown in the letters of Paul to his wayward communities: "insisting in season and out of season," committed to impinge constantly on his flock and its enemies, driven by the objective "terror" of the Holy Scriptures. (p. 206)

Finally, it is from Paul that Augustine learned what we have called the eschatological solution to the theological problem of the connection between this world and another, to the entrepreneurial problem of the connection between actual present possibility and hope and expectation. Theologically put, Paul provided a model of the dynamics of the apocalyptic, namely, revelation and its presence in this world; entrepreneurially, the dynamics of strategy and planning. In each case the problem is how we can reconcile ultimate hopes with the necessities and disappointments we actually encounter. What I have been calling the purist solution is to radically separate what is actual and its disappointments from what is ultimately possible and its fulfillment. But when prophecy fails us, what are we to do? I have been suggesting that the purist solution, at least in times of potential institutional growth, is likely to be disastrous since it isolates entrepreneurial actors from their markets. Such pride leads to the decline of institutions and to the abandonment of larger responsibilities. From the point of view of the community or consumers, they too are excluded from what they very much want.

A theological interlude: Paul insists on the reality of the apocalyptic. Yes, we live in this world, but in this world we do have evidence of what might be ultimately achieved; and what we have here in this world makes sense only in terms of another world. We may well be disappointed or be impure or troubled, but that does not exclude us from what is ultimately possible. Rather, imperfection sets the occasion for our being aware of what is possible.

Apocalyptic means revelation, namely, the particular detailed truth. God's word comes to us in language we can understand, flawed and incomplete as that understanding must be. But it is God's word. That particularity does not deny us access to that other world; rather, it is the only way we could have any such access.[41] That we are sinful (and here I may be reading Augustine into Paul) does not deny us access to the ultimate; rather it is a sign that we are connected to what is ultimate. (Otherwise, we might be said to do meaningless stuff, as do objects.) We shall understand the meaning of revelation only in the fullness of time, but revelation is available for us, now. The dynamics of "not yet" includes what we shall become. This world is God's providence, whatever its imperfection. For, again, imperfection is a sign of Providence and possibility. The church is for those of this world.

The entrepreneur must insist on the reality of the apocalyptic. She must address what is actual, the world as it is now. Yet the ultimate message, the hope and vision and the possible, is just as real, just as powerful, not at all unrealistic. Myth redeems history; larger vision informs, gives meaning to, and motivates actual action.[42]

To shift to the language characteristic of business education and practice: if marketing is having what other people want,[43] and strategy is saying how those wants are to be owned up to by you, then Paul is saying that marketing and strategy not only go together, but they redeem each other. Marketing is redeemed from unfocused desire, strategy is redeemed from irrelevance. To be committed to practical nitty-gritty problems and details is to be committed to a synoptic and even transcendent sense of your mission as well. To be committed to the church is to be committed to revelation and apocalypse, no matter how everyday is to be the occasion of one's churchly task. That everydayness is the only way one could be in revelation.[44]

Paul's problem was how to make Christianity available to those who were not perfect: whether they were Christian Jews who were abandoning, often reluctantly, their rituals, or they were pagans who from the Judaic point of view were ritually unclean to begin with. For a movement to grow it must be able to incorporate just what it would have formerly rejected, and to incorporate that impurity in such a way that it is not polluting, not delegitimating of the ultimate values, not seen as selling out. This is why the eschatological solution is of such practical interest.

To legitimately incorporate otherness is just the problem of the entrepreneur who must grow out of a deep insight into a larger more diverse world and meet the needs of that world, even if that world is rather more unfocused than is the entrepreneur. Authentic vision and hope are here never defeated by actual difficulties and impurities; rather, they are given meaning by those struggles and challenges.

There is another solution to the problem of being in this imperfect world. If the Pauline solution (and through Augustine, modern Christianity's solution) to ecclesia or community is both apocalyptic and ecumenical, the rabbinic solution (what we now call Judaism) to having had one's homeland destroyed and so being thrown out of the Garden is ritual definition and an acknowledgment that revelation or theological doctrine is not realized without apparent contradiction in this world. Hence there was in about 200 CE both an extension of the rules of ritual purity so as to define the Judaic community and the growth of rabbinic law to deal with the actual particular problems that community encountered, especially within itself and in its relations with outsiders.[45]

Pauline Christianity and rabbinic Judaism may be said to come from the same source, the in-effect postlapsarian fate of Judaism once it is tossed out into the impure Roman world. And their solutions are functionally the same—namely, to make peace with what were once taken to be pollutions, so that those impurities do not deny the providential character of the everyday world. Paul's apocalyptic and eschatological solution does not free him from the in-effect rabbinic or pastoral or juridical demands that are fully present in this world, demands that must not only be reconciled with revelation but actually employ revelation in their resolution. So Paul in his epistles is still using all of his talents as a Pharisee, and Augustine still uses all of his secular rhetorical gifts. Whatever the theology, the demands of actual organizations force both a theocentric or authoritative reference and a pastoral practice. While Christianity might want to distance itself from the rabbinic solution, in fact it had to face the same problems posed to the rabbis, and its solution in actual practice, by its most effective practitioners, is roughly of the same sort.

Management is both transcendent and everyday practical.[46] And the growth of entrepreneurial endeavors depends on not denying either fact. So, for example, Paul's problem was not so much to say how the gentiles might be saved, for that was already possible in Judaism. Rather, "[Paul's] claim that the saved Jews and gentiles could form a single new community and freely interact was more innovative [than that circumcision was unnecessary for gentile salvation]. The issue was not how the gentiles could be saved but how to eat with them and marry them." [47]

Paul's problem in making the apocalyptic practical was to redo Judaism so that one did not have to be Jewish to become Christian. So he had to address practical issues of ritual as they were understood in actual practice. Again, Paul thinks as would a rabbinic Jew, at least in his methodology.[48] He solves particular problems of ritual, problems about circumcision or dietary rules, rather than working out coherent and systematic theological argument, so as to make Jewish Christianity more inclusive (and in effect avoiding much knottier and more resistant theological issues). In the end, that particularistic problem solving is exactly what Augustine self-consciously does for his flock as a follower of Paul, although Augustine is also a very great systematic theologian.

Augustine learns from Paul how to be an apostle, a person whose task is to deliver a message.[49] That message has to be understood by its hearers and listeners in their own terms; it is a message addressed to their problems in their society. The message is radically particular and contingent. And because the message is so situated, the Jewish context is pervasive for Paul, the Roman context is pervasive for Augustine.

When an invention is made or an entrepreneurial idea is realized, it is built from what the entrepreneur will eventually deny or see as wayward. As a Pharisaic Jew, what else has Paul to work with but Judaism and its early Christian developments? As a philosophically trained rhetorician, what else has Augustine to work with but ancient philosophy and rhetoric, besides of course the Christian tradition, a tradition inevitably touched by all these profanations. Augustine writes a confession to take stock of his traditional heritage and put it in its place. But a confession is only part of the story, a part that emphasizes discontinuity and transformation. Imagine a philosophic or rhetorical or Neoplatonist or Manichaean or even Donatist account of Augustine (to choose the range of Augustine's enthusiasms); or imagine a Jewish or Gnostic account of Paul, as convert and apostle. Whatever else, such accounts would surely see much more continuity than might be allowed by the confessor himself.

Augustine learned a very great deal from Paul: how to become a Christian, how to be an authoritative and missionary bishop, and how to create a growing church. He self-consciously takes Paul as a model of the kind of towering figure he does become, and from Paul he takes permission to be that figure. Yet Augustine is not a mere copy of Paul. Rather, he takes from Paul what *he* needs, models himself after Paul, sees in Paul a prefigurement of his own life. Technically, Augustine as he presents himself is a typological or formal repetition of Paul. That Augustine learned from Paul must be understood in this rather more holistic and encompassing way. And, as we have already noted, Paul is a typological repetition, too, in his own way, but now of the prophets of the Hebrew Scriptures. (Or in Christian terms, the *New* Testament is a typological repetition of the *Old* Testament, as we might expect from the use of the modifiers *new* and *old*.)

So it might be asked, what is the reader supposed to learn from the kind of discussion we are engaged in here? We learn from others and the stories of their lives, including how they learned from others how to be the persons they are, how to be the persons we shall be. What we learn is a way to conceive of ourselves, and so to act accordingly, here in roles to some extent distinctive to entrepreneurial endeavors. So we are literally encouraged, and so we become articulate about how we are to enact our missions.

Augustine keeps returning to Paul for courage and articulateness and theological technology (about hope and the apocalyptic, for example). When we read a biography we might come to understand the life in terms of how we ourselves might fulfill the tasks that person takes on. I have been speaking of Paul to enlarge on what I have been saying about Augustine and entrepreneurship, and to show how an actor (say, the reader) might be rationally inspired by another figure. From Paul, Augustine learned how to be the St. Augustine we have come to recognize in Pauline terms.

Prophecy and Creation

Learning from others is an exercise in humility; we are never original or the first in a line. We are a typological repetition of these others, our predecessors now taken as our prefigurers. That might well give us the courage of our convictions and commitments, for we can see how we may fulfil those commitments. Still, while we do not avoid what we have already learned, the implications of that learning are more diverse than was ever expected. And so there is substantial room for invention. The creativity of the entrepreneur is always more than that entrepreneur could conceive prospectively. For the entrepreneurial idea speaks through the person. Such a person is a prophet, one who is literally influenced by God.

Students are much troubled about whether they have the essence of creativity, whatever it is, and how they can have more of it. Surely, they might increase their creativity, breaking down cognitive and emotional resistances and barriers, just what teachers can do for their students.[50] Still, mastery is a primary task of education. There are no useful resistances to be broken down if there is no mastery. Creativity is the premium for being a master of a craft, having been trained in its canonical skills, having studied within the tradition of its masterpieces. Then, whatever one makes, whatever does actually happen, one might be creative (or not).

Creativity cannot be explained by mastery, even if mastery is a desideratum for creativity.[51] Moreover, creative acts are not only objective, the production of extraordinary institutions and objects; they are also subjective in the transcendent and ecstatic experience of the producer. Creativity is acts of prophecy.

While Moses is perhaps the archetypal prophet within the Western tradition, recall that Paul in his apostolic calling is such a prophet and so is Augustine as he has come to interpret himself at that moment of conversion related in the *Confessions*. They receive a message from God, they are dumbstruck by it, and their response to God's care for them is a mission they take upon themselves. In prophecy God cares for you, is affected by what you do (and correspondingly you are affected by his call): what Abraham Heschel calls "pathos" and "sympathy," respectively. God is absolutely present to you; God speaks through you.[52] And it is by means of your response that what God speaks is realized in this world. Not only is there revelation, there is the response to revelation, the prophetic act.[53]

As the prophet goes out into the world on a mission, the prophet's and the world's mode of speech is in prayer. So the prophet speaks and God listens. Prayer occurs within that mission; it is not abstract or isolated; it has meaning within that prophetic message. Prayer is the way the prophet and others can be within revelation, within a covenant. Entrepreneurship is in the grips of the world and its prayerful response, as much as it is in the grip of the entrepreneur.[54] Does the world respond to her mission? Has she found and developed a market for her endeavor?

How could the entrepreneur possibly be considered a prophet? Does God speak through the entrepreneur? In a way that Paul or Augustine would understand, the answer would seem to be yes.[55] The structure of entrepreneurial creativity is rather like the prophet's calling and mission, both in revelation, the entrepreneur's (or God's) idea, and in response, the entrepreneurial endeavor. If the prophet is sometimes ordered to violate the ritual law for a higher purpose, so, too, do entrepreneurs find themselves violating the conventional rules and processes. As for who it is who speaks to and through the entrepreneur, I have no answer, largely because entrepreneurs have no simple answer. But it is clear in their reports that entrepreneurs are often spoken to and cared for, and they do respond to that message with a mission.[56]

In Jewish thought, the Messiah will come when we are not focused on him or her. So, too, revelation is a matter of God's grace. Revelation dramatically focuses the prophet on the particularity of the moment. The prophet is called to order and to an order. God speaks and the prophet listens.[57] And through the prophet, the divine imperative and message and oracle is conveyed to a community. That message is sacerdotal and magical. They are words that transform the world, immediately by their being heard, mediately in their being realized.[58]

The ancient Hebrew prophet's conversation is a much more nuanced interchange than was experienced by Paul or Augustine. It is an ongoing conversation. Not only is God absolutely present to the prophet, God is present for the prophet (again, pathos and sympathy). God feels for what the prophet does; God is affected by that person's actions. Reciprocally, the prophet is open to the presence of Another. And her mission presses her into the world. In the end, this is no private conversation.

The prophet finds herself with a task, that of spreading the word, ensuring its receipt, fulfilling its powers in this world: a task of dominion. The prophet also finds herself in an ongoing relationship with another, coming to understand the meaning of that dominion: a task of redemption. Again, prophecy is revelation and response, engaging in the particularity of the message, and so prophecy is dominion and redemption.

The experience of creativity is nicely characterized by this prophetic dynamic. The creative idea employs us as its vehicle, but it would be presumptuous to claim it as our own. Such a gift, as is revelation, demands a response from us, and that response is crucial if the idea is to have a life of its own. The acts of creativity are dialogic, our talking to another who listens to us much as we listen to her. We are pressed into the world, forced into the marketplace.[59] In sum, the phenomenology of creativity is a typological repetition of the phenomenology of prophecy.

Entrepreneurs institutionalize creations. They take what is thought to be contingent and make it necessary. They sacralize what is mundane. So contingency becomes revelation. Moreover, the history of prophecy reflects a tension between the prophet and the institutionalization of prophecy, between revelation and church. A prophetic religion is subject to new and overturning prophecies, that ongoing conversation with God, while a religion that becomes institutionalized is rather more public and codified. Put differently, is our sacrifice (entrepreneurial creative destruction, for example) commemorative and eucharistic, reviving the prophetic moment and overturning convention; or is our sacrifice redemptive and expiatory, living off that moment?[60] Do we have Gnostic Elijah or covenantal Moses?[61]

Augustine and Paul institutionalize prophecy, insisting on scriptural canon, creedal authority, and episcopal hierarchy.[62] These institutionalizations, as dominion and redemption, are perhaps crucial for entrepreneurial endeavors that want to preserve their legacies. For they force the entrepreneur to take seriously marketing, strategy, and corporate organization. But once we ask how we might motivate such an organization of people, how we might get them to march together, then we must turn to the Mosaic-Israelitic story, as we shall in the next chapter.

An Apologetics for Hierarchical Authority?

To take entrepreneurship seriously we have to pay attention to its most unmodern of features: big decisions and election, illiberal authority, the redemptive character of rewards, prophetic creation, and errancy and tragedy. And its moral dilemmas, as in sacrifice and creative destruction, are not to be finessed.[63] What might well seem irrational or contradictory to modern thought actually works, and works quite well.[64]

Sacrifice, creation, and judgment are awful. And hope and prophecy transcendently herald the future. (They are proleptic, to use the theological term of art.) The ideas we have discussed incorporate the apocalyptic and the proleptic. Under a religious and a theological understanding, entrepreneurship's phenomenology is natural, and education for entrepreneurship is practical and traditional.[65]

From the Donatist (and more generally Gnostic) point of view, what I have been describing in this chapter is an apologetics for hierarchical authority and violence. Augustine takes the moral freedom characteristic of the story of Adam and Eve, the choice in the Garden, and turns it around. It becomes a story of original sin and compulsion, and hence the need for churchly and episcopal authority to control uncontrollable passions.[66] What is private, sacred, coded, exclusive, and direct is shown to be less productive than what is public, institutional, inclusive, and mediated. From a radically secular and conventionally rationalist point of view, my employment of God is also an invocation of external authority.

Moreover, the violence employed by Augustine through Roman state power seems to be intrinsic to what he is doing. Entrepreneurship here requires deliberate creative destruction. As in Augustine's description of such violence as parental discipline (corrective punishment, a "softening-up process," "teaching by inconveniences"),[67] that violence is taken as natural if regrettable. And it is justified. And so Augustine becomes used to it.

Finally, episcopal hierarchical authority, which judges scriptural canonicity and the creedal genuineness of members, is here enshrined.

Entrepreneurs do assume authority so their judgments prevail. This does not mean that their assumption need be accepted by us. The authority of an entrepreneur is understood as authentic through the entrepreneurial endeavor and just how, in detail, it proves itself and just how, in detail, we find ourselves going along with it (or not). Revelation is particular, in detail, and it might be false. An apologetics is not a moral justification.

Entrepreneurs are perhaps as tempted as anyone to say that they made it on their own. Actually, those who have comparatively little experience are more likely to believe this. Such pride is not only wrong, it leads to disaster.[68] To speak of God, and authority, and state intervention is to remind us of just how we do make it. Such humility is simply practical.

I am driven to this religious mode of description by actual reports and experiences of entrepreneurs. The value of this description, besides its verisimilitude, lies in its capacity to lead us to sufficiently complex ethical discussions. Put differently, the rhetoric of entrepreneurship and its practice require destruction and tragedy if there is to be creation; there must be sacrifice and mortification if there is to be redemption and dominion.[69]

What we have yet to analyze is how authority is worked out between the authoritative figure and others: Moses' problem. Or how people come together when there is no church: a covenantal moment. To that story of leadership and judgment we shall now turn.

2

Commitment
Moses and the Israelites as a Story of Binding, Sacrifice, and Mission

Prophecy and Its Obligations. How to Follow a Story. Binding and Leading, The *Akedah* and the *B'rit,* Resistance, Backsliding, Marching. Stigma and Scapegoat. Sacred Acts of Judgment, Compassion, Righteousness, Covenant, Sacrifice, Mission. Story and History.

Prophecy and Its Obligations

Prophecy is no ordinary conversation. It is awe-filled, it is frightening, it is impossibly demanding. That revelation is dreadful, in its particularity, its consequences, and in its being addressed to you. And your response is a transcendent act that requires your violating the everyday prudential or moral rules in outrageous ways (for why else would there be prophecy?). At first, Moses resists prophecy; he must be instructed in its ways in very great detail. His people, the Israelites, as they become a people, must learn to hear a truth that will drive them into the desert for a promise that seems to be a curse as well. To see how things ought to go, to have a hopeful vision, to enter into an entrepreneurial endeavor, is no free blessing; you are then engaged in what surely appears to others as a treacherous life. To have faith in yourself, or for others to have faith in you, might well be madness.

For the Donatists (or the Jews), the ecclesiastical inventions of Augustine and Paul, which I have eulogized in the last chapter as inclusive authoritative institutions, are misrepresentations, slanders, and calumnies. They are opportunistic moves, personal attacks presented as theological and institutional justifications for the destruction the church would wreak upon those whom it would presume to succeed. Moreover, to treat those inventions as progress is to ignore subsequent church history in which there are regressions to Donatist (or Gnostic or monastic) ways. Such a story of progress is a triumphalist fiction that denies its own overturning, which often occurs quite soon after the fiction was confected, as Augustine feared on his deathbed.[1]

For Jews, their task is the fulfillment of prophecy; the Augustinian attack is to deny them the authenticity of that task. Augustine would allow us, but not himself and his episcopate, to avoid the awfulness and hence the fulfillment of the demands of prophecy in the name of individual salvation, and so the Israelites would not be a people. But the consequent cost is that we might well avoid prophecy's challenge and be disheartened and discouraged in the name of ecumenism.

For the Jews, in Mosaic or in rabbinic times, the ecclesiastical and entrepreneurial problem was not one of progressive growth, as such, but rather one of boundary and definition: How are we to be a committed people in a world that is otherwise unbounded and destructive by its diversions and entrancements? The Pauline Christian solution is no solution, the Jews might argue. For in the name of ecclesia it denies history; it denies by expungement just what defines a people. It substitutes or at best makes preeminent the spoken word of the bishop and his rhetorical and casuistic skills for the authority of history, story, and sacred text. It substitutes revisionist claims of faith for memory and for ritual observance of history.[2] Pauline Christianity is a misrepresentation of authority, moving it from history to the present, from God to men, men who pridefully claim to interpret God's wisdom. And they are not even fully authentic prophets through whom God might well speak.[3] For the age of prophecy is over.

Put practically, the Pauline-Augustinian ecclesiology does not create an organization that is in its members committed to its purposes. It harbors too readily the doubters and the go-alongs, as Augustine was only too aware. If we want an entrepreneurial organization, not simply a growing one, Augustine does not tell us how to go about achieving it.[4]

It is perhaps just those features characteristic of Judaism that Augustine and Paul deride, such as particular and pervasive rituals and a capacity to be polluted by unclean outside forces, that make for the kinds of commitment needed if an organization is to act entrepreneurially. Instead of an eschatological church everywhere present, what we might need is a more parochial institution: what is motivating here is a distinct and unique heritage that one must then fulfill. The Israelites, and the Jews who followed them, are not antiquarian artifacts, but rather the models we must emulate. So, for example, Exodus themes are pervasive in political revolution throughout modern history.[5]

What is perhaps most foreign to modern readers about the biblical rendering of the Israelites' story is its details and the importance that is attached to each and all of those details.[6] Whether it be in ritual observance or in biblical commentary, every little bit counts, and it counts immensely in ways we can never fully anticipate. That is the nature of revelation, especially when it is a long, complex, repetitive, typological, and seemingly contradictory story, as are the Hebrew Scriptures. Such an apocalyptic is not readily to be picked apart for sayings, for each picking apart brings along with it the rest of the story. The survival and triumph of the Israelites and presumably the Jewish people cannot be epitomized by a series of reasonably abstracted policies and programs and rules.[7] *This story* in its particularity is all that counts. History is legitimating, and we must take on that history whole if we are to inherit its authority. What we now take as miracles or as tests of those people are also for us miracles and tests, to be understood as they are understood in the text: as too demanding moral and meaningful events, events that are given deeper meaning by reference to other such events in the story. To hope to avoid such uncomfortable details is to deny the history: whether it be by looking for the essential truth, by getting rid of supernatural elements, by finding those parts of the ritual from which we are to be freed (rather than by asking how we might now observe that ritual, an unavoidable interpretive problem given changing circumstances), or by hoping we might think our way to the truth.[8] This is a redemptive revelation, a particular and detailed account of our heritage and of our becoming who we are.

Actual entrepreneurial endeavors succeed in their details, in their particulars, in precisely how they go about what was done. We might like to believe we can identify the crucial moves, others being less relevant and in that sense arbitrary. But it is not at all clear that such crucial moves would have worked if we had not also made all the not-so-crucial moves and mistakes along the way.

The Israelite heritage seems inflexible. The atavistic quality of the Israelites' story is repulsive to Paul because it excludes the pagans (who still might be saved according to the Israelites);[9] and it is problematic for Augustine, as he sees it reflected in the Donatists, because it does not accord with the inevitabilities of state power. Of course, Exodus says that to accept the inevitability of state power is to be enslaved.[10]

The Israelites' atavisms are perhaps just the moves that have to be made if there is to be a Jewish people, if there is to be a viable endeavor. To argue that other moves might have worked is a lovely act of pride. What we would presumably learn from such pride, were it to prevail, is that we know better than history and story, that we can get around the irrelevant details. What we do learn from the Israelites' story and from Moses is that the details, the roundabouts, the inefficiencies, the errancies, are crucial to the endeavor's ultimate ongoingness. Such a history is not even a rite of passage, a formal and transcendent ritual that occurs at one time, and then life goes on ordinarily but now transformed. Vigilance and careful attention are for all time, not just for one moment. This is a history that is lived every day, its obligations and temptations ever present.

To live out a story, in detail, is to become a people; to tell the story, in detail, is to assert and find out the meaning of being a people. And to read or hear such a story is to take what seems arbitrary, inconsequential, and merely nominal and make it necessary, significant, and sacred: to have a truth that speaks to our needs, to find a purpose within chaos, in effect to have been spoken to in a language that leads to authentic action.[11] Now, Moses is surely too big a figure for any of us to be like him. But no matter, we have his tasks of binding a people, giving it meaning, leading it to its destiny, and justifying both its trials and its mission. (Recall that "justify" means putting things in their places; it does not imply approval or fairness.)

None of this is counsel to hypervigilance and righteousness. For we could not know which details really matter; scrupulous ritual observance does not free us from contingency. That is why there are other rituals to free us from that scrupulousness.[12] Rather, this way of speaking is a counsel to pay attention to the particulars, the exact progressions and backslidings as such. Prophecy is frightening because it demands our full attention. School's in session; the lessons are in everything and everywhere. Or, as Abraham said when he heard God's word, "Here I am" (in Hebrew, *Hineni*), as later Moses did as well.

How to Follow a Story

A question that I have already addressed in chapter 1 and that will recur in each chapter is, How am I to learn, what am I to learn, from the stories and analyses you offer of Augustine or Moses or Paul or Oedipus or mothers? How am I to follow in their footsteps? Just how am I to follow a story in my own life?[13] We can follow these particular stories because they really are open to our interpretations; we have come to understand ourselves and to have selves at all and to understand what we might do in just their terms. To follow a story is to have the appropriate expectations, and to have such expectations for these stories is to be a person within our culture.

Moreover, we can and do deliberately follow stories, both as a keeping-track-of and as a fulfilling-in-our-lives, because "following" lies in the actual details of how a story is fulfilled this time. The necessity of those details this time (revelation) is only appreciated when we reveal those details in our actual detailed and particular doings. The stories' structures of motive and cause, generic and formal though they be, make sense only in their specific detail. The persons we have become are in part a consequence of our learning those stories. We are trained in our educations to follow them, whether in folk tale or in literature. There is no need to assume that there is some God as screenwriter doing the archetypal work; we do it, by the way, in just how we become educated members of a community.

Surely, some of the analytic categories I discuss are sufficiently abstract and portable yet applicable and grounded, such as "big decisions," that they will fairly readily apply to some situations one encounters. But I am making a much more significant claim in telling these stories. I mean to keep in mind their original narrative and literary form so that we might put ourselves in actual places in those stories, places defined not simply by abstract formal rules but primarily by an organic integrity provided by the story as it is told, namely, we put ourselves in roles defined in those stories.[14]

So how are we to learn to follow a story? Traditionally, we are to master it through repetition and enactment. We learn a story inside and out, again and again, through rituals that are partial reenactments and through exercises, such as rites of passage, which are meant to free us to hear the messages of that tradition. Given such mastery, you do recognize yourself in that tradition's terms, in part because the self you have become is defined by the experiences and tests prescribed by that tradition. You do not ask, What would Abraham do? You know already, because you have come to see yourself and your situations in terms defined by that man of faith and his cosmos. To retell stories as I am doing here, highlighting particular analytic features, is meant to so educate the reader, to encourage the reader to reread her life and the world itself in these terms. Still, the exercises here are rather meager when compared to traditional training regimes. I have set up a description that I hope the reader finds sufficiently powerful to take what was once inchoate or misunderstood experience and name it in actual practice.

In sum, you come to understand yourself as the person you are by following a set of stories.[15] A self is the repetition and integration of the stories heard, enacted, taken to heart and mind. You do not become the person you are through your experiences, but through the stories you tell yourself about those experiences. The difference between stories and everyday experience is that stories are deliberately meaningful, deliberately orderly. Stories are specific, detailed, concrete, driven by our sentimental involvements and motives. So we take experience back to ourselves through the stories we tell. The stories are not meant to send us abstract messages and lessons, although that is what they may do. But those messages are only understood when we name our own situation in terms of those stories.[16]

When students ask, How am I to follow the story of Moses? the proper reply is that you will follow it whether you wish to or not. The crucial task is to make that following your own. It could be a mechanical and formulaic appropriation, and some of the time that is right and enough. But some of the time you must learn to follow a story in a way that it demands for you and your situation. Now, if you know the tradition's stories already, you have the advantage of understanding the world roughly but at least provisionally in those stories' terms. Here authentic action is a repetition of the tradition, in your own way: *initiative is imitative.* And the imitation of Augustine or Moses or Oedipus truly "throws" us into the world authentically.

To take on a story authentically is to focus that story's meaning on what we are doing. If anxiety is an absence of focus, a lostness in the world, then to authentically take on a story, to appropriate it as your own for your situation, is to bind that anxiety and endow it with a particular meaning. Such binding is the possibility of becoming something that has its own integrity.[17]

Binding and Leading

Not everyone believes that where they are is Egypt, that there is a promised land, and that "the way to the land is through the wilderness," or that to get from here to there we must join together and march.[18] Some believe they are already in the reasonably comfortable City. Others find it hard to conceive of a promised land at all. Others are not only not drawn to the wilderness, they are terrified of its powers. And others would not think of joining together; they find the prospect of marching in file demeaning. But entrepreneurs know that they are in Egypt and that there is a promised land. They are attracted to the wilderness despite well-warranted fears. And they learn to join together and march.[19]

In Egypt there is as yet no institution for you as an entrepreneur. To have a good idea, even a well-worked-out good idea, is a curiosity, surely to die of its own accord. How are you to institutionalize and so make necessary and conventional what is at best a vision or a calling or a promise, an unenforceable one at that? I take this as a problem of *commitment,* our being bound to each other and to an idea and its realization, when there is nothing much to show...yet. Moreover, in this way of thinking, the resistance and backsliding and sacrifice we shall encounter along the way must be given their fullest significance, rather than be dismissed as meaningless fluctuation or as bad fortune. Here is an entrepreneurship that demands a commitment that is sacred, and so resistance is forgivable; a commitment in which loss and struggle, to be taken as sacrifice, are necessary and educational; and in which mission is motivating and objective, so that the entrepreneur is an agent of a mission.

In the first chapter we emphasized the heroic dimension of entrepreneurship, the development of an institution or a product as the consequence of the entrepreneur's doings and undoings. Here we ask, how do people, including the entrepreneur and coworkers and customers, find themselves joining and participating in an endeavor? The entrepreneur may well be defining needs that are already present and providing a solution to those needs, being a midwife of necessity that is defined by larger forces, whether they be God or a market. Moses takes this role. Yet, if the people do not respond authentically, commitment does not occur and the enterprise is in trouble. Will trial, resistance, backsliding, and sacrifice create the situation that demands response and that allows for commitment?[20]

Coaches of team sports take it upon themselves to create an authentic team out of a ragtag group of characters who mistakenly believe they are a team already. Commitment may come from shared tribulation of training camp and shared moments of exhausting success. And it helps to win, and to win together, and to see that winning as a team accomplishment. Value is created in those moments. The coach's task is to show the members how to appreciate that moment of being together. They have to be able to understand the answer to Why are *we* here? Why have *we* been elected? Why *us* now?[21] These are matters of election, covenant, and struggle.

The entrepreneur's task is to set up a sacred boundary, one defined by detailed and ritualized observance of rules, rules the nascent people have come to understand through their own tribulation, in which violations are dreadful and more-or-less forgiven. Within such a boundary there now might be the more mundane and practical tasks of leadership.[22] No one can lead us to the Promised Land if we are not committed and bound to such a project. And to be so sacredly committed and bound allows for an entrepreneurial organization.

The Akedah and the B'rit: The Binding and the Covenant

The story of Abraham's sacrifice of Isaac and the story of Moses and the Israelites are so well known and so deeply embedded in our culture that I could not get away with an abstract summary like that used in chapter 1 for Augustine's life. We know these accounts in one interpretation or another as well as we know anything.

The story of Abraham and Isaac (Genesis 22) has come to be known within the Jewish tradition as the Akedah, the binding of Isaac: "Some time afterward, God put Abraham to the test.... Abraham took the wood for the burnt offering and put it on his son Isaac...They arrived at the place of which God had told him. Abraham built an altar there; he laid out the wood; he bound his son Isaac; he laid him on the altar, on top of the wood. And Abraham picked up the knife to slay his son."

That same story is also known as the sacrifice of Isaac, or in the Christian commentary by Kierkegaard in *Fear and Trembling* (1843), as the test of Abraham. In Judaism, the test is a proof, showing that the bound are righteous. Namely, God tries only the righteous.[23]

That binding is a literal binding before sacrifice. It is the sign of commitment, a commitment defined by sacrifice, a sacrifice that is a test. Binding, sacrifice, and test are sacred acts, given meaning by a larger and transcendent purpose, here a covenant (the B'rit) between God and Abraham, and then between God and a people. Binding, sacrifice, and test are acts that define a people. But they work only if that larger purpose is authentic and motivating and enduring. Otherwise there is only desacralized oppression, murder, and prudence (rather than binding, sacrifice, and test).

As contrasted to the episcopal problem of chapter 1, or the presbyterial problem of chapter 4, the binding of Isaac represents the congregational problem, the problem of how to create a sacred community in terms of the voluntary commitment of each of its members: a commitment to each other and to the community and to the sacred meaning that is taken to define that community—a problem of binding and bonding and bounding.[24] How shall we act together? As we shall see, this is the task of the Israelites in making the Sinai covenant among themselves: again, a task of binding, sacrifice, and test.

The Abraham story is sometimes presented as a choice between obedience to God and prudential or moral considerations. Now, if we are not bound, then obedience to God might seem like a problematic alternative to prudence and morality. But once we are so bound, and about this Augustine was deeply correct, then obedience becomes much less problematic. It is a demand we then come to expect ourselves to fulfill and sometimes to fail. But how are we to be bound, committed, entrepreneurial—so an institution, a people, or a firm arises out of what appears to be nothing? We must march together.

Resistance, Backsliding, Marching

Before we might be bound among ourselves, we have to begin marching out of Egypt. Then we might exhibit resistance and backsliding, and that is how we shall learn we are a people.

Only when we are "on the way" will there be an understanding among ourselves of our situation, of what is possible, of what we might hope for, one that allows for commitment.[25] Before that, the commitments we might make are abstract. They are more like a children's pact among themselves, not at all tested, their meaning more in the realm of fantasy than of hope and action. Still, even on the way, we are not yet very realistic, not at all sure what it is we are committing ourselves to; we do not know what those commitments will demand of us. Of course, were we to be sure or to know those demands, we might refrain from commitment, from marching at all. For there to be a binding we have to be sufficiently on the way so that we have some sense of what we are up to, but not know so much about the prospect that we are completely discouraged. Hence, any story of binding is a deliberate back-and-forth flow among resistance, backsliding, and marching forward; and binding takes place at some point in the middle. Abraham's test (the binding of Isaac), Moses' test (God trying to convince Moses to take on a prophetic life, and Moses' trials in the wilderness), and the Israelites' test (the Golden Calf) come at the right time, in the middle, so that commitment makes sense yet is not precluded by absolute horror and by the fear of prospective events.[26]

Still, how did the Israelites get into this mess, this awful situation from which they are forced to march and so become a people? As we have come to expect, human freedom and temptation does a good deal of the work. The Israelites are said to have been enslaved as a consequence of abandoning their more sacred task for wealth. The pharaoh offered them a chance to become richer, making more and more bricks, and that temptation eventually led to their not being paid for what they had originally volunteered to do for a wage. So the Israelites justify their enslavement to material idols, in the story they tell themselves of their history.

In general, people have good reasons for choosing a path and a way of life, one that later they might take to be oppressive and errant. That way may provide them with satisfactions, despite its manifest inadequacies and problems. Is not every way inadequate and problematic, to some extent? they might ask themselves. Egypt is not so bad, especially when the prospective alternatives are rather less known and more risky, and we might not be able to return to the life in Egypt were those alternatives to prove to be pipe dreams. A better idea is just that, an idea, not a potential reality. Or so they tell themselves.

Consider the children's story *Two Bad Ants:* Two ants on a night expedition with their compatriots to bring back goodies to their queen decide not to return to their nest. All the goodies are out here. Why go home when there is delicious sugar so readily to be had? "'Why go back?' one asked the other. 'This place may not feel like home, but look at all those crystals.'"[27] Eventually daytime comes, the ants are almost toasted, drowned, and eaten, and in the end they are exhausted. Perhaps there are lots of sugar crystals here, but home offers the redemptive act of feeding the queen, not to speak of its being home. These ants will never be Israelites.

What gets the Israelites to consider marching is no idea, no prophet, no insight. Rather, they are being toasted, drowned, and eaten. And there is no place they can go back to. In the end, they are driven out by external circumstances, literally acts of God. Whatever the resistance they sensibly feel about moving is overwhelmed by the horrors of their situation.[28] Eventually, pharaoh goes too far, even for the remarkably compliant Israelites. Violently, they are forced to move, in a ragtag mixture of vanguards, laggards, murmurers, disparate in their commitments.[29]

The temptations to backsliding, delay, and denial remain ever present. Just outside the Promised Land, the Israelite spies betray Moses' vision by badmouthing Canaan, telling frightening tales of the Land so as to discourage the Israelites from entering it. But then, of course, Moses also betrays his own vision in his rough treatment of the stone.

A group must be thrown out of its former, seemingly comfortable, perhaps oppressive and errant ways—if it is to march, if it is to create an organization that in its actions is eventually seen as entrepreneurial, so that it is on the way to a promise that for the moment is just that, a promise. Markets might disappear, perhaps slowly but still surely, so that even meager opportunities become barren of the breadcrumbs we are used to (what are often called fair returns on investment). Or we become bored, incapable of focusing on the successes we have achieved, the anxiety of boredom throwing us upon the world's possibilities. Or, in fact, we are actually unbearably oppressed, pharaoh having gone too far, being too blind and stiff-necked to ever become reasonable; he even ignores plagues that would suggest to the less stiff-necked that they are going too far.

Between oppression and actually moving, there will be feelings of anger, fear, and pride, feelings that are motivating so people actually do move, feelings that are binding so people do recognize themselves as a people through their shared experiences and the stories they tell themselves about those experiences. These feelings are seen to be meaningful, transcendently so; they are no mere complaints or transient emotions. In the context of an overarching story, the people are motivated by circumstances that affect them and that they choose to engage. It is a story they tell to themselves so they understand what they are doing in their moving and marching, and so they understand themselves as a people sharing and participating in a story.[30]

So, eventually, we decide we really are in Egypt. Egypt is a place of the soul, not of the intellectual and rationalizing mind. Our hearts are borne down upon and they are heavy. And so we might become disheartened. Yet we can discover that we might march, that we might march together, for we recognize in some others kindred souls who are also in Egypt. Moses and God, with help from pharaoh, did this work for the Israelites, so the Israelites might march together. Now, an entrepreneur might think she could do it for a group. But not much can happen unless God is on the entrepreneur's side and creates that external environment that oppresses yet in the end frees the soul, and that allows acts of mutual recognition and movement. How do the people come to feel oppressed and unsatisfied? An employment they once took as attractive, they now recognize as without recompense and as enslavement. Such a reversal almost surely requires that God be on our side, educating us to see ourselves as a people enslaved.

In effect, God is that autonomy of the world that leads us into our history and our salvation. For the Israelites or for the entrepreneur, there are apparently arbitrary external circumstances (discoveries, inventions, acts of God) that in their cumulation and articulation create awful situations that the Israelites or the entrepreneur may use to get themselves moving.

I will later discuss the nature of the promise, the presumed payoff or reward or redemption the Israelites are to receive, and the role of a mission in the Israelites' march. Here I want to emphasize that people march as a people as much for a temptation as for anything else, the temptation being the milk and honey that characterizes the Land, what eventually proves to be a fetishistic obsession. The concreteness of their oppression, of their seeming abandonment by God, is so palpable, so undeniable, that the people might be drawn to a transcendent but material prospect, that vision of milk and honey, rather than to a short-run practical solution in Egypt.[31] Many promises have been offered to these people, and they have learned to be rightly skeptical of them, conservative in their hopes, practical in their solutions. Perhaps the corporate product line is getting old, but it does return an almost decent profit. There is a tradition that cannot readily be ignored. We are not going to get rich quick, even with a struggle. But when profit and tradition have abandoned us, we might begin to listen and to hear and to march.

My theology here is neither redemptive nor prudential nor prophetic. People do not move because of ultimate meaning, or incentive, or promise. People move as group that might become a people because they are driven by unbearable external circumstances, as they understand them. And they are driven as a ragtag group, incoherently, unsurely, and resistantly. But they do move.[32]

Such a possibility of moving then allows for marching, backsliding, and resistance. There is now a direction that we might follow and from which we might deviate. Such marching, and backsliding and resistance, too, is just what continues to define a people: a moving that becomes a marching together. To be unbearably oppressed now might focus us on where we might go. Given such a focus or interpretation of our unbearable situation, then we might have a march rather than a rout. Such a march has its own dynamics. Marching in line encourages disciplined observance and thus commitment among would be stragglers, for someone is nearby to put stragglers back in their places. Doubters are dragged along, in part because they do not have the courage to go it alone. On the other hand, if there is marching there can be murmurers, a subgroup of the people who find among themselves that they do not share the movement's focus; for what is not-yet, what defines the mission, is, as far as the murmurers are concerned, an unachievable and impractical fantasy. And so they come to worship the more immediate idols, real gold rather than the milk and honey of a promised land. Finally, if there is marching there will be resistance, for the desert is harsh and its demands unreasonable. To ask for more, and then more again, as does the desert, seems ungrateful. Yet, of course, sacrifice is by its nature unreasonable. Moreover, the memories of Egypt become embellished with gold, so the hope for the Promised Land seems misplaced.

Once we have gotten a putative people to move and march, and so to backslide and resist, we might hope to get them to march directly forward. But the march in the desert is a peregrination; it does not move forward.[33] Only later might we say which direction could even be considered "forward," given the trials that cannot be avoided. In this sense, the march, as it is done, in detail, is fully necessary. There is no straightforward or efficient path.[34] That the details and the history are necessary, that to change a detail is to change the history, is our recurrent theme. We cannot be sure which of our actions are the efficient causes: whether in fact it is just the last thing we did that worked, or perhaps we need to do seven or eight things and they add up willy-nilly so as to be effective.[35] So not only do we not know what it would mean to march forward, we cannot say much about what in the end gets the march going.[36] This is revelation, a history we are given in which every detail matters.

Moreover, the march gets going in fits and starts. The detailed dynamics of binding do not derive from a central figure, even if that figure is the source of the idea and is a great motivator, as was Augustine. There is no master entrepreneur who leads a charge. Rather, binding takes place among the marchers and with the entrepreneurial idea. Binding is a covenant: a people is being created among themselves.[37]

Entrepreneurs show a people how it will see itself defined in terms of a promise or mission, the land of milk and honey. That process of definition of a people, that is, of a group coming to see itself defined as a people, is as significant as the mission itself. And the dynamics of binding, why we might act together, how we come to learn that mission, and our actual acting together are realized through the details of the mission, that wandering in the desert. So we work out the tasks of solidarity on the road to commitment: tasks of binding, sacrifice, and mission.

What makes binding possible? What makes commitment effective rather than merely formal and ritualistic? When does "going through the motions" actually do something?[38] We might get a hint of an answer to these questions by asking, Why might form and ritual not work at all? Form and ritual do not work when we are skeptical of their powers so that we do not believe in their efficacy, and we are prophylactically inclined: deliberately explaining away by rather more mechanical means any signs of the rituals' effectiveness, and suppressing and stigmatizing those of the people who believe otherwise or who remain unsure.[39]

It would seem that binding, sacrifice, mission, and ritual can work when they are seen to be moments within a larger story, a story we come to take as fully meaningful and transcendent, as a sacred story. It is a story we tell to ourselves, and the story is taken as the meaning of what we are up to. Form and ritual then will possess the power to transform us, so that when we listen we hear a call that not only motivates us but is also authentic. So we are encouraged, heartened, driven. Binding is not a sequence of isolated events; it is a ritual process within which those events take place.

Stigma and Scapegoat

In that story we tell ourselves, binding is possible, commitment takes place, and ritual works, as an immediate consequence of particular marked sacrificial moments, in time and in history. Historical though they be, such moments are outside of time, ecstatic, grace-filled, and providential.[40] Within a people's story these moments not only make historical sense; they are also taken to be the epitome of that story. They may be moments of decision and choice, as in Augustine's conversion story. But even more likely they are moments of stigma and sacrifice and covenant. The task of solidarity is to create a sequence of such moments within a story that binds a people, a story they tell among themselves of the proofs of their worthiness and of the electedness of their mission, a story that in fact makes them worthy and elected.

Yet on the way to becoming a people they have been wayward and divisive and skeptical, perhaps even reasonably so. The people's sensible and prudent acts are in retrospect seen as mistaken, prideful, and sinful. So binding requires a way of sacrificially purging ourselves of pride, collectively rather than individually: the sacrifice of the three thousand, each a "brother" of a Levi. Also, a scapegoat figure is needed to absorb transgressions and so permit fulfillment of the promise. The Israelites stay with Moses, they are led by him, insofar as he is that scapegoat figure. Through Moses the Israelites become the people with the destiny they eventually come to possess.

Moses can see but not enter the Promised Land. His transgressions are exemplary and archetypal of his people, whether they be resistance to prophecy or a lack of faith as in striking the stone. Moses' achievements will be overcome; by his sins they must be. The Israelites will enter the Promised Land, to then err and fail in their own ways, ways Moses could not stop before and cannot stop later.

Why are entrepreneurs often left behind? Why must they be left behind? The pathetic figure who once was a great and creative destroyer is now out of touch, abandoned by history and her flock. If she insists upon continuing to be the entrepreneur within her organization, there is at some point something unseemly in her unwillingness to transcend her original role. So if and when she is actually physically feeble, she is made to pay the price for her pride. She is not Lear, but she is made to suffer as Lear does. The entrepreneur is humiliated in her frailty, rather than honored and protected. And so the next generation of entrepreneurs learn their lessons.

The entrepreneur must be left behind, it would seem, for only then can the entrepreneurial endeavor have a life of its own. This might be phrased in managerial terms, as the transition between entrepreneurial and corporate management. But management is not the issue. The transition would have taken place much earlier than it does, if the problem were only one of management. Rather, the entrepreneur must be left behind to absorb the cost of sacrifices that are creative destruction in actuality. Like Moses, the entrepreneur must be a scapegoat.[41]

The entrepreneur is consumed by her achievements. But as a consequence there is a people, an organization, that has a commitment and a life of its own, its members bound to each other and to a mission. No one would choose to be a scapegoat, and perhaps with scrupulous care one could avoid such a role. But then that careful person would come to be seen as a marginal figure rather than a liminal one. What makes Moses—and Jesus, later—so poignant is that he cannot avoid becoming a scapegoat. He knows what will happen to him; he does not choose it, but he comes to understand that this is his role.

The entrepreneur is a pathetic figure just because as an entrepreneur she shall be a creative destroyer, but in so doing she is also destroyed, by forces exactly like herself. Insofar as the entrepreneur wants to avoid an inconvenient mortality, she is to be disappointed, sorely and decisively—think of Moses toward the end of his life, still wanting to enter the Promised Land. And, rather than simply being punished for her errancy, she is a scapegoat. She absorbs the errors of her enterprise so it can go on less pridefully, now rather more conventionally or even corporately. Along the way, as a scapegoat, the entrepreneur makes possible commitment and binding to her mission.

Scapegoating allows for the detailed acts of binding so there can be solidarity. Namely, binding takes place through violations of the rules, which violations are then seen as signs of a greater mission. But those violations must be redeemed so that the bond is a sacred commitment, a commitment that is not to be destroyed from within by its profane history (its being founded in violation, as such). Every revolution has to deal with the violence it employs, which then must somehow be stigmatized and made unacceptable.[42] It is now a past that need not be relived. The scapegoat absorbs and encapsulates that violent and disruptive history, in effect redeeming it.[43]

Sacred Acts of Judgment

We are taught to act together by struggles and sacrifices we could not survive alone and do not survive except as a people. The wilderness is the great teacher for the Israelites, "the school of the soul."[44] There they learn that the covenant is offered to them as a people, not individually. One by one in their acts of commitment, they make a covenant among themselves and God. Yet it is as an elected people that they covenant and march. No entrepreneurial project will work without that acting together as a people, just because in being entrepreneurial it demands more than can be expected incrementally from adding on a few more souls.[45] And as a people, we learn to recognize a project as valuable and meaningful through sacred acts of judgment: acts of compassion, covenant, sacrifice, and mission.

Compassion

Why must we wander in the desert on the way to the Promised Land, with all the peregrinations and missteps, rather than following the stars or employing dead reckoning? Because we are to be educated: to compassion, to covenant, to sacrifice, and to mission. We learn compassion so that we might learn to live by the law, as a people, so there might be solidarity among us. So we might be those Israelites, who made living by the law the creative art called Talmud.[46]

The world is small and we must be generous toward each other. It is not that resources are limited and we shall be inundated by our garbage, as proclaimed by some ecologists. Rather, it is wild out there, especially on the heath and in the desert, outside the limits of the city.[47] We need each other. If we are mean, we find that that meanness might come back to haunt us. That haunting return is not a matter of retribution that is rationally controlled by accounting and fairness; rather, it is almost arbitrary in its implications, and not all of them are destructive.

Moreover, we must be generous because there is room enough to live together, and so we are judged by how we make our space within that room. That the world is small means we need each other, but it is not so small that that need is unavoidable and determines our responses to it. We can miss our calling or deafen our ears.

Compassion is feeling another's suffering as if it were your own, and acting on that feeling to aid the sufferer.[48] How are we to be compassionate, and even more, how are we to be generous? Compassion may require that we not be analytical, that we not join issues, that we not bargain or negotiate. Issues may not demand a resolution now, decisions might be deferred, two opposed values may not be a resolvable conflict. Acts of analysis disrupt just that tacit social order, solidarity.[49] So we figure out what to do without the disruptive presence of a trail of analytical stigma. We are respectful of the spaces a people has provided among its ongoing activities and beliefs, spaces that allow for community and commitment. We find new spaces, in homilies that allow the conventional stories to persist even if they are less attractive than a new story, a story that may eventually take over. Eventually. And unprepossessingly.

Not only do we not join issues, we temporize. We keep talking, we wait, we backslide. The longer we wait, the longer we wander in the desert and the wilderness, the more likely there will be a way out. We might perish in the desert. So we must have confidence in history's providence, that eventually things will change in just enough ways so that what to do next is clear. There will be an opening for action.

Temporizing allows us to be further engaged and educated, those modes of engagement almost always contributing to the final resolution. But we do not know how they are to contribute, and they may even prove destructive. We need a way of waiting around that keeps us in shape, and so capable of hearing a call at the right moment. So we wander in the desert under providential guidance.

What seems impossible, in time becomes workable. We know this from retrospective historical accountings. In time, in the accumulation of events and in growth and development, there are new combinations, new formulations of our task. What was once monstrous and awful is now just what we need to do next. All the while the people do suffer, plaintively wanting answers and resolutions, as they are warranted to want. Again, what proves striking, but remains unsatisfying as a prospect, is the productivity of history, the answers we would not have conceived of, the resolutions that abandon the constraints and taboos we once took as rigid and necessary. There needs to be a godly providence and a sacred mission to bind our anxiety.

A recurrent theme in diplomacy and politics is that timing is everything, joining of issues is a strategic move, and so one is constantly looking for an opening. It is worthwhile to buy time. One must also know when to close a deal, concede what was once thought to be vital, make the little gesture or grand move that saves face, the move that bespeaks authority through humility. These are gift relationships, in which there is never a complete balancing. There is always residual debt and gratitude. And so we go on together.[50]

To have compassion is to leave as much as you can on the table, just because it is yours, and surely not to take the last crumb from the table, again just because it is yours. Eventually we all are needy, and to gather your marbles and leave the game puts you out of the realm of mutual consideration and care.

Compassion requires our appreciation of the incommensurability of the various realms of others. For you to take my last crumb to complete your banquet is to mistake your desire for a need, to have no sense of your place in the world. That crumb may be all that I can offer, and it is to be taken as an ultimate gift. And not just symbolically. In fact, it is an ultimate gift.

Righteousness

We act by in-effect violating the conventional rules—bending them, going around them, finding ways to take hold of those rules that pay attention to their intentions but in new ways, ways we had not conceived before. Such casuistry attends to the specifics of each situation and so makes it possible for us to find avenues for action.

In a bureaucracy, the regulations and the hierarchy set the stage for action. Those who work in bureaucracies possess a very fine sense of how to play on that stage so that the work gets done. Any structure that survives always has a back stage on which the hard problems are played out, and a front stage on which easy problems are solved and upon which those persons who stray too far are publicly chastised. The Israelites went through the desert to discover the structure of that stage they had been assigned, to discover how the rules were meant for them, both front stage and back stage. How was the Torah to be theirs?

Rules are instruments for joining an issue when we want to do so, for legitimately temporizing, and for allowing gracious resolutions. Those who insist on being righteous in the sense of literally following the rules (rather than strictly following them) are given minor tasks. They will not get the important work done when it has to be done. The truly righteous follow the rules religiously, with compassion and grace and invention and providential wisdom. So the discipline provided by the rules allows for our autonomy. Within the discipline one may achieve glory or ignominy. Investing yourself in a role, you then may transform it. So Augustine and Moses discover.

Still, how do we deal with the conniving, the corrupt, the niggling, and the rigid: namely, the bullies? Compassion's advantage in these situations is that it cannot engage in the bully's game. Surely we are wary and careful and even afraid. But when we are presented with the bully's imposing presence, we temporize, refuse the conflict by presenting another stage for action, and offer the bully means of saving face.

Courage, guile, and humor are appropriate responses to the bully (here proverbially male). Courage outlasts him, yet defeating him is unlikely, for he defeats himself. Through our guile we feed him what he wants, or what he thinks he wants, yet we can reserve what is valuable to ourselves. Humor is perhaps the only way of dealing with his presumption. Of course, we do our best organizing against the bully and trying to defeat him. But we do not want to let him set the stage for action, for that stage is mean and not very roomy. We can be triumphant without humiliating those who lose, so they may join us in our efforts, perhaps not at first, but in time they may.

Covenant

I have been describing how binding and commitment become possible, how the scapegoat figure allows for the election of a people whose history is filled with errancy yet is redeemed. There is, eventually, a time when the trials and wanderings that are their education teach them how they might be a people. So the entrepreneur might leave a legacy of an ongoing institution, the entrepreneurial endeavor having a life of its own, one not determined by its mistakes and errors. But just how are we actually to bind ourselves? The Israelites, when they have been made ready, make a covenant among themselves and with God. That sacred act in history defines one mode of binding.

At Sinai the Israelites make a covenant, accepting the law and their mission as they understand it then.[51] In this axial moment in their history, they become committed, absolutely and sacredly, to an enterprise, and so they are bound. The covenant redefines the Hebrews as Israelites and Moses as their prophet. They are a people. What was once a notional idea now becomes a commitment: what might have happened otherwise, now must happen *this* way. The covenant is revelation, the Torah. What was once a practical and technical and rhetorically powerful plan is now something they live by.

It would seem that the Israelites become a people through a document. Moreover, while the document is public and practical and monitory, its ultimate meaning is hidden from them, to be revealed in history and in the coming of time. The document provides material evidence of a particular commitment; it is a relic that allows for prayerful respect. That document becomes known as a sacred document in the story the people tell of themselves. In actual entrepreneurial endeavors, often it is written on the napkin of the restaurant (or the packing of the take-out food) in what we in retrospect see as the convocation place of our endeavor.

When we make a commitment, we know that we are doing a significant historical act. People sense it and say it. But it is in retrospect, in the telling of the story, that the event becomes not only a marked moment in time but a sacred moment (rather than, for example, a misprision of history). Only in that biblical coming of time do we understand the sacredness of the act, the significance of the covenantal document. It is a sacred relic or fetish, not a piece of parchment or a paper napkin.

Covenants are not contracts. Covenants are not partial, they cannot be bought off piecemeal, there is no compensation for their violation. They are not analytic devices or legal instruments. Even if they are freely entered into by their participants, they are not deals or arrangements among free individuals, mediated by law and economy. Rather, covenants are among committed individuals and are mediated by God. Covenants are sacred acts and documents. That sacredness allows commitment and binding that encourages the transcendent action demanded of entrepreneurial endeavors.[52]

Covenants are subject to defilement and pollution because they are sacred.[53] There must be vigilant concern for the breaking of such commitment.[54] Impurity and mixture desecrate a people and so weaken and destroy it. Heresy is not mere annoyance; it attacks the possibility of the historical fulfillment of the promise made in that covenant. No wonder that otherwise lithe and wily entrepreneurs will become brittle and intolerant given the prospect of pollution and heresy. Pollution must be cleansed, heresy must be rooted out. Compromise leads to disaster.

Yet compassion demands that we avoid pejorative and absolute designations such as pollution and heresy, so that we have diplomatic room enough to do what we must do to be effective and successful. An abstract rule or law cannot be allowed to justify a lack of compassionate inventiveness. So the covenant must be read both casuistically and sacredly, deliberately avoiding literalism and opportunism.

Once we might achieve a covenant, we realize how fragile is that achievement. Pride, thinking we are God (clearly a God more effective than the Hebrew Bible's), might allow us to believe we could root out heresy when in fact heresy is ineradicable, as one senses at moments in the first half of Augustine's career as bishop. And particular heresies prove eventually to be a saving resource, as for Augustine's church in later centuries. Practically, of course, effective prophylaxis of heretics by authority might destroy the covenant by decimating its membership, like the terrifying legacy of Gnosticism. In any case, the covenant has its own integrity. The crucial problem is the abandonment of God by the people. For the entrepreneur to take on God's work is to abandon his own, which is to actually live within the covenant. And compassion is needed still, as Augustine or Moses have to learn again and again.

Say that we were to make a covenant, a sacred commitment among ourselves and the entrepreneurial idea. The sacredness of that commitment allows the authority expressed in that covenant to inform our action, and so we are to be under the providence of the entrepreneurial idea.

Entrepreneurial endeavors are characterized by the unsettledness of authority, the uncertainty of what is true and of the source of that truth. (Otherwise, we would have altogether more conventional endeavors, where we know ahead of time or might rationally and prudently speculate about which path will thrive and how we ought to organize the enterprise.) Now, the entrepreneur might think she is in charge; at least, she is on to something. But experience will tell her that something more is going on. She is in the grip of an idea, a people, and a market, which have their own autonomy and authority. How are we to understand this fluidity of authority within entrepreneurship?

Of course, authority is located in God. But what could we mean by such a statement in this context? If we focus on the authority located in the entrepreneurial idea itself, we understand both the fluidity of its appearance among us and its definiteness as we apprehend it, namely, our experience of creativity.

The authority resident in the entrepreneurial idea, or in God, does not fully authorize any person. No one, prophet or not, can claim to be fully in touch with that idea or with God.[55] Authority does become present in our covenantal or sacred commitment. But how that authority is present, in detail, is not at all settled when we make the covenant. Rather, we are then free to pursue the idea, to enter seriously into the entrepreneurial endeavor. Under the covenant we are within a space in which our action can be focused and make sense, compassion is possible, and we might be effective rather than lost. We are on to a meaningful project.

To summarize: The sacred commitment provided by a covenant, by a commitment to ourselves and to God through a document, allows the authority expressed in it to inform our endeavors and endow them with meaning. Yet the commitment provided by a covenant is not merely our coming under a sacred provision. There is enormous and it would seem necessary collective sacrifice as we become a people. Such struggle and suffering are perhaps an artifact of our taking on difficult tasks. But struggle and suffering are justified only when they are seen as sacrifice, part of our education, and such justification is never very comforting.

The actual world is rather imperfect, and in imperfection lies hope and possibility. The promise of a covenant, of an entrepreneurial idea, lies as much in that mundane promised land and in those errant if elected people as in anything transcendent and godly. Our task is to attend to the sacred and the profane.

The value of these sacred notions, such as covenant and sacrifice, lies in their capacity to name the world so that we may pay attention to what we sense is practically important. In naming the world we are transformed, largely because we have taken what was implicit and inchoate and diminished, and made it something we might consider, employ, and make even more real for ourselves. The test of these ways of thinking about what we are up to lies in their capacity to deliver the world back to us in such a way that we are more effective, more aware of openings for action and invention.

Sacrifice

Binding makes it possible for there to be a people; a people's mission is their conception of how they shall be remembered; and sacrifice is the path from binding to mission. While sacrifice is needed for binding, what is most curious is that, once there is binding, sacrifice not only continues but perhaps intensifies. Why, when we are now a people under a covenant, must there be further sacrifice and suffering? Why must the Israelites continue to wander in the desert and be in the wilderness, and for so long? Why, once we are organized and have a plan, must there be so much errancy and loss?[56]

Entrepreneurs learn, as does Moses, that there is good reason why we go through the desert. The wilderness is the "school of the soul."[57] From sacrifice and suffering we learn to be who we are. From such experience comes memory and an indentifying story to be told about what we went through, as well as lessons to be drawn about humility before God and about the necessity for community. We are not in control of the entrepreneurial idea, and to be effective we shall have to march together.[58] These are lessons that it seems cannot be learned in any other way.[59]

Entrepreneurs are neither rational nor secular. They understand that suffering is meaningful, that the desert and the wilderness is meant for them, no matter how much they despise it. Those meanings are to be revealed in the actual detailed wanderings their endeavors must follow. In that particular history they and their projects are worked out. Of course, entrepreneurs have to be wily and prudent, but they know that none of that will in the end prevent sacrifice or ensure success. Their actions, as efficient as they may be, lead to the sacrifices that might make their endeavors fruitful.

Moreover, entrepreneurs know that the desert and the wilderness are not the city, with its progress and its scientific management. In the desert, the city's rules and powers might well be upturned and reversed, and there are no superordinate rules that tell when that "might" applies. So conventional financial or market analyses might be deliberately ignored or inverted, indications of potential failure might be taken as nascent opportunities. Through the entrepreneurial idea or the covenant one accepts an outlandish regime, as did the Israelites accept the Mosaic law. To others, this is a dramatic move, an act of faith. But to the entrepreneur, who is paying attention to details others deliberately ignore or do not even know they are missing, there is good reason to read the rules differently, to value the world anew. In this sense the entrepreneur is rational and secular.

Entrepreneurs appreciate that the wanderings in the desert are surely wanderings (a peregrination that it would be nice to avoid were it possible, which it is not). The wanderings are never rationalized as merely a straightforward path over what just happens to be a very peculiar terrain. Yet the wanderings reveal a coherent story, one that would fall apart if entrepreneurs were to edit out the bad parts. Entrepreneurs want to get to the goodies as efficiently as they can; they are not martyrs. But they are as well not so perfectibilist that they believe they can avoid errancy and the consequences of that errancy, namely, their education. What they and their cohort learn in that education is how to be a people with a mission, bound to each other. In that learning they do their work.[60]

To be in the desert means that we shall lose our way. Even if there are signposts, we are quite sure they could be read in more than one way. This is the eschatological interpretation of the apocalyptic, to use a phrase from chapter 1. Namely, we are on the way, but that way and its meaning are revealed as we go along. In this world, revelation is not so obvious we might not mistake it for error, nor is it so distant we ought give up hope. To be in the desert means that we shall be tested. We shall be visited by those "inconveniences" Augustine talks about. How else are we to know we are in the desert but by its problematic hospitality? Those inconveniences shall demand that we deviate from our covenant.

Cities are the places of justice and order; wilderness is sublime only to the city dweller, and only as an idea at that. To be in the desert is fearful. The struggle and suffering is almost unnameable. To be in the wilderness is to encounter surprises you cannot classify or justify. There is awe and terror here. Struggles are against what is essentially unknown; suffering appears arbitrary and meaningless.

Moreover, whatever the education to be provided by loss, trial, and suffering, to be in the desert is also to live with violence. There is awful killing for infractions or waywardness.[61] This is an unforgiving world, its discipline too stringent to seem anything but arbitrary.

Yet to be in the desert is to be subject to sacrifice, just what is meaningful and redemptive. Loss, trial, suffering, and violence are in the end not arbitrary. The terrors and horrors become part of a story; anxiety is fully significant. There is revelation and redemption. Such a story justifies these horrors as being "along the way," necessary for *this* story. But the story does not claim that there need be compensation for the horrors. Rather, they are part of a whole that may well terrify us. In fact, it ought to. To be in the desert, to be an entrepreneur, is dreadful. There is nothing prudential about it. Rather, being in the desert is what we are drawn to. That being overturns history, and itself is overturned in time.

Why do we wander, why do we suffer? That is just the way we become who we shall become. Through the memory or the story of that wandering and suffering we recognize ourselves and so we stay committed and know who we are. It is through the celebration of sacrifice (reading the Torah, the Eucharist) that the history that defines us continues to define us.

Errancy and sacrifice are part of our education. To be humiliated before God is not sadism, but rather the way we understand the precise meaning of our commitments. Pride may well go before the Fall, but then in the Fall we have the chance to become willful and purposeful. And so we might fulfill these commitments rather more devotedly. To err, to make interestingly big mistakes, will allow for our virtue and forbearance, likely again to serve us well.

To be trained for a mission requires that we be educated in adversity that in the end must be meaningful, not just cruel. The trials in the education of a physician or a scientist might seem sadistic, but if they are seen as part of a ritual of commitment that leads to the humility that creates courage, then we might justify them. Of course, and this is crucial, we have to believe that that commitment is an authentically sacred one. If we are within a people, we come to that belief in part through the trials we are put through, and in part through a rather more public judgment of the meaning and value of the entrepreneurial endeavor, whether in prayer, in professional service, or in the marketplace.

In our telling stories, the meaning of what we are up to and our judgment of its value are subject to argument and conviction among a people. Stories are told and have a life only within a people. Stories are judgments that are articulated in their being told and retold. Whatever characteristics mark us as a people are to be learned historically and biographically, and in that learning we are transformed, each of us, to be of that people. So, for example, there is no efficient way of teaching a people humility, to educate an entrepreneurial endeavor to its limits and opportunities. Rather, it must be humiliated and then subsequently relive that humiliation, and in so reliving it a people is educated to the demands of a mission. Because the humiliation is collective, whether in front of our compatriots or in front of God, it is not simply cruelty or being bullied. We are to be educated to be a people in God's eyes. We are to be educated to be an endeavor in light of the entrepreneurial idea.

Sacrifice is to be understood collectively, a sacrifice for a people, understood by that people as an act that enables them to become a people. Sacrifice is not an arbitrary untoward happening. Violence and education make sense only within a collectivity. Otherwise, they might well be murderous killing and solitary fantasy.

Practically, sacrifice actually does specific work for the people. Think of a sacrifice fly in baseball, which is both a sign of team commitment and a help toward winning a game. Symbolically, the sacrifice is a sign of the people's ultimate election, in effect absorbing the disruptive and profane forces that would otherwise destroy the people. The internal dissent (say, about God or the entrepreneurial idea), the differential losses among the people when some idea is chosen and another is abandoned, the differences between those who prove themselves in the tests and those who backslide, the struggles only some must endure (and some endure better than others)—all these divisive facts are to be healed by sacrifice that provides for a decisive moment of community.[62]

The entrepreneur cannot prevent sacrifice or even control it. Sacrifice must happen if there is to be a people, and when it does happen it is a product of that people's historic actions, actions through which they become a people.[63] Sacrifice is actual, practical, and communal, not abstract or intellectual or individualistic. The stories of sacrifice are real and terrifying and incomprehensible. Of course, to be so judged and sacrificed is the very greatest of grace-filled honors. We are being taken seriously indeed. Here education is a life-and-death matter. To recognize such a necessity, such a powerful claim that collective life might rightly demand from us, is to recognize that the desert and the wilderness, as we find ourselves experiencing them, are the way to the promise and the mission. So we are freed from fantasy and allowed to work on the serious problems that make us a people.

When I reread what I have written here, I find it frightening. To a liberal mind, violence and sacrifice are extraordinarily problematic notions, especially when justified as collective. But the Mosaic/Israelitic story is frightening. And so is entrepreneurship.

While the Israelites' story as they present it has a triumphalist quality in the Torah, it is somewhat more problematic in the Prophets and the Apocrypha. We latterly know that the rest of their history has been not at all straightforward. There is a long history of doubt, of messianic fervor,[64] of abandonment. Some may well feel they have been bound into errancy, sacrificed only to be murdered, having a mission that makes their existence even more fragile than it was under pharaoh.

Entrepreneurial endeavors may ruin, mislead, disappoint, and destroy. There can be false prophecy, redemption that is dreadful and ugly, broken covenants, mistaken elections, and abject humiliations. Not only do things not work out, but they form a coherent story that tells us we were meant to become victims: wandering forever, suffering that is awfully meaningful, responding to deceitful promises.[65] Modestly, we expect milk and honey, and we receive at best a rocky road, at worst despair and hellishness. To have once been resistant to sacred entreaties or to the appeal of an entrepreneurial idea might well have been prudent, or so it now appears. Maybe we shall never be a triumph.

Among the Israelites there have always been those who have so felt their heritage and legacy. And among entrepreneurs and their committed followers there has been at times the sense that they had gone too far, asked for too much, and were surely pipe dreaming. At best, this is a tragic story rather than farce, victimage being a well-attested role. But to be the victim or the sacrifice would seem to apply to others, not to ourselves. *They* are creatively destroyed, *we* merely stumble and get up. But our humiliation may be rather more complete. That only makes sense if we have a mission.

Mission

If all we wanted were milk and honey, namely commodities, we might not have to march. Recall the two bad ants; those crystals might be imported. Foreign trade would do nicely to provide for our needs, as Adam Smith advises. So we might be bought off, the necessity to march no longer empowering. But if we want a *land* of milk and honey, a promised and so blessed land, an ideal of redemption, then we do have to march. We are engaged in a mission.[66]

To have a mission is to take ownership of what is already there for the taking. Whatever the mission (say, the Torah), it has been offered before to others, and earlier to us. But that mission has yet to be adopted authentically, remaining available long after it first became needed, long after it was first known.

For Abraham, binding and sacrifice literally set the occasion for mission. For Moses, and then for the Israelites, the story is much the same. But we have to be ready, we have to have been made ready, to be able to acknowledge a mission. Only when we are ready to act in response to a particular occasion or a call might we be able to take ownership of a mission. What is remarkable, and perhaps only God can speak about this with the requisite empirical evidence, is how resistant people are to taking on a mission, to accepting an election, even if that mission and election seem to be just what they are asking for.

The trials of the Israelites may be seen as ways of softening them up, so that when they are offered a mission they are ready to act in response rather than in blindness and resistance. Even softened up, many of the Israelites want to abandon the mission when their hopes are presumably denied, when the going gets rough. To live out an election is no mean task, and it is perhaps no wonder that they might lose heart. That is why a people is elected in that sacred way through test and covenant and sacrifice, so that their binding is rather more than resilient, it is transcendent.

An entrepreneur alone, or Moses alone, is a pitiful picture without a people who in their diversity and complexity take on a mission and make it realizable. Why are *we* here? is the question that must be asked, if what happens is to be transformed into a mission that engages a people. Then events become meaningful, desires are motivated, and capacities are actual. To have a mission is to come alive. But as we can see in the Hebrew Bible, and in the characters of folk tales or of television mission programs,[67] the people have a tendency to goof off, to prefer the easy if uninteresting life, to want to throw in the towel. They must be called again and again, and be called together; in acting together they are transformed.

For a television serial to work, we need to know that the characters will get together as a team every week. And to get them together every week is a challenge, for they do not team up so readily. They need to be recruited, called, prepared (say, by an exciting vacation with a lover, a vacation that is infinitely more barren than is their life with their teammates). They are called, but then they need to be reminded who they are, why they are here, and what they owe to each other. They are agents of a mission that is given to them by a deus ex machina or a God who understands sin only too well.

While the entrepreneur is often presented as a protagonist who moves the world, to the entrepreneur the world is the source of movement. The world calls the entrepreneur to a mission. Whatever autonomy and direction the entrepreneur may exhibit, she has the uncanny sense that she is an agent of a larger task, her action being an enactment of a demanding role for which she has been put on stage. The Israelites, and subsequently the Jewish people, are sometimes presented as an arrogant and triumphalist people.[68] But, of course, they have been elected to a role, a role they keep abandoning only to have it thrown back onto them. The Israelites are humiliated into accepting just the mission they keep resisting. My point here is not to plead for the entrepreneur or the Israelites, but rather to describe the actual dynamics and phenomenology of how we are educated to a commitment.

Missions are stories a people tell themselves, composed stories, with beginnings, middles, and ends: leaving Egypt, wandering, the Promised Land. To be an entrepreneur is not a mission; to be an entrepreneurial endeavor, a specific one, is such a mission. (Moses is Moses for the Israelites, while he is a very different, rather more ordinary figure when he is among the Midians.) Missions are specific projects, matters of detail and mistake. Entrepreneurs might have all the faith in the world in themselves, but without a specific project to which others might be committed, the entrepreneur is not a serious figure. He must be acting in response to a call or an entrepreneurial idea.

For the Jewish people to see themselves as the fruition of a redemptive story they keep retelling to themselves is for them to acknowledge that they have been missionized. Their lives are set within a story they have been given. To be an entrepreneur is in this sense a humiliation of pride, for our freedom is now understood in terms of purposes we do not command; our endeavor and our selves are part of a story that we have been given already, even if its detailed outcome awaits our action. That such a story repeats itself typologically and prefigures its outcome does not say just how it works out, and it is in the how that we actually live. So while entrepreneurs might not be enslaved to a corporate structure, their freedom is rather more terrifying in its monitory demands. God is no ordinary boss.

By their nature, missions demand discipline and courage, for they demand sacrifice rather than prudential consideration and action. Courage is that binding ourselves for sacrifice. Then we might well act, and if we are as fortunate as are Isaac and Abraham, a ram might be killed rather than ourselves, but not always. Missions also demand focused attention and action, and discipline is that justified but drastic limiting of our field of attention that then allows for a paramount consideration that is the mission.

Covenant, sacrifice, and mission are sacred ways of describing a people, naming a way of life that is sometimes tragic, sometimes heroic, almost never fair. So a mission draws us out of routine and everydayness, marking what we do as transcendent, taking some ordinary plot, one we have seen many times before, and endowing it with the uniqueness of redemptive revelation: a story by which we shall come to understand ourselves, through its specificity and intendedness for us.[69]

Such tragic and heroic contingency is scary and exciting. Yet, to be an agent of a mission, to be educated to commitment and mission through a struggle so that we learn that we cannot do it alone and must be a member of a team or a people, to view struggle and sacrifice in the collective and redemptive terms defined by a covenant, to take on an election—to be an agent of a mission endows fear and excitement with focus and meaning. Justification lies in the story and the struggle, and not in any payoff or outcome.

I do not mean to celebrate the tragic and heroic and horrifying vision I have been sketching. Killing and sacrifice are no fun for those who are killed, or even for those who are spectators, whatever the catharsis. A liberal and prudential point of view might be more gentle and fair.[70] I am less sure such an account, liberal and rational, will capture the experience of the entrepreneur in a way that would be recognizable and morally cogent.

Story and History

The covenantal moment when a people is created is a verbal birth. It is a moment of grace and election mediated by a founding document, a document that is received as a divine Providence. Such a founding is often taken as paternal: God the father, Moses, the Founding Fathers of the U.S. Constitution. (I mention this as preparation for chapter 3, where the founding is maternal.) The founding demands leadership of high order. An agenda has to be set, people must be gathered, and they need to be moved, actually and emotionally. They must pass a series of seemingly arbitrary tests to prove their worthiness to fulfill their transcendent purpose and to educate them to their redeemed status. So there is struggle and mission, as well as Providence and strategy.[71] Founding is historical, enacted by a particular people in their lives. And it is only a beginning. The actual problems and tasks of entrepreneurial endeavor remain.

The stories of founding are presented as historical narratives, repeated and retold and elaborated upon. The tests and struggles and setbacks are not something that may be avoided, at least if there is to be a story that justifies the triumphs and the failures of a people. The tests are crucial to the founding's effectiveness as an account and a source of further commitment.

Commitment derives from those borderline or liminal moments we share, when all was presumably lost and we needed each other to get through (or, for that matter, from those shared but often fleeting ecstatic moments of triumph).

Historical founding and story are not separated here. The founding story of Moses and the Israelites is itself an act in history. Other than Abraham's binding of Isaac, the story is the exemplary act of revelation, the giving of the Torah on Mount Sinai.[72] Accounts of entrepreneurial endeavors are both history and story: how it all happened, and how we shall understand ourselves as an ongoing endeavor through our retelling that account.

We are committed to each other because we have chosen to be so committed, to be such a people, to acknowledge who we are. Yet our choice is seen as providential. We are committed to each other and to our collective selves through that covenantal document (Torah, Constitution), whose original is the sign of the moment of founding, and whose continual reinterpretation (Talmud, law) is the means of that commitment. The Mosaic story is historical in what it tells and in how it was received by the Israelites. Commitment comes from a ritual return to the moments of history and the moment of the story's reception.

Commitment is of two sorts. The first is the process through which we come to see ourselves as a people. The second is the everyday work we do if we are so committed. Of course, they can be identical, the everyday acts of commitment being ritual reenactments of the founding moment. But I think it is helpful to keep in mind that founding and infancy eventually are settled, and we do act differently, when those moments of founding are memorialized rather than relived.

3

Devotion
Mothers and Their Children

Bringing Up Baby. The Entrepreneurial Role. What Mothers Know. To the Nursery. Another Visit to the Nursery. Development and Tragedy. Integrity and Sacrifice. Letting Baby Cry. Autonomy and Mission.

Bringing Up Baby

Entrepreneurial endeavors may become ongoing institutions with sustaining markets. They take off on their own and they are inventively responsive to what the world actually desires. Such a process of maturation is exemplified by how an infant takes off from her mother and makes her place in the world. Here the very great tragedy is when an infant or an enterprise is lost rather than committed to the world or the market. If, in the last chapter, commitment was a binding of a people to itself and to an idea, here binding is that capacity to connect autonomously with those who are genuinely other than ourselves. How does an entrepreneurial endeavor grow from a dependent and precarious infancy to autonomy, from a rather limited relationship to markets to actually meeting the needs of a world, a world the endeavor will learn in its weaning to be not at all identical to its fantasies?[1]

As I indicated in the introduction, this chapter is exceptional in that the figures I discuss are everyday rather than heroic, and the texts that guide the inquiry are psychological rather than literary or religious. Moreover, the empathy and identification required here are in our culture more likely to be available to women. But in order to launch an enterprise, I suspect we have to be mothers.

Healthy babies are in business to start with.

> Now, of course, a provident nature has insured that almost any baby who is born with intact equipment will learn to walk and to talk, even if he has had the misfortune to get a mother who ranks low on the Zweibach Scale [of Maternal Warmth]. This is just about what Hartmann means when he speaks of the "autonomous functions of the ego" and the guarantees for adaptive-

> ness in "an average expectable environment." But if a baby is born with a deficit in his equipment [say, blind from birth] the "average expectable environment" has some built-in hazards. The minus on the side of "state of adaptiveness" will require plusses on the side of a mother who will have to substitute for the deficit and take over the role of facilitating adaptation where the intact equipment would have virtually guaranteed it.[2]

It seems that most entrepreneurial ideas are not quite so healthy, and they need and must elicit from the entrepreneur "plusses" if they are to thrive. Moreover, the entrepreneur brings her own history to each endeavor, and some such histories are haunting and tragically inappropriate to that endeavor.

> In every nursery there are ghosts. They are visitors from the unremembered past of the parents; the uninvited guests at the christening. Under all favorable circumstances the unfriendly and unbidden spirits are banished from the nursery and return to their subterranean dwelling place. The baby makes his own imperative claim upon parental love and, in strict analogy with the fairy tales, the bonds of love protect the child and his parents against the intruders, the malevolent ghosts.
>
> This is not to say that ghosts cannot invent mischief from their burial places. Even among families where the love bonds are stable and strong, the intruders from the parental past may break through the magic circle in an unguarded moment, and a parent and his child may find themselves reenacting a moment or a scene from another time with another set of characters....
>
> But how shall we explain another group of families who appear to be possessed by their ghosts? The intruders from the past have taken up residence in the nursery, claiming tradition and rights of ownership. They have been present at the christening for two or more generations. While no one has issued an invitation, the ghosts take up residence and conduct the rehearsal of the family tragedy from a tattered script.[3]

In these passages, Selma Fraiberg is describing the deepest problems we might face in binding ourselves to the world. What if, at just the crucial moments, we as infants require in the service of development, as well as a felt need, to reach out into the world but do not see it as "there" and whole, possessing an integrity we might recognize? We shall not make the moves that allow us to grow. Correspondingly, what if the moves we make as mothers do not work, do not bring our children into our world? Our intuitions and devotions fail us. How are we as a family to grow? What if at just the crucial moments we as infants must protect ourselves from the ghosts of our protectors, just when we have the fewest resources? We shall make moves whose consequences are protective, but they are also perverse and destructive for ourselves. Or, again, what if we as mothers find ourselves driven almost demonically by our own histories, doing what was done to us, knowing too well—but in the end not at all really knowing—how to respond to the situation we find ourselves in?

Can we allow ourselves to learn from our babies how to mother them more effectively? Can we give ourselves over to their legitimate authority? Can we learn how not to let the ghosts take over for too long? For successful entrepreneurship, we must learn how.

The paramount tasks for the entrepreneur are those of commitment and transformation. We shall learn about such commitment and transformation from ordinary infants, and from infants blind from birth, and from their mothers. How does autonomy develop in the context of desperate need when survival is an issue? How are babies and their mothers responsive to their differing needs? How do they discover solutions, or fail to discover solutions to adaptive problems that are particular to themselves, problems most mothers and their infants usually do not face, problems that are not part of society's standard repertoire?

Moreover, what might it mean that a baby or an entrepreneurial idea is "good enough" (to use D. W. Winnicott's phrase), so that it would allow for the mother or the entrepreneur the possibility of success? How are mothers and entrepreneurs transformed in their actual lives by the intimate presence of a baby or an entrepreneurial idea so that they are no longer determined by their ghosts and histories?[4] Finally, just how are baby and mother, entrepreneurial idea and entrepreneur, attuned to each other, so that they work together more or less well?[5]

The big secret is that mothers and their infants have become made for each other, in suckling, tactile pleasure, regard, smell, and devotion, whether bottle or breast feeding. There is here no explicit binding, no covenant, no sacrificc, no mission. Infants and their mothers are also made to become autonomous, separate, on their own, the child a "going concern" from the very beginning (Winnicott's phrase). We need those adaptive inventions, but in the end if we are fortunate there is some version of that ordinary availability of endowments, what we sometimes call Providence.

Such a model of commitment suggests to the entrepreneur just how necessity and need are the mother of invention. What is needed is already present in the entrepreneurial idea and the world; to pay devoted and pleasurable attention to one's situation is the essential attribute. Success is contingent but perhaps not so tenuous as is often portrayed. Of course, that entrepreneurial idea may not be good enough, but we discover that inadequacy only through devotion and attention.

Bonding, growth, and autonomy are natural here. Babies are going concerns. Not only is bonding already present when mother and infant first encounter each other, but bonding implies in the situation of the mother and the infant an agenda of separation that is defined by growth and autonomy. Of course, the entrepreneur has to acknowledge in his practice that he is in the realm of mothering, and such acknowledgment takes one out of the realm of competition and creative destruction and into a realm where regard for the other is critical, a realm of love and marketing.

Entrepreneurs are devoted and present to the moment and so they discover adaptive solutions for when they and the world fail each other. The infant or the entrepreneurial idea runs this show, by its neediness and its surge toward autonomy, the entrepreneur enacting, in his own need and inventiveness, its needs. While this might sound abstract, that is just how it feels when we are engaged in an entrepreneurial endeavor or when we are mothers. We are the agents, individuals that we are, of something bigger. We are transformed by our babies.

The Entrepreneurial Role

What analogy am I insisting upon here? In chapter 1 the entrepreneur was modeled after Augustine, the endeavor after the development of the church. In our consideration of Moses and the Israelites, the entrepreneur is educated and guided and chastened by God, as is his object or endeavor, the Israelites.[6] Theirs was a mode of commitment—of sacrifice, of covenant, of test, of prophecy, of mission—in which the entrepreneur, the entrepreneurial idea, and the people are mutually engaged through a story they tell themselves and reenact as their history. My purpose in this chapter is to describe another such mode of commitment.

Moses believes his task is much like that of a nurse carrying an infant (Numbers 11:12).[7] He is a founding father touched by a people's burp, barf, blood, and bowel. We might also expect that a more everyday, less metaphoric version of family life, where suckling is palpable and weaning is poignant, and where development is wrenching, might tell us something more about the dynamics of commitment. That dynamics rather than any single role will be our focus here.[8] To identify with a situation rather than with one of its actors is perhaps a godly demand. But that is just what we must do if we are to understand commitment of this sort, a commitment that is essential to entrepreneurship.[9]

Moreover, entrepreneurs do not command their situations. Moses does not command his situation, bound as he is by God to the Israelites. Mothers do not command their situations, bound as they are to their infants.[10] Such binding is both anxiety-provoking and enormously gratifying. For a mother to stay on the same side as her baby is no trivial commitment, at least in actual stressful life.[11] To understand the infant's position is frightening for ourselves, and to be fair to the infant is often to displace our own desperate interests. Adrienne Rich has written about it most poignantly.[12]

> I remember a cycle. It began when I had picked up a book or began trying to write a letter, or even found myself on the telephone with someone toward whom my voice betrayed eagerness, a rush of sympathetic energy. The child (or children) might be absorbed in busyness, in his own dreamworld; but as soon as he felt me gliding into a world which did not include him, he would come to pull at my hand, ask for help, punch at the typewriter keys. And I would feel his wants at such a moment as fraudulent, as an attempt moreover to defraud me of living even for fifteen minutes as myself. My anger would rise; I would feel the futility of any attempt to salvage myself, and also the inequality between us: my needs always balanced against those of a child, and always losing. I could love so much better, I told myself, after even a quarter-hour of selfishness, of peace, of detachment from my children. A few minutes? But it was as if an invisible thread would pull taut between us and break, to the child's sense of inconsolable abandonment, if I moved—not even physically, but in spirit—into a realm beyond our tightly circumscribed life together.

What Mothers Know

Fraiberg's and Winnicott's descriptions of mother and infant in interaction ring true. That experience of mother with infant has a reality and a facticity that insists upon itself despite our defenses, prejudices, and ideologies. The mother's and the infant's inner lives are defined not only biographically by their backgrounds, even the infant's, but more so by the ecology of the immediate environments they provide for each other. It is an ecology manifest to anyone who is willing to open his eyes in the nursery, an ecology that then shapes the development of mother and child.[13]

As for the ordinary devoted mother, to use Winnicott's phrase, say, a mother who was brought up by a mother, her task is to "hold" the baby so that the baby becomes real for himself.

> I suggest, as you know I do, and I suppose everyone agrees, that *ordinarily* the woman enters into a phase, a phase from which she *ordinarily* recovers in the weeks and months after the baby's birth, in which to a large extent she is the baby and the baby is her. There is nothing mystical about this. After all, she was a baby once, and she has in her the memories of being a baby; she also has memories of being cared for, and these memories either help or hinder her in her own experiences as a mother...[and she] is ready for an experience in which she knows extremely well what are the baby's needs. You will understand I am not simply referring to her being able to know whether the baby is or is not hungry, and all that sort of thing; I am referring to innumerable subtle things,...I am contented to use the word *hold,* and to extend its

> meaning to cover all that a mother is and does at this time [as in "holding the baby"]....She cannot use even Spock just at this point where she feels that the baby needs to picked up, or put down, to be left alone or to be turned over, or where she knows that what is essential is the simplest of all experiences, that based on contact without activity, where there is opportunity for the feeling of oneness between two persons who are in fact two and not one. These things give the baby the opportunity to be, out of which there can arise the next things that have to do with action, doing and being done to. Here is the basis for what gradually becomes, for the infant, the self-experiencing being.
>
> All this is highly tenuous, but repeated and repeated adds up to the foundation of the capacity in the baby to feel real. With this capacity the baby can face the world.

An inchoate venture might be launched, and failure can be instructive rather than disabling.

> When these conditions obtain, as they usually do, the baby becomes able to develop the capacity to have feelings that correspond to some extent with those of the mother who is identified with her baby; or shall I say, heavily invested in her baby and in his or her care. At three or four months after being born the baby may be able to show that he or she knows what it is like to be a mother, that is a mother in her state of being devoted to something that is not in fact herself....
>
> In time the baby begins to need the mother to fail to adapt—this failure being also a graduated process that cannot be learned from books. It would be irksome for a human child to go on experiencing omnipotence when the apparatus has arrived which can cope with frustrations and relative environmental failures. There is much satisfaction to be got from anger that does not go over into despair.

Can the enterprise encounter the world's demands? Yes, if it has been well launched.

> Any parent here will know what I mean when I say that although you subjected your baby to the most awful frustrations you never once let him (or her) down—that is, your ego support to the baby's ego was reliable. The baby never woke and cried and there was no one to hear. In later language you found you did not try to put your child off with lies.
>
> But, of course, all of this implies not only that the mother was able to give herself over to this preoccupation with the care of her infant, but also that she was lucky. I need not start to enumerate the things that may happen even in the best-regulated families.[14]

Again, the mother and infant are immediately a going concern (notably, a commercial term). The mother and infant are ready for each other. That ongoingness then makes it possible for the baby to have its own autonomy, to be devoted on its own, to grow. Growth will surely involve missteps that mother and child recover from, most of the time. Mother continues to be available just as baby gains "the capacity to be alone" (Winnicott). And yet there can be tragic failures in this process. While there are errors from which we can adaptively recover and grow, there are also tragic errors from which we recover only with the greatest of effort and good fortune and which, even then, we are not likely to ever forget.

Babies and their mothers are morally devoted to each other, sometimes failing but never in need of blaming:

> It is necessary for us to be able to look at human growth and development, with all its complexities that are internal or personal to the child, and we must be able to say: here the ordinary devoted mother factor failed, without blaming anyone....some of the failures of development that we meet sprang from a failure of the ordinary devoted mother factor at a certain point or over a phase....
>
> But I have one special reason why I feel we must be able to apportion aetiological significance (not blame), and that is that in no other way can we recognise the positive value of the ordinary devoted mother factor—the vital necessity for every baby that someone should facilitate the earliest stages of the processes of psychological growth, or psychosomatic growth, or shall I say the growth of the most immature and absolutely dependent human personality.[15]

Entrepreneurs know, from their actual experience, just these facts about devotion and tragic failure. Winnicott's insistence on the facticity of experience, beyond theory or formal rule, is of enormous moral import. Whatever Winnicott the pediatrician knows, he knows from the consulting room: watching babies and their mothers, talking to them, playing with them, and thinking about them in terms that are therapeutically effective.

We are sometimes tempted to avoid this kind of knowledge. For Augustine, mothers' testimony to their own experience of infants is to be dismissed. If only mothers were to think clearly and logically! he might suggest. Mother and infant are acting out roles given to them by God; there is no authentic interaction. The infant is isolated, and in that sense the infant is not a going concern when he is newborn. And the infant and his mother are sinful. Here is perhaps one of the most famous passages from the *Confessions,* book 1, where Augustine insists on these points. It is Augustinian theology (a ghost?) in the nursery.

> So I was welcomed by the consolations of human milk; but it was not my mother or my nurses who made any decision to fill their breasts, but you [God] who through them gave me infant food, in accordance with your ordinance and the riches which are distributed deep in the natural order. You also granted me not to wish for more than you were giving, and to my nurses the desire to give me what you gave them. For by an impulse which you control their instinctive wish was to give me the milk which they had in abundance from you. For the good which came to me from them was a good for them; yet it was not from them but through them....For at that time I

> knew nothing more than how to suck and to be quietened by bodily delights, and to weep when I was physically uncomfortable.
>
> ...Little by little I began to be aware where I was and wanted to manifest my wishes to those who could fulfill them as I could not. For my desires were internal; adults were external to me and had no means of entering into my soul. So I threw my limbs about and uttered sounds...
>
> ...What sin did I then have? Was it wrong that in tears I greedily opened my mouth wide to suck the breasts?
>
> ...I have personally watched and studied a jealous baby. He could not yet speak and, pale with jealousy and bitterness, glared at his brother sharing his mother's milk. Who is unaware of this fact of experience? Mothers and nurses claim to charm it away by their own private remedies. But it can hardly be innocence, when the source of milk is flowing richly and abundantly, not to endure a share going to one's blood-brother, who is in profound need, dependent for life exclusively on that one food.[16]

Again, what a mother or nurse might know is dismissed by Augustine. Only objective others, theoretically informed, can observe what is really going on.

> [A]s I have heard from the parents of my flesh, him from whom and her in whom you formed me in time. For I do not remember....That at least is what I was told, and I believed it since that is what we see other infants doing. I do not actually remember what I then did....That is the way of infants I have learnt from those I have been able to watch. That is what I was like myself and, although they have not been aware of it, they have taught me more than my nurses with all their knowledge of how I behaved. (§ 7–8)

The baby's world tells Augustine about human nature: "for I see in that child what I do not remember in myself" (§ 10).[17] Yet Augustine's denial of mothers' knowledge allows him to distance himself from his own experience of childhood.

We might well be resistant to an infant's actual world, the dependence and vulnerability and impotence and love and intimacy it reminds us of. And so we become objective, and it seems scientific and what is now called managerial, denying what mothers and infants know.[18] So we deny ourselves what entrepreneurs know.[19] Such resistance is that ghost in the nursery that can also enter the proverbial garage where an enterprise is born. Actual entrepreneurs must know about holding. All I shall be doing here is saying out loud what entrepreneurs as mothers have already learned.

To the Nursery

To understand what it means for an entrepreneurial endeavor to go off on its own and to be placed in the world, we have to understand what mothers and infants know, in the language adequate to the nursery (and not the language of the prophet or the bishop or the manager). It is a language of necessity and need, devotion, intimate knowledge, discipline, emergency, and particularistic and historical problem solving.[20] And, while bonding, growth, and autonomy may formally parallel the Mosaic-Israelitic binding, sacrifice, and mission, they represent a very different world indeed. It is to the nursery that we must return.[21]

Again, your baby is a going concern, your baby knows what she wants, she wants what is good for her, and she knows how to train you to be a good mother.[22] You are seduced into being a good mother, and if you are failing, baby will take you to task and further train you. Correspondingly, you know your baby, you give meaning to what she does, and how you respond constitutes what she is up to.[23] In actual fact, you know your baby intimately. Her needs are not expressed as demands but as necessities that define both of you. If you try to avoid that intimate knowledge there will be disaster, a moral failure to acknowledge a relationship both of you are given the moment you are together and separate the first time.[24]

Entrepreneurs are in these ways intimately involved with their endeavors, their babies, and in that intimacy they define their project by their staying with it.

The tasks are to "put on your oxygen mask first," so you can take care of your baby; to show up on time; to pay attention, be ready, be there in the present (rather than "losing it"); and, again, if you can, to "stay on the same side as your baby, for he wants to please you (you are his world) but he does not always know how."[25] Babies, even your own, are often not so interesting, and sometimes they are downright boring. But it has to be done, and what counts is doing it, whatever it is that needs to be done. The intimacies of the moment cannot be abstracted away, or there will be disaster in bringing up your baby. Concrete necessity and devotion and intimate knowledge are fundamental.

Moreover, whatever else mothers or entrepreneurs are doing with their crying babies, they are solving problems of a very different sort than are assigned in school homework. When your baby is hysterical with crying, you discover that nothing matters and everything does. Either nothing will work, or just about anything will make a difference. The situation feels decentered, and robust and overdetermined. And if it is just the last thing you do that works and focuses your child and brings her out of hysteria, that last thing will not work as the first thing the next time. These are situations that are worked on, not problems that are solved. History matters here. The history of failed attempts and comfortings sets the stage for what finally does work, this night. In your best moments you know that it will not go on forever. Whether it be diaper rash or loose bowel or crying, there will be a resolution. Yet waiting it out and so doing nothing, in effect a null hypothesis that any intervention is worse than doing nothing, is not at all morally acceptable much of the time.

Here most advice and schooling is useless. Advice is useful before one has a baby since it comforts anxiety. But later on, advice mostly induces guilt, unless the advice is of the sort that recommends trying something else, without claiming much for that next option other than it is the next one. The real value of advice, in any case, is that it provides a line of action that then can be abandoned for another.

Situations of motherhood or of entrepreneurship are not only complex, but they are so overdetermined in a tight overlapping historical-social web that the attempt to isolate factors or causes is likely to make action seem either hopeless or arbitrary. The task is to follow some prudent advice and so be provided with both confidence and a natural set of questions, rather than to optimally choose which advice to follow.

I have more than once switched baby's gender in my description. Mothers know that gender matters enormously. You do not know how to treat a baby who is without one. Similarly, entrepreneurial endeavors are particular, not generic, and must be addressed as such. Your baby, this particular baby, will educate you.

Your major task as a mother is to bring your infant into the world, so that he can be a member. And so your child becomes disciplined, initially fitting into your life. He comes to recognize your authority through the joys of participating in a much larger life than he has when he is first born.[26] Through his acquired discipline your infant learns to be effective and have his own authority. The constitution of society is here a matter of authority and membership, what Augustine in particular understood.[27]

Your life with your baby is perhaps highly scheduled and predictable but not bureaucratic. For it is all of a piece and not at all modular and interchangeable. The flexibility you surely have with your child, and he with you, is a product of an ongoing conversation rather less formal than negotiation and bargaining. Like entrepreneurs, you have learned to pay attention to the details, the everyday peculiarities that allow for opportunities others do not appreciate.

The good-enough mother is devoted to her child. That means that diapering time is what counts, at least as much as any other times. Again, it's all of a piece.[28] There is a Latin phrase discussing original sin (proverbially attributed to Augustine) to the effect that we are born between urine and feces (referring to the location of the vagina). I take that to mean that we are unavoidably bound up in everydayness.

Time is not something to be allocated and used efficiently. Rather, there is never much breathing room, there is always more to do, and what counts in the end is the responsiveness mother exhibits. Necessity gets you through what you must do, and so you discover what does not have to be done.[29] Moreover, emergencies and overloads are occasions for extraordinary and heroic effort. They are not random fluctuations. The world falls apart, or together, totally.

Time here is narrative and historical. Development comes in stages. A large number of subtasks need to be active and in place for a single task, such as walking, to take place. Stages of development are real, and markers of development are socially transformative: when your baby walks, at that point he becomes a new kind of person within the family.

The usual story of time in financial-commercial life would seem to be about a commensurable linear unit (different times made commensurable by discount factors, e^{-rt}). But time here is defined by necessity and emergency and development (as in the discussion of compassion in chapter 2).[30]

Motherhood is the existential truth of the present; it is concreteness and immediacy. Do this today, now, in this situation; and then do that, then, in that situation. Moreover, every modern mother is a single mother. So most mothers report of their experience. You are on your own. No wonder there is a romanticizing of motherhood, when the appropriate response in retrospect is perhaps one of anger, ambivalence, devotion, and wonder. Motherhood insists on those murderous feelings you sometimes have toward your beloved children, as Adrienne Rich describes: children insist on themselves just when you have a moment to yourself; the ambivalence you feel, avoiding their need so that you do have that moment alone; the tremendous relief you feel when you share your most outrageous feelings (of eros as well as thanatos) toward your children.[31] That is why the operative categories must be necessity and need, devotion, intimate unavoidable knowledge, discipline, emergency, and particularism. Someone has to bring up the children. And, it seems, that has to be a mother.[32]

Entrepreneurs have to be mothers, and they will recognize their situation and themselves in this description. The rest of this chapter is an attempt to further stake this claim. There will be adaptive problems, ghosts in the nursery, calls for devotion—and they must be recognized as such. What we want to understand is just how commitment is affirmed and so leads to growth, the transition from being a going concern to being an institution, the kinds of failure that encourage such development, and why problems along the way are distinctive to each stage of development.

Another Visit to the Nursery

We so often wish to avoid these facts of life, to deny motherhood's palpable reality, that I provide here more than one accounting of them. Readers who do not feel the need for such instruction might skip to the next section.

Some phenomenological facts:

You are educated by your baby (and so marketing is authentic). Your baby knows what she wants, whether it be to eat, sleep, rest, play. And you know your baby, when she needs comfort and how, what works for her at this time. You have a real sense of where she is. Such intimate knowledge is objective.

Your baby will train you to be a good parent. She knows how to seduce you into being good, and being good at it. Babies want and know what is good for them. To avoid her demands is to court disaster. (Your entrepreneurial baby will educate and so transform you, so the endeavor may begin to grow.)

Management is paying attention. So you pay attention to her and you are there for her. Details matter. Little things are fully significant in each context. You track where she is and where you are—and she does the same. It's all there, in the present, on the surface, and all you need do is be with it.

Of course you will lose it. Life is busy, and paying attention is so absorbing we sometimes flee from such intensity and intimacy. But if you pay attention, then your baby will know even more about what she wants. You'll just know it.

Development is natural. What is remarkable is that your baby develops; those abstract stages described in books about child development (or about business) go along with actual events; and it does appear that your baby is advancing in steps. She can become a person in richer ways, and that richness is not incremental but it seems is holistic and actual and experienced by you and by her as deeper.[33] When she can smile, or gaze, or walk, you and she become involved with each other in qualitatively different ways. Also, stages of development imply degrees of mutual autonomy; you are part of each other and then not so much so.[34]

Devotion is management. Life with your baby is of a piece. Changing diapers is a pleasure along with feeding and loving. They are the same. There is no set of costs to be arrayed against a set of benefits, no way of separating the clean parts from the dirt, a dirt that is intrinsic and legitimating. (I take it that entepreneurial work is women's work, as that is conventionally understood, as much as it is mothers' work.)

What gets you through all of this is necessity. And there is of course tomorrow when things will be better or different. Mood swings, feeling trapped, being trapped, days when nothing works and what you do only makes your baby crankier and more hysterical—all have a tomorrow, and necessity gets you through them today.

You do not manage your time, and there is no breathing space. There is always more to do, and no time to clean up adequately. There is no balancing act here. Rather, you do what you must and what really matters. And stuff is left behind. Your baby is just yours. That is enough, as long as you realize that your ambivalence and devotion are of a piece. Again, they do not balance or cancel each other, but both are present and real.

Immediacy is vital; balance and order are luxuries. It is not a matter of weighing her needs as against yours, or of self-sacrifice. Rather, again, you put on your oxygen mask first, help her on with hers, and pray—while changing a diaper or giving her a pretzel. Practical necessity is the paradigm, not efficiency and trade-off. You cut corners to survive, but the lost corners are not so important.

Guilt. Advice often assumes that context is abstractable, and that you are managing yourself and your baby and your time. The books you read are helpful before your baby arrives, since they provide you with something to do (not reading, but something to do in your various fantasies). It seems like you could pull it off. But when your baby comes, the advice is mostly irrelevant, literally.

What works for your baby and her needs are situational, and situations and histories are complicated enough so that it is not clear what is the case in point at this moment. Advice may be applicable, but there is too much of it. What probably is true is that consistency of a sort does matter, and taking some advice focuses your action and thinking, and so you pay better attention and can learn from your baby.

Loss and giving up the reins. The erotics of mother and baby (touch, smells,...) is intense, more intense than a lover or spouse. This is the big secret, and why husbands never recover from being sent out of Eden.

Mothers are often trapped by the erotics. But this is a deeply satisfying trap. This erotics is the way your baby learns to love. Intimacy and independence are not opposed; they are conditions for the possibility of each other.

Having become so attached and involved with your baby, you then have to learn to grow up alone, as will she. Alone with the joy, and with the risk that something will happen to her. For it will. There is now the possibility of loss.

Launching an enterprise. In sum, a mother provides a world for the infant in which the infant finds that she is omnipotent. She has a desire, and it is soon realized. The breast or bottle appears, her imagination seemingly sufficient to magically bring it about. The neediness of the infant, the natural authority of mother in interpreting those needs and thereby fulfilling them, and her devotion or caring allows mother and infant to be committed to each other. A mother provides the chance for her infant's power, for the creation of reality, and for the growth of autonomy.

In Augustine's eschatological description of Christianity in the *City of God,* Christianity has always been present, only to be realized in its fullest form in recent times. In the biblical account of the Israelites, they are a people from the beginning, since Abraham and his covenant with God is a prefigurement of the Sinai covenant. Now, too, babies are a going concern as soon as they see the light of day. A baby is fully present to the world, fully involved with it, suckling and feeling and being in the world of her mother, bringing along that world in such a way that the world will take care of the infant and lead her to growing up. The milk and the loving are already there for the asking. Babies know what they are to do. Mother's task is to respond to that knowledge. For baby and mother, the authentic task is to pay attention to what's up and to respond.

For the entrepreneur, the lessons to be drawn from these phenomenologies of the launching of a new enterprise are threefold: to be a going concern is a given, and the problem is to "hold" the enterprise as it takes off on its own; such holding is detailed and particular and it demands our devotion, as well as good fortune; and, the contingent character of such launching, whether it be in the product or the existence of a market, requires that we not ask too soon whether the product or the market are real. Following Winnicott, the product is a "transitional object," neither just an entrepreneurial idea nor just another commodity on the market.[35]

Development and Tragedy

The play and interaction of mother and infant are intimate and specific. Babies present us with truly urgent demands, those of life and death, of eros and thanatos. So we need to be on site, in touch with our baby or our enterprise. Launching an enterprise requires that its specific needs for its further development be taken care of at the time they are needed.

Sometimes there are tragic misses and slippages, such as for the infant blind from birth, and then we need those adaptive solutions, those moves that demand our creative inventiveness (at least until they become widely adopted clinical practices). Insofar as we find such solutions, the enterprise might take off again on its own. For infants blind from birth, Fraiberg and her collaborators found solutions to making the world "there" for the infant, so he would have sighted hands rather than blind ones: to "reach on sound," to have "midline organization of the hands." "We reasoned that for every developmental failure in the blind autistic[-like][36] child there should be a correlate in the development of all blind babies in the form of a unique adaptive problem posed by blindness. The difference between the autistic blind child and the child in the 'normal' group should appear in developmental studies in which one group found the adaptive solutions and the other group met a developmental impasse."[37]

Entrepreneurial success or failure is a matter of adaptive solutions to developmental problems.[38] Such a developmental perspective demands we actually respond to need and to slippage. We cannot simply pay off or compensate for our errancies; for, again, moments of need and slippage are times of profound motive, not simply erasable events. Insofar as we are responsive, there will be not only a return in the long run but an immediate response in pleasure and liveliness.

> [A]t every point where vision normally provides incentives and lures in prehension, the blind infant reaches a developmental impasse; sound does not provide an alternative adaptive solution in the early months.
>
> Our problem in devising "an education of the hands" in the guidance program was to facilitate adaptive hand behavior by exploiting the intact systems, by providing exteroceptive "lures" to substitute for those normally provided by vision....
>
> To promote midline organization of the hands, we and our parents developed strategies to bring the hands together. Where vision normally provides the lure, we found substitutes in everyday experience. In feeding, we encouraged our mothers to place the baby's hands on the bottle....With the hands placed upon the bottle we provided one lure to midline engagement of the hands with a "pleasure bonus" in the experience of feeding itself.
>
> We encouraged patty cake games and other hand-clapping games with rhythmic chants, which provided their own "pleasure bonus" for midline engagement of the hands (where vision would have guaranteed the spontaneous untutored engagement).
>
> We created an "interesting space" at midline—"furnishing" a space that is empty for the blind baby when he is not in immediate contact with a human partner....
>
> Similarly, when the baby achieved independent sit, and enjoyed sitting on the floor, we "furnished" the near space of the floor with interesting and

> intriguing objects which could be "found" at midline, and also at various points in the arc which represented his reach space.[39]

More abstractly:

> We employed game strategies to bring about midline organization of the hands and reciprocity between the hands, the essential conditions for all later stages in adaptive hand behavior. With the collaboration of our parents we provided both interpersonal exchanges and experiences with toys to create a maximally engaging and interesting surround in which the hands, now organized at midline, could reach out and make contact with persons and things within range and obtain rich, polysensory experience in exploring the qualities of persons and things. Where vision normally lures the child to discoveries of his surround, we created the conditions under which persons and things could provide tactile-auditory lures. (p. 276)

Such lures are not abstract behavioral cues. They are temptations to actual pleasure and involvement and meaning.[40] Marketing, the enterprise's involvement with the world out there, is just what makes entrepreneurship real, what makes the going concern into an institution. Entrepreneurial ideas are more or less blind at birth, and the entrepreneur must find a way for them to reach out and move forward.

> Through the enhancement of the blind baby's surround, through providing the lures of persons and things "out there," the child who had postural (maturational) readiness for mobility and an elementary concept of the object in space had the incentives for creeping and for walking. Under these circumstances sound could now substitute for sight in providing a distant lure for initiation of the mobility pattern....
>
> This, then, is not "training," a method commonly employed by educators of the blind, but a form of guidance which derives from the developmental principles we had uncovered in our research. If the developmental principles are not available to the parents or the educator there is great peril for the baby in finding the route toward mobility. Clearly, if a baby has not yet demonstrated "reach on sound," all efforts to entice him to creep with a distant voice or sound will fail....
>
> An educational program that is attuned to developmental principles needs to take into account the impediment of blindness to "reach on sound" and to provide the blind infant with the incentives for initiating mobility. Then it can confidently wait for the baby to "invent" mobility for himself. (pp. 278–279)

Those solutions, peculiar as they might seem until they actually work, gave the child the thereness of the world, a thereness that is ordinarily available visually. Most importantly, again, they gave the infant pleasure, the pleasure of the world, and that is ultimately motivating.[41] A going concern that is growing is imbued with pleasure, and insofar as we solve adaptive problems, the newly available possibilities for pleasure are motivating.

Enterprises have a life of their own. Insofar as one engages that liveliness, they will respond. That response will come from those who work in the enterprise and those who are its market. The task of the entrepreneur is to provide for the average expectable environment and for the adaptive solutions when that environment offers profound hazards. Then the world will be there for the enterprise and it may flourish.

I take what I have been saying here as descriptive of what entrepreneurs actually do, and as encouragement for entrepreneurs to continue in their mothering roles. These are the actual tasks of effective entrepreneurs: on site, in the middle, concrete, and urgent.

It is not cutesy metaphor to speak of babying an enterprise. To hold a baby, or to hold an entrepreneurial endeavor, demands close and sensitive attention. For there to be a market, a binding with the world, there must be adaptive solutions when there are slippages and failures. These solutions are ontological inventions that alter the natural objects and moves in our world, not just devices for making up for mistakes. Moreover, growth and development are within a contradictory moment when a going concern is and is not independent, is and is not on its own. Such a moment is frightening, since dependency and abject failure are palpable possibilities.

The entrepreneur or the mother allows safely for what is in-between, what is and is not separate from the matrix in which it is growing. Commitment and compassion mean that we do not judge independence or cash flow or market, at least not too soon. To ask early on whether the entrepreneurial endeavor is real or a fantasy is to miss the point, to misconceive of what we are up to. What is ordinarily taken as prudential and sensible behavior, such as careful planning, must be denied by the entrepreneur if the endeavor is to have the chance to go off on its own.

The archetypal scene here is perhaps the binding of Isaac. Is Isaac to be sacrificially killed or not?[42] Abraham does not ask the question. He knows his duty. Those who try to analyze his behavior philosophically will, if they take their own advice, be failures for sure. For that contradictory in-between is just where Abraham and Isaac must be.

Let us see how Winnicott describes these in-between or "transitional" phenomena. Then we might say something about creativity and play, the essence of that in-betweenness of entrepreneurial endeavor.[43]

> It is well known that infants as soon as they are born tend to use fist, fingers, thumbs in stimulation of the oral erotogenic zone, in satisfaction of the instincts at that zone, and also in quiet union. It is also well known that after a few months infants of either sex become fond of playing with dolls, and that

> most mothers allow their infants some special object and expect them to become, as it were, addicted to such objects....
>
> I have introduced the terms "transitional objects" and "transitional phenomena" for designation of the intermediate area of experience, between the thumb and the teddy bear, between the oral eroticism and the true object-relationship, between primary creative activity and projection of what has already been introjected, between primary unawareness of indebtedness and the acknowledgement of indebtedness ("Say: 'ta'")....
>
> I am here staking a claim for an intermediate state between a baby's inability and his growing ability to recognize and accept reality. I am therefore studying the substance of *illusion,* that which is allowed to the infant, and which in adult life is inherent in art and religion. (pp. 1–3)

And in entrepreneurship.

> [T]here may emerge some thing or some phenomenon—perhaps a bundle of wool or the corner of a blanket or eiderdown, or a word or tune, or a mannerism—that becomes vitally important to the infant for use at the time of going to sleep, and is a defence against anxiety, especially anxiety of depressive type. Perhaps some soft object or other type of object has been found and used by the infant, and this then becomes what I am calling a *transitional object.* This object goes on being important. The parents get to know its value and carry it round when travelling. The mother lets it get dirty and even smelly, knowing that by washing it she introduces a break in continuity in the infant's experience, a break that may destroy the meaning and value of the object to the infant. (p. 4)

> The intermediate area to which I am referring is the area that is allowed to the infant between primary creativity and objective perception based on reality-testing....[A]t some theoretical point early in the development of every human individual an infant in a certain setting provided by the mother is capable of conceiving of the idea of something that would meet the growing need that arises out of instinctual tension. The infant cannot be said to know at first what is to be created. At this point in time the mother presents herself. In the ordinary way she gives her breast and her potential feeding urge. The mother's adaptation to the infant's needs, when good enough, gives the infant the *illusion* that there is an external reality that corresponds to the infant's own capacity to create. In other words, there is an overlap between what the mother supplies and what the child might conceive of. To the observer, the child perceives what the mother actually presents, but this is not the whole truth. The infant perceives the breast only in so far as a breast could be created just there and then. There is no interchange between the mother and the infant. (pp. 11–12)

The illusion is just that nonjudgmental space in which growth and invention may happen.

> The transitional object and the transitional phenomena start each human being off with what will always be important for them, i.e. a neutral area of experience which will not be challenged. Of the transitional object it can be said that it is a matter of agreement between us and the baby that we will

> never ask the question: "Did you conceive of this or was it presented to you from without?" The important point is that no decision on this point is expected. The question is not to be formulated. (p. 12)

Compassion allows us to play.

> The thing about playing is always the precariousness of the interplay of personal psychic reality and the experience of control of actual objects. This is the precariousness of magic itself, magic that arises in intimacy, in a relationship that is being found to be reliable. To be reliable the relationship is necessarily motivated by the mother's love, or her love-hate, or her object-relating, not by reaction formations. (p. 47)

> I have tried to draw attention to the importance both in theory and in practice of a third area, that of play, which expands into creative living and into the whole cultural life of man....I have located this important area of *experience* in the potential space between the individual and the environment, that which initially both joins and separates the baby and the mother when the mother's love, displayed or made manifest as human reliability, does in fact give the baby a sense of trust or of confidence in the environmental factor. (pp. 102–103)

There is an in-between, a neutral space, in which development takes place. In that space there is no tight market, no financial test, no asking if the nascent project is or is not real. The entrepreneurial endeavor is to be treated as it is, not as success or failure or on the way. This illusion, for that is what it is from the point of view of the disciplines of finance and accounting and management and strategy, is just what is necessary if there is, eventually, to be a corporate institution. The entrepreneur has to allow for this illusion. Then the enterprise or the infant may develop the capacity to be alone, namely "the experience...of being alone, as an infant or a small child, in the presence of mother. Thus the basis of the capacity to be alone is a paradox; it is the experience of being alone while someone else is present."[44] This capacity to be alone allows the infant to discover himself as real, rather than as an instrument of external stimuli. The mother's presence has provided a reliability that allows the infant to be alone. In such a state there is play and creativity rather than anxiety and compulsion. The task of the entrepreneur is to create that neutral space so that the enterprise has the capacity to be alone, to be creative—an illusion that in the end serves reality.[45]

Continuing in this vein, I shall ask what it would mean for an enterprise to miss adaptive solutions, to have insufficient good-enough devoted mothering that might hold the enterprise, to be haunted by ghosts, to have inadequate neutral space.[46]

Modern education in business and the professions would seem to push aside just those phenomena that are transitional, especially if they are associated with religion, family life, or art. Perhaps transitional phenomena are featured in a course on creativity or teamwork, or experienced in an orientation program, or discussed under a rubric such as ethics. But the conventional scientific content of such education remains comparatively untouched; in effect, it is without illusion.[47] It is also without prophecy, that rubric under which I discussed creativity in chapter 1. The dialogic space between God and prophet is just that neutral space I have described. We are not to ask if the space is sacred or profane, this- or other-worldly. So there is room for play.

Transitional phenomena (play, creativity, prophecy) are fully present in actual practice. They acknowledge the irreducible problematic otherness of the world. One cannot act as a mother without an infant, as a bishop without a flock, as an entrepreneur without an idea and a potential market. And to think of the entrepreneur as a mother or a bishop or a Mosaic leader, one must immediately have in mind that curiously demanding autonomous otherness of the world that makes for the neutral space of transitionality.

Integrity and Sacrifice

The infant is now on the way to being a toddler. She is not quite so immediately dependent, the enterprise might eventually go off on its own.[48] Along with such growth, there is possible failure and sure sacrifice, a structural sequence that with good fortune leads to further autonomy. Each step makes the next one possible within a life's pattern we discern as she grows and makes choices and is influenced by the world she lives in.[49]

Her education is civilizing because it gives her the chance to belong to society, to exhibit discipline and achievement, mastery and skill. Education teaches her how to appropriately employ a repertoire of talents in a complex and subtle world. To do things correctly, in manners and conversation and comportment, is membership in society. Being able to do what her parents find significant makes her more of a person in the family; for her, it is a pleasurable fact of life.[50] Discipline is learning to be articulate in the society, and so one needs to be corrected when one makes an error. So character and courage are perhaps the most important qualities for the child.[51] Will she be virtuous, meeting the challenges of fortune with dignity and autonomy, the challenges of sin and temptation with temperance and humility? (I have been describing robust mature institutions that might exhibit corporate social responsibility.)

Children do possess integrity, discipline, and virtue, and that allows them to develop, with all of the progressive implications of "development." That integrity also allows them to experience sacrifice, incompensable loss in the service of that development. Put differently, the entrepreneurial endeavor has a life of its own, and that life is centrally about sacrifice in the service of transformative growth.

If all goes well enough, the process of bonding leads to its rupture. The breast or bottle is no longer available so magically. The child becomes real for himself and in the world, by the way freeing his mother from some of the devotions and tyrannies she has allowed. Enormous anger and frustration now can be expressed, by mother and child, without being murderous.

So growth and development is also destructive and sacrificial: destructive, because what was appropriate at one stage is counterproductive later on; sacrificial, because there is incompensable loss nonetheless, the loss of closest intimacy with mother, even if it is for the better. No wonder, as entrepreneurial endeavors begin to take off, there is often internecine bloodletting and war. Weaning, even as its rewards are realized, is anxiety provoking.

There is no way out of sacrificial loss, except through memory and forgiveness, namely, through an entrepreneurial myth, a Bildungsroman, whether it be Augustine's *Confessions* or the Hebrew Bible. One of the great skills of entrepreneurs is knowing how to remember and to forgive.

There are much greater tragedies than sacrifice. To be abandoned is one of them: to have no good-enough devoted mother who holds the enterprise, to miss adaptive solutions, to have no neutral space, to be inhabited by ghosts. In each case, the child or the enterprise is driven from development to pathology. To be abandoned and not to be held is to fail to develop the capacity to be alone and so be real for oneself. It is not to be autonomous. It is not to have help in inventing adaptive solutions that again would lead to autonomy and so one is forced to be on one's own in an awful way. And to be abandoned is to have one's space for play and invention rigidified too early or to be invaded by agendas having nothing to do with you, fulfilling others' fantasies rather than your real needs. To be abandoned developmentally, to have to do it on your own, is disastrous. It is an ironically free enterprise. No one does it, and survives, on their own.[52]

Sacrifice may be ritualistic. But it is actually felt and understood as appropriate and necessary as development works itself out. We sacrifice what we are doing in the service of what we want to do next, that wanting driven by the pleasures of autonomy and growth.[53] We give up what we once took as most dear, for an excitement and interestingness that, too, becomes eventually most dear to ourselves. It, too, shall be given up in turn. And at each stage we become prepared for what is next. Such a logic of development is about the evolving capacity to be alone, to be on one's own in the presence of mother and then when she is not there. Who enacts these sacrifices? Both the mother and child, both the entrepreneur and the entrepreneurial idea.

When we speak of child development in terms of ages and stages we understand that "age" is a label we place on a structure of successive stages, each one more or less necessary for the next. Development's patterning might be adaptively routed around, but its functional demands at each stage are rather more incontrovertible. The next stage depends on them. Enterprises not only grow but they mature, and there is no substitute for maturation, and so no substitute for mothering, at least if we want pleasure rather than pathology.

When baby is ready for what is to come next, then it helps for mother to know what to do. An experienced mother surely knows, even when she does not know. "[Toni's] mother was an experienced mother. In spite of her feelings of guilt and fears for the future of her blind child, she was a woman whose motherliness responded to need, and this baby who needed her in special ways evoked deep tenderness in her."[54] Just at this moment it helps to have some advice, to have some methods for proceeding. Fraiberg's descriptions of her child-guidance devices for these moments of adaptive blockage and need are so poignant in that they are methods that an ordinary devoted mother could use in her own way. She will now be rather more inventive than before, since things have begun to work a bit. Having sacrificed a whole way of being, now perhaps perceived as pathological, mother and baby are ready to go on. The blockage is eased, and there is takeoff once more.

Letting Baby Cry

Devoted attention to the moment, to the concrete and the immediate, allows you to become unstuck. You discover how what you already know might be useful, but in a context that violates the conventional rules or is off by a bit.[55] When mother and baby are stuck, so that neediness becomes an awful tyranny, they must discover developmental solutions. Baby is ready for what will come next but is blocked by his own defenses and coping devices, only to be released by actual developmental progress.

So, here I am, afraid to spoil the child, and he's screaming (with fear, teeth, gas?). It has been going on a few nights like this. A new trend? Forever? Until he's eighteen? I always need to remember that it will change, whatever it is.

False starts. He awakens at 11:30 P.M. screaming. (I will not give a detailed description of the screaming. Let it be said that there are very different kinds of cries, screams, whimpers, and sobs, with rather different powers and anxieties.) Nothing works, nothing that worked last week seems to be comforting. So, out of desperation and to kill time, we watch television for a while. He focuses. After several false starts, when he cries hysterically every time he is about to be put down, or after thirty seconds—although from another point of view these are the right starts—he goes back to sleep. There is no conversation, no direct comforting. All I am doing is holding him, a holding that is crucial. Those false starts—too little television? too soon back to bed?—are what get to me, if I believe there is a right answer. Rather, there is an interplay of his needs, my intuition, and my desire to get it over with, and memories of those two-hour bouts when I let him cry and was going back and forth, up and down with him. Perhaps we need false starts, trials and errors, to find out when we are ready to go to bed. And eventually the last thing we do works.

The first of those nights I feel murderous. I shout (quietly), "F— you." Things then get much worse, more hysterical, more frightening. He needs comfort and consistency. I am not quite comforting him so much as holding him resentfully. So there is guilt, once I am quieter and feel what I have just done. What he needs is firmness and discipline, and I need to acknowledge my anger and appreciate his frightened and frustrated position.

When to respond? When am I willing not to bear his crying? When am I willing to believe there are patterns, and we shall ride this one out, rather than panic at what is happening? ("Will it go on forever?" is the sign of panic.)

What is funny is that a month later it all seems like ancient history. Surely he has changed, and surely he still gets up sometimes. Yet the texture and the meaning are different. I am under less pressure, he is more manageable, and I feel for him better. And his teeth are in! His diaper rash and loose bowel are over. The awfulness is forgotten, actively forgotten I bet.

But the frustration and problems return a few months later, when he is fourteen months and I am tired. There is a pattern when I am angry or tired, he frustrated or demanding.

Regulating and caring. I do not get very far when I think in terms of behavior and punishment and spoiling. I become ineffective, angry, frustrated. I am not tougher than he is, for I am not so frightened, not so determined to grow up. It is not fun to hold him resentfully, even if some of the time I may have to do that.

He has real needs. They can be responded to, although perhaps not met. His desires are legitimate, even if he and I do not know how to fulfill them. At these times he needs to recenter himself and his body, calm down enough to find out that he feels tired. When he does so he can be a big boy, that rather mature happy child that he can be. But there will always be diffuse unfocused energy, sobbing, crying, out of control. (And what does "out of control" mean?)

Eventually we both become pros, knowing what to do, talking to each other. He is happier, delighted, reassured by his place in the world. And so am I. Yet then something happens. We are no longer in touch. I always think he has changed or someone did something to him. But perhaps my mood is different and he is responding. Still, it is curious how I think of him as the center of change. Eventually we are once more in step. That I might track him smoothly, or he me, does not continue. The disruptions lead to new plateaus, and the modes of tracking are themselves developmental and not universal, and so we need to keep reinventing new tracking modes.

Solving problems. Should you let baby cry? One current consensus is yes. Go in and comfort him, check out if there is a "real" problem, and leave. In a few nights he will not cry, or will at least comfort himself and go to bed. Or go in every five minutes and comfort him, but do not lift him out of the crib, be brief... Of course, he is not to go to bed with you. If you do not teach him "independence," he will pay and so will you. None of this is sadistic. It is not the strategy to pursue when he is ill or newly frightened. Rather, it is to set up a pattern of all-night sleeping. You are giving him a chance to be a disciplined member of the family, giving him a chance to take charge of himself.

Every parent knows that crying comes in many forms. Fear is different from physical pain which is different from terror. Sobs and shivering, after a half-hour bout of screaming, are for me the most scary moments, that screaming being so obviously out of control, his being so frightened. Does he feel my comforting? Or are things so bad he needs to cry it out to start getting in touch? And what is "crying it out"?

Limits to caring. Of course, there are times when I am exhausted and I cannot cope, or frustrated by my attempts at calming him, or I am too angry. I must go inside and eat something, regain my energy and center and composure, and so I let him scream (assuming no emergency). And I may just give up out of exhaustion.

Can't I just put out more? the devoted self-sacrificing mother. No, unless it is a life-and-death situation. Otherwise, and almost always it is otherwise,

I need first to put that oxygen mask on myself. I have to assume he will do OK, be permanently scarred by love and by being ignored, my doing the best-enough I can so we can go on as a family.

Communication and hypothesis testing. I have been leading up to another view of letting baby cry. Crying is his mode of talking to me, and letting baby cry is a permissive letting. It is to hear his crying as meaningful, not something to be gotten rid of but to be responded to. What that meaning is, is sometimes unclear. And so I respond the best I can, and my response gives meaning to what he does. That response may be adequate to the situation, or not. It will surely change his mood and how he feels. In particular, how he feels about being responded to in the way that I did will very much affect his mood. I can make things much worse. But it is not fair to invoke a null hypothesis at this moment, and say that things might have gone that way in any case whatever I did or did not do. That is rather more skeptical than is allowed by our experience and our sense of ourselves.[56]

Returning to how my response elicits and sets up the meaning of his cries, here is another example. He transfers food from his right hand to his left and drops it over the side of the high chair. (He cannot so easily drop it off the right side since a wall is in the way. Or is he a lefty?) I have become righteously angry and frustrated, firmly saying no! Maybe he is being defiant, and so what? More likely what is going on is, No I do not want this to eat, or, Let's play and see what happens. He has begun to look overboard a while afterward, not for the dropping stuff but for the dropped condition. Two weeks later, dropping food is no longer the issue. (Always, one must describe situations in their present, with all the hysteria and fear. That it does go away and then there is something new does not efface how awful that present can be.)

My response offers meaning to what he does, and he may offer another meaning, here play rather than defiance. Then I am back to responding. At least I get away from trying to control him. (Sometimes the issue is actual danger, and then protection is in order.)

Testing regimes and matters of control and error. By the way, there is no Rubicon, once crossed, that then determines future behavior. If this time you go back in to him when you should have let him cry, you may well breach a training regime and there will be setbacks–if what you are up to is a training regime. But usually much more is going on, like learning to break the rules when necessary and still be disciplined.[57] If that is so, acceptable violation of the rules and the invocation of new ones is subtly dependent on the situation, its urgency, its meaning. When something more is going on, the training metaphor misses that moreness.

Another way of putting it: We may well repeat past errors, although we do not have to. But if we do so we will repeat them in new ways. That we are condemned to repeat history does not say how it will repeat. Repetition is a way of coherently telling a story of our disparate modes of sin.

History, management, witness. Crying is not managed. It is dealt with and responded to, borne, suffered, witnessed, alleviated. The last thing I did, the one that finally works, works because of all of what I did beforehand. Our responses to each other are historical, to what we have done over time and not merely to what we did just now. And how we interpret what we did just now is also historical.[58]

When my baby wakes in the late evening screaming and shuddering with fear, and not just crying, I expect we shall work it out together. There is no answer. But we do know what to do. Tonight is a new kind of upset, and he cannot put himself together as he ordinarily does. So my usual talents fail me, and so do his. We are lost, or so it seems. No policy works, and it is not clear what the issue is. Eventually we both are exhausted and fall asleep. But the next time I turn on the light, we play while he sobs, and in two minutes he rubs his eyes and wants to go back to bed. We have invented a once-in-a-while second goodnight. The issue is not my treating him, or being firm, or giving in to him, as it is often portrayed in some of the baby books. Rather, how do we reconstitute ourselves so that we can go on?

Baby's crying is not so easily managed or fixed or repaired. Rather, we try one thing, then another, and then another, and something finally works; and it is that sequence of failures and successes that matters and eventually works. "The last thing we do is what works" says that history matters, that what led up to the present prepares us for it. And it says that change is conversionary, as I described it in chapter 1. Eliminating all or even most of the seemingly ineffective or wrong moves is a lovely fantasy. That fantasy has little to do with what I must do tonight.

Although we shall eventually establish new effective patterns, no single fix works reliably. It does not work in some slightly different context. In trying out the various remedies I change my baby's mood and my own, perhaps exhausting him and me along the way. Of course, it might have worked just as well to have done nothing, but, again, that null hypothesis is hard to accept as a way of being caring. Life is a contaminated experiment, and I will never know for sure what made the difference.[59] That does not prevent my doing better, and my finding patterns of action that work well most of the time.

In these contexts, good advice may be of three sorts: Try this, then try that, then try this, then take a break,...highly provisional suggestions, offered nonjudgmentally, meant as reminders of what might work, suggesting new avenues for action after we have exhausted our own list and ourselves, helping to shake us out of our own traps. Even more useful is a theory about what baby is doing, feeling, and experiencing, and suggestions for action based on that theory. If baby is taken as a soulful and disciplined creature, with authentic motives, someone much like us, the theory will allow us to have a feeling for him that puts us in his place. If that theory is also about ourselves and what we are experiencing, it will make even greater sense, provide the comfort of recognition, and give us courage.

What works depends on the moment, past history, this baby's character, details that are fully loaded with meaning and in fact are multiply meaningful. The artist Robert Irwin describes the relevant experience, but at the racetrack in pari-mutuel betting: "The thing about the race track is the incredibly wide range of information that has a bearing. If you're going to have a chance there, you have to achieve the discipline necessary for keeping track of all of it. The one thing more than anything else is learning to pay attention....and then *it's like you run your hand over the race*."[60] The metaphor is bearing witness and testimony, care and devotion. We meet the challenge of fortune with virtue, so that we and our babies make the best of what we have been given. Fortunately, babies are going concerns, willing to train their parents to treat them in just the right way if the parents will pay attention.

Some lessons. Actual entrepreneurial situations are meant to attack our prescriptions and prohibitions by their details and ironies. A sensible systematic method proves inapplicable or its conclusions are contrary to our mission. Those uncontrolled experiments that are our entrepreneurial projects are the ones most subject to fortune, to fate, to the gifts we are not to anticipate. We are to rise to the occasion, be virtuous, meet contingency on its own ground, making the best of it.[61]

Yet your baby is on your side; she is not simply a problem out there. So she will work with you, especially insofar as you show her how. The solutions to adaptive problems are to be found on site, your retrospectively seeing in the tradition of prescription and prohibition a justification for what in the end works. It takes an extraordinary quality of character to stay with the situation, to attend faithfully to what is needed, when the situation is one that you would rather extinguish. Such devotion to the present is rewarded, but that is not apparent as you are trapped by problems that seem insoluble and that subject you to tyranny. Such devoted motherhood, while authentically pleasurable, is also too demanding. Fortunately, you are bound to your baby (and to your enterprise). Such binding allows you to do more than you would have conceived possible for yourself.

Autonomy and Mission

If binding and sacrifice lead to mission, as we saw in chapter 2, so bonding and development lead to autonomy. To have the capacity to be alone, to be real for oneself, is to allow the world its own otherness and to be responsive to that otherness. The infant has become a child with a rich subjective self.[62] The enterprise is separate from the entrepreneur and responsive to its markets. If marketing is having what other people want,[63] that ability "to have" only comes with a sense that others are different from you and so must be engaged. Otherwise, a firm is either isolated from its market or slavishly following it. In each case, the firm is in serious trouble, in the first case because what it produces is no longer indulged by the market and there is presumably little in the way of sales, in the second because market makers will dominate and capture the major returns. To have a mission that is not in touch with a community is to be either isolated or only marginally effective.

The baby or the enterprise becomes autonomous as it develops the capacity to be alone. Mothers make infants powerful by providing them with the reliability that allows them to go out in the world and receive pleasure from it. Once that happens, the infants are launched, for they hunger for that diverse pleasure while still returning to mommy. And firms are made powerful by their entrepreneurs' giving them the support they need early on so that they too can go out in the world and begin to receive the pleasurable response of market. Once that market is revealed, the rewards from intimately interacting with such a market are authentically motivating.

If an internalized mother empowers infants, what we as outsiders see is a disciplined child who knows how to be with others.[64] That discipline leads to membership in the larger community and to its interesting rewards. If an internalized entrepreneur empowers an endeavor, what we as outsiders see is a responsive institution or firm that is involved with its market in an inventive, satisfying manner. In each case, baby or enterprise shows what we call courage and character, integrity and authenticity.

What if, however, there are ghosts in the nursery and in the entrepreneur's garage? Mothers and entrepreneurs might well find themselves "identifying with the aggressor," taking the role of the forces that would destroy their babies, and so harming their infants and endeavors. For the mother that aggressor might be her mother who hurt her. For the entrepreneur such an aggressor might be the demanding and damning analytics of modern abstract finance and marketing. Still, the moral demands of being a mother may be invoked as a mission in the service of autonomy, the mother in effect saying: "I would never want that to happen to my child."[65] "But Mrs. Shapiro persisted, gently, and made the crucial interpretation. She said, 'I could imagine that as a little girl you might be so scared, that in order to make yourself less scared you might start talking and sounding like your [frightening] mother.' Annie said again, 'I don't want to talk about it right now.' But she was deeply affected by Mrs. Shapiro's words….[Eventually] Annie was able to say, 'I don't want my child to be afraid of me'" (p. 132). And so the mother, if she is offered a sympathetic ear may be able to fight off those ghosts, much as a prophetic mission (God's ear) saved the Israelites from their own temptations and so led them to freedom.

Mothers or entrepreneurs must put to the fore the pain and suffering of being impotent and little and vulnerable. (Recall the pathos that characterizes prophecy.) This is experienced most brutally by new enterprises in highly competitive, overly monitored systems.

> [T]hese [parents who are possessed by ghosts] are the parents who, earlier, in the extremity of [their own] childhood terror, formed a pathological identification with the dangerous and assaultive enemies of the ego [say, their parents]….[But for these parents who have been able to ward off those ghosts] the pain and suffering have not undergone total repression. In remembering, they are saved from the blind repetition of that morbid past. Through remembering they identify with an injured child (the childhood self), while the parent who does not remember may find himself in an unconscious alliance and identification with the fearsome figures of that past. In this way, the parental past is inflicted upon the child. (pp. 134–135)

What we have to protect ourselves against is the same school of hard knocks that we have survived. The way to protection is through memory: "I would never let my child go through what I went through" (p. 135). That mothering, that devotion, that sacrifice of repetition in the service of growth and autonomy, that allowing for a neutral space, that ability to hold the enterprise, that ability to freely provide adaptive solutions—all of which might be spit out, as was milk, by the child—is the greatest lesson the entrepreneur can learn. But it is a very hard lesson to master, and as we discuss Oedipus in the next chapters, that difficulty will become tragically clear.

4

CREATIVE DESTRUCTION
Antigone and Oedipus, Courage and Technology

Creative Destruction and Pollution. Tragedy and Civilization. Courage, Devotion, Loyalty, Resilience, Perversion, A Phenomenology of Courage. Why Rome, Jerusalem, and Athens? Incest, Parricide, and Abandonment. Errancy and Contingency, Statistics, Fortune, and History. Pollution and Problem Solving.

"[T]he process of industrial mutation–if I may use that biological term–that incessantly revolutionizes the economic structure *from within,* incessantly destroying the old one, incessantly creating a new one. This process of Creative Destruction is the essential fact about capitalism."[1] So Joesph Schumpeter describes how, in the matter of course, entrepreneurs rend the fabric of society in an unending sequence of overturnings, violating the rules, destroying the conventional institutions. They have an unnatural commitment to their projects, loyal to them even when it would seem prudent and rational to follow another, perhaps more conventional path. Entrepreneurs must be blind, their insights about their project in effect balanced by a systematic incapacity to see impossible difficulties and destructive side effects.[2] The violations and destructions they enact are to them simply necessary, their own courageous acts being just what they must do, merely on the way, a juggernaut that will naturally have some folks jump under it to be ritually sacrificed.

What does it mean to be such a creative destroyer? Why is entrepreneurship so destructive? How does such destruction later heal, so reestablishing a tradition?

Creative Destruction and Pollution

A story of modern entrepreneurial endeavor driven by technological invention might go as follows:

> A technological invention, discarded by its originators for its ominous implications, is then, as a foundling so to speak, adopted by innocents. The

> invention proves fortunate for them. But in time, having been modified to avoid harming the innocent, it destroys its original inventors—all the while proving more and more technically successful, even being readopted by and enriching the culture of its originators. Eventually, side effects of the adopted invention become dominant in that original culture, and in time the invention is discovered to be the culprit; its readopters (namely, its original inventors, who were once its rejecters or discarders) now become in their own eyes culprits, the invention also being its own corruption. They are all blind, or so they believe, for did they not once foresee this outcome?
>
> Still, inventions breed successors, which then vie for dominion (not merely compete for markets), only one of which is dominant and fully adopted, the others being outcast yet retaining their own partisans. The authority and power and dominion of the original tradition and its invention escapes any of the successors. That original tradition eventually dies out, in effect compensating for the harm and even the good it has wrought. This compensation allows for the reestablishment of a preinvention, premodern "traditional" culture.
>
> Still, the successor inventions remain in conflict, none having authentic authority, and in time they, too, do each other in, none achieving dominion or market. The world is now rather more primitive, and in such a world conventional forms of authority, based on power and blood, are in conflict. Who shall inherit the authority that once was appropriated by that remarkable, revered, and feared original invention? Traditional blood ties are perhaps morally superior to those of power; and personal loyalty and devotion rather than technical efficiency may well play a practical role in the protection and launching of an uncertain invention. But blood ties tend to lose to power in actual conflict and realpolitik. In its triumph, power is revealed for what it is—undisciplined, violent, illegitimate, and ultimately unjustified in its own eyes. And it, too, will be defeated by a successor outcast invention, so beginning the story once more.

Much of this story reads as an epitome of commonplaces drawn from jeremiads about technology, invention, and entrepreneurship in modern society.[3] It reveals an ambivalence about creative destruction and technology, indicating the not-so-linear nature of progress. There are, to be sure, rather upbeat, more linearly progressive stories, but I think they read well only to those who have not experienced any interesting struggles or failures, or who have chosen to forget having experienced them. And that forgetting generally proves disastrous in time. My concern in this chapter is, What do entrepreneurs learn from such an awful story? (Answer: they learn everything —and that only encourages them all the more.)

In this story creative destruction has no end and there is no protection from creative destruction's eventually engulfing you. Savagery lurks, in a world where contest leads to annihilation rather than where competition leads to division of a market.[4] Yet to be so perpetually and recurrently wrenched from tradition and origin makes for a surprising and interesting albeit alienating world. And to be so unredeemed is to be forced to be practical, to be responsive to actual contingencies rather than living in fantasy. Moreover, to be so ignorant of your origins, a consequence of such recurrently disruptive change, is to be in the end dangerous to yourself. Adoption that is not understood as such and is thought to be natural is likely to be undermined. We might expect that matters of loyalty and devotion and commitment are crucial in such a self-consuming world, one in which conventional ties are questioned and disrupted.

If motherhood is a model of launching an enterprise, then to be taken from your mother is a wrenching separation corresponding to the tragic in entrepreneurship.[5] Such tragedy will be the story of innovation, invention, and questioning of the established order.[6]

To be wrenched from your mother recalls Augustine wrenching himself from Monica, and Moses being abandoned and exposed by his mother as was Oedipus by his. Such wrenching makes the issues of commitment rather more problematic than we have seen in chapters 2 and 3, since there is good attached to being wrenched and set free.

I have deliberately imported into this story a discourse that is rather more warlike than marketlike. To be wrenched from your mother, that awful scene in tyranny and war, is what I am talking about here when I speak of invention and adoption. It is a model of creative destruction. Creative destruction is not just a lovely birth. It is killing or at least denying the mother and father as well, and perhaps the reestablishment of a new family.

From the point of view of the entrepreneur, my story is perhaps still too abstract, my interpretation mythic and psychological. I have described personified technologies ("invention breeds successors"), but not entrepreneurial actors who are driven and motivated. Even if technology may be taken to be a disrupting insemination, a pollution that transforms a society, an incest that starts a new line, real actors do that polluting and incest. What do they actually do, and does it at all correspond to killing the mother, to pollution, to incest? (Answer: entrepreneurs in pursuit of their idea inadvertently destroy their own tradition; they mix what was once unmixable, namely, in those new combinations of the means of production; and their seminal ideas bear fruit in unconventional places.)

Similarly, if there is to be reconciliation and redemption for large and tragic losses so that such losses are not totally unredeemable, then who or what institution enacts that reconciliation? Who absorbs the losses, in effect, and allows the entrepreneur and the system to go on? (Answer: as I discuss in chapter 5, we have a cure or medicine of commercial bankruptcy provision or of biblical jubilee rather than a traditional scapegoat.)[7]

Finally, in a society in which alienation—that continuous overturning of alliances and conventions—is so productive, as it is in modern society, how are we to be loyal and devoted to an institution, how are we to be traditional? (Answer: commitment defines just those areas we take as beyond overturning, for each of us has untouchable or sacred places. Entrepreneurs are in this sense unavoidably traditional.)

As we shall see in this chapter and the next, pollution, redemption, and devotion characterize entrepreneurial actors and their world, and it is in this sense that entrepreneurship is a sacred, premodern, premarket endeavor, even if we nowadays revere it in commercial or capitalist terms. The abstraction, myth, and psychology here are simply descriptive, at least to the practicing entrepreneur. I hope the description feels right, even if the terms of reference are not the usual ones.

Put differently, entrepreneurial activities wrench us away from our homes and hearths and mothers, offering instead ideas and solutions and technologies. So we develop modes of reconciling ourselves to such disruption, modes of reestablishing a sense of tradition and orderliness, modes that in effect offer a sacrifice for incompensable losses, a social therapeutic or cure. What is demanded of the entrepreneur is the capacity to contest others, putting himself on the line through courage and loyalty: courage that could never be understood as competition, which is always defined in rather more narrow terms and contexts; loyalty that could never be understood as investment, for here there are no such rational returns.

Tragedy and Civilization[8]

It would not be surprising to use agonistic discourse were we in a society in which war and honor were ever-present issues, in which armies were central to civic virtue, in which catastrophe (meaning overturning) and catharsis and passion were close at hand. In fact, the story I told at the beginning of the chapter and the questions I asked about pollution, redemption, and devotion are an epitome of Sophocles' Oedipus tragedies (*Oedipus the King, Oedipus at Colonus,* and *Antigone*):[9] Oedipus is the original technological invention (for he is the great problem solver, more or less out of nowhere); his originators are his birth parents Laius and Jocasta (of Thebes); his adopters are Polybus and Merope (of Corinth); his technical success is solving the riddle of the Sphinx; the plague in Thebes is the side effect; the readopters, Jocasta and Oedipus, kill and blind themselves, respectively. The successor inventions are Oedipus's sons Eteocles and Polynices, and

Oedipus eventually dies redemptively at Colonus. Finally, the successors Polynices and Eteocles kill each other at the Theban gates, and Antigone and Creon claim authority through blood and through power, respectively, with Creon eventually challenged by successors to Polynices' followers. In the following, I have opened up this story with the above keys.

> A technological invention (Oedipus), discarded by its originators (Laius and Jocasta) for its ominous implications, is then, as a foundling so to speak, adopted by innocents (Polybus and Merope, of Corinth, who are childless). The invention proves fortunate for them. But in time, having been modified to avoid harming the innocent, it still destroys its original inventors (Laius, to start with)—all the while proving more and more technically successful (solving the riddle of the Sphinx), even being readopted by and enriching the culture of its originators (marrying Jocasta, good times in Thebes). Eventually, side effects (plague) of the adopted invention become dominant in that original culture, and in time the invention is discovered to be the culprit (discovery scene in *Oedipus the King*); its readopters (namely, its original inventors, who were once its rejecters or discarders) now become in their own eyes culprits (Jocasta and Oedipus), the invention also itself being its own corruption. They are all blind, or so they believe, for did they not once foresee this outcome?
>
> Still, inventions breed successors (Eteocles and Polynices, Oedipus's children and brothers), which vie for dominion (not merely compete for markets), only one of which is dominant and fully adopted (Eteocles), the others being outcast yet retaining their own partisans (Polynices). The authority and power and dominion of the original tradition and its invention escapes any of the successors (Oedipus curses both his sons). That original tradition eventually dies out, in effect compensating for the harm and even the good it has wrought (Oedipus, at Colonus). This allows for the reestablishment of a preinvention, premodern "traditional" culture.
>
> Still, the successor inventions (Eteocles and Polynices) remain in conflict, none having authentic authority, and in time they, too, do each other in, none achieving dominion or market. The world is now rather more primitive, and in such a world conventional forms of authority, based on power and blood, are in conflict (Creon and Antigone). Who shall inherit the authority that once was appropriated by that remarkable, revered, and feared original invention? Traditional blood ties are perhaps morally superior to those of power; and personal loyalty and devotion rather than technical efficiency may well play a practical role in the protection and launching of an uncertain invention. But blood ties tend to lose to power in actual conflict and realpolitik. In its triumph, power (Creon) is revealed for what it is—undisciplined, violent, illegitimate, and ultimately unjustified in its own eyes. And it, too, will be defeated by a successor outcast invention (the Epigonoi, sons of the followers of Polynices, the Seven against Thebes), so beginning the story once more.

The sacred and the tragic represent crucial features of entrepreneurial endeavor. We shall examine Sophoclean tragedy as a key to the dread of modernization, showing how our model, here tragedy, provides a phenomenology of what entrepreneurs actually do. Notably, tragedy itself is the act of creative destruction, its actors in Greek being *agonistai* (contestants), the lead actor being the protagonist.[10] Let me give the full text of something I paraphrased earlier.

> Ritual [here think of corporate order] tends to be conservative and affirmative of the cosmic and social order. Tragedy [here think of entrepreneurial endeavor] is innovative, polysemous, and deeply questioning of that order. The myths embodied or reflected in ritual are basically unitary in meaning. Those of tragedy are complex and problematical, open to new interpretations, focal points of conflicted points of view and divided values....
>
> The tragic hero has the task of confronting the most violent divisions within himself, enduring his *Selbstenzweiung*, the experience of his self as contradiction and conflict. This experience is the riddle which he presents to himself. He becomes conscious of a self which is also his enemy. Rather than evade or repress this vision, he suffers its full consequences. His life becomes an open existence with his evil double, his dark shadow. As the unity of the tragic polis [or civilization] divides to admit a potential savagery, so the king/hero (or queen/heroine), the guarantor of the civic or domestic order, divides and opens to reveal violence, destructive passion, blindness. But through the course of his suffering he compels this other self [the polluting self, the self that reconfigures the means of production] to stand apart and become visible in its separateness.[11]

Tragedy here is the account of innovation and destructive transformation. The abiding question will be, In what sense are the consequences of such transformation to be borne: as redemptive, or retributive, or occasional?

The parallels with earlier chapters are rather rich, and they indicate further why tragedy, as Sophocles defines it, is so powerfully suggestive for our concern with entrepreneurship. Sophocles lived for most of the fifth century (496-406 BCE), the time of Athens's triumph; yet he died just before the "barbarian" Spartans invaded Athens much as Augustine died just before North Africa fell to the Vandals (here also we might think of Moses dying just before reaching the Promised Land and its tribulations).[12] So Sophocles lived just before the fall from grace and the sacred, as did Augustine and Moses, when heroic acts might still be celebrated over prudence. And to celebrate entrepreneurship as I have been doing requires such a commitment to the heroic. To deprecate entrepreneurship, to view it as too violent to be worth bearing, is to give up the heroic for the prudential.

Moreover, for these model entrepreneurs the disrupted relationship to their parents is fundamental. It is the narrative and personal motive for the stories I tell about them. As we might expect from chapter 3, growth toward autonomy is weaning from mother. But here the disruption is altogether more profound. Again, Augustine is fascinated by weaning, and he must in the end sneak away from his mother. His father plays the most minor of roles in the story he tells of himself in the *Confessions.* Moses and Oedipus do not know their parents, and that ignorance is the crucial fact in how they survive at all, and how they are marked forever in their actions. And Antigone, who will not become a mother, becomes in effect the mother to Oedipus, her father and her older brother. These "Oedipal" issues are not about marrying your mother and killing your father. Rather, they are about a willful denial of knowledge. We force ourselves not to know so that we may break with convention.[13] It is a denial that allows one to act decisively and powerfully: entrepreneurially, I would claim.

We all have problems with our parents, no matter how ritualized; that is how we grow. Sons have got to make peace with a mom who has had to reject them, yet with whom they have been most intimate, and with a dad whom they might well want to conquer or kill. Entrepreneurs make a curious peace with tradition, one that transforms the mythic eros and thanatos in conflict into an enduring institution. Such a commonplace about civilization and its discontents becomes in the hands of the entrepreneur the actual mechanism for creative destruction. The technological trick of invention, the one that allows you to marry your mother, along the way killing your father (that is, incestuously recombining the means of production, along the way putting others out of business), depends fundamentally on being ignorant of the truth while being technically quite adept. But it is just such ignorance of the forbidden and such technical skill that is entrepreneurship. Technical skill sets us up for self-discovery, as is surely the case for Augustine, Moses, and Oedipus. (For Augustine the technical skill is rhetoric, for Moses it is prophecy, for Oedipus it is riddling.) These skills set the stage for a savagery that is as well the interesting postlapsarian world.[14]

Sophocles and fifth-century (BCE) Greece are taken to represent war and savagery and violence, rather than the rational and thoughtful self-control of the world of the fourth century, the world of Plato and Aristotle.[15] In such a world of blood and birth and pride and vanity, for that is how the fifth century echoes the eighth of Homer, loss is not simply coming in second in gentlemanly competition.[16] Rather, who is to be dominant, on top? Loss, in such a world, is humiliation and castration.

Creative destruction is serious and awful business—for Augustine, for the Israelites, for Oedipus. (Notably, Antigone is not to be castrated.) But it is in Greece's internecine battles for power, what might be called controversies about the structure of a presbyterium of conflicting governors (in contrast to Augustine's episcopal world and Moses' congregational world), that courage is a dominant motif.

To redeem the claims I have been making as simply phenomenological description, I examine *Antigone* and *Oedipus the King,* and in chapter 5 *Oedipus at Colonus,* and so allow to actual entrepreneurs a sufficiently powerful language to speak of themselves in terms of the traditions of courage, technology, and redemption. No one writes a play such as *Colonus* (or, correspondingly, *The Tempest*) as merely a ritualistic way to make peace with the world toward the end of life, although the plays are about such a peace. Rather, Sophocles and Shakespeare and even Moses want to say what they have come to understand about the tragic, the sacred, and the salvific. By a sense of impending horror, they are driven to say just what must not be known explicitly if the entrepreneur is to be an entrepreneur when he or she is younger.[17] Yet at the same time, the young hero or the entrepreneur surely knows the archetypal story, the tragedy, and knows that he shall not avoid its consequences—even if he hopes for a family romance, with rather more protective parents and a more perfect and fair world. Such an ambivalence, of knowledge denied but already possessed, of a mother you do not know but nonetheless in effect recognize, is not a contradiction for the entrepreneur. Rather, it is just what motivates entrepreneurship: courage permits us to die; technology frees us but allows us to pollute ourselves; and redemption is the occasion for the next disruption. I take entrepreneurship to be driven by the desire for an interesting, surprising world. It is a defense against boredom, a resolution of anxiety.

Courage

Antigone has come to be the model of courage, and Sophocles' version of her in *Antigone* is the archetype.[18] Why is this woman our model of courage, a woman who is cursed never to bear children,[19] and why is courage defined in such a political context? Why is courage defined for us by this ancient Greek work of the fifth century BCE?[20]

Recall, for the moment, that Antigone is Oedipus's daughter (and half-sister), and that she with the help of his other daughter and Antigone's sister, Ismene, in his blindness guides him to his resting place in Colonus on the outskirts of Athens. In *Antigone* her brothers, cursed by their father to kill each other, have just done so, one defending Thebes, the other attacking it. The loyal Eteocles is buried properly; the traitorous Polynices is unburied, attacked by the elements and the animals. King Creon, Oedipus's successor and Antigone's uncle, so decrees, for "our country *is* our safety" (l.

211). Antigone, devoted and loyal to her family and the gods, proceeds to violate that ruling, is caught, magnificently resists Creon, and is condemned to death. The gods are not pleased. Creon eventually sees the error of his self-righteous ways, as did Oedipus. But Antigone is already dead, Creon's son (and Antigone's fiancé) is also dead; Creon's wife then kills herself as well.

Entrepreneurs, like tragic figures in general, may well know everything tragic I say in the story of technology that begins this chapter. Tragic figures do know their fates, at least abstractly and formally, if not in exact detail. Such knowledge motivates and energizes rather than depresses the entrepreneur, as it does also the tragic figure, and neither ignorance nor an idiotic pride ("It won't happen to me") accounts for this motivating power. To repeat an earlier question, Just how are the consequences of tragedy to be borne? To the tragic figure, the abstract structural account of pollution and redemption that I tell, that story of unending retribution, is treated as a fact. But for the moment its exact relevance is not at all obvious.[21] One might find a way of going around its inevitabilities, perhaps fulfilling them symbolically.[22] Moreover, it is in the details, in the revelation, that I am an entrepreneur. I could not understand the story's meaning otherwise, and so I must act in the concrete.

I am defined by the tragic, but in a way that I make my own. So, to be wrenched from mother is to be autonomous, rather than to be unredeemed and problematic. To be devoted and loyal is to be focused on what matters in a project, rather than to be dominated by externally denominated pollutions. To be barren (as Antigone must be) is to be beyond even symbolic castration, beyond being defined by women's role as against men's, by women as against men. Namely, Antigone's devotion to her family is extraordinary, not readily defined by her being a woman. To be a pollution, as is Oedipus, is to see pollution for what it is, something you live with every day, not something to be extirpated.

Entrepreneurs do not see themselves as outside a system of market and a structure of historical tragedy. But they are not defined by system and structure. One might call this their foolishness or their pride. In the actual doings of entrepreneurship, there is a lightness of being despite the inevitabilities of market and tragedy, there is a sense of being just right despite the fact that others might judge you as having gone too far and so being irrational. Antigone feels just this lightness, especially when she compares herself to her sister Ismene, who is in the end trapped by prudence and convention, and her uncle Creon who is paralyzed by righteousness.[23] Antigone's sacred obligations, still fully meaningful to the world of fifth-century Greece, give her courage. They define her actual tasks. She transcends the idiocy of tragedy, its automaticity, by what she must do. She is foolish, defying the gods as Creon represents them politically, because she must be. The sacred is a motive and a justification for doing what others perceive as merely foolish.[24]

This woman, defined by her familial obligation to her father and her brother (and not to a husband or children), for us represents courage by how she redefines convention and social role, beyond prudence or bravery. We learn from Antigone that the entrepreneur transcends system and structure through her particular actions, which are justified by the situation at hand rather than through some master plan, method, or abstract narrative and mythic structure. Also, the entrepreneur is not disturbed much by violation and mixture, for she has lived with them always (as has Antigone with Oedipus). She is outraged and disbelieving when such violations become the occasion for extirpation and ejection rather than opportunities for justice and devotion.

Antigone's power is hers because she operates on a different plane than Creon's hierarchical one.[25] Antigone is not defined by men and their order. She possesses a power that would not be hers were she playing a conventional win-lose game. Her compassion and apparent mixture of gender qualities allow her insidious room for action. So, too, the entrepreneur possesses a power: to make a space on another stage while elsewhere the conventional others do themselves in.

Antigone teaches us these lessons by her acts: by her actual devotion, loyalty, and resilience; and by her compassion and her comfort with mixture. She is obsessed, parochial, unreasonable, and necrophilial; yet she is also focused, defiant, not to be castrated and not to be annihilated. Her commitments make her into a creative destroyer. She is the downfall of the conventions—namely, of Creon and his wife, Eurydice, and his son and Antigone's fiancé, Haemon—and the determined protagonist of her project. From the point of view of the conventions of her city she is foolish and a traitor; from the point of view of the sacred she is righteous and a heroine. She shows us how vulnerable are the conventions to determined resistance, how they collapse under an attack that denies their legitimacy. But the costs of such resistance are very great indeed. Not only does Antigone die but so does what would have been a fruitful future for her (although her father knew this would be the fate of his daughters). This is no happily-ever-after story of the triumph of the entrepreneur. As we have seen in earlier chapters, there is no reason to believe the entrepreneur gets to any promised land. What is profoundly attractive about the entrepreneur is that insistently ironic quality of creative destruction. While it would be lovely to "make a killing" and retire on your earnings, the conventional story about the successful entrepreneur, such killings are perhaps more tragic than we want to believe.

Death is very close in this Greek world of war and sacrifice and honor. To be living dishonorably is to be dead. So I take it that Antigone is a model of courage not so much for her martyrdom, but for her devotion and loyalty. To be courageous is to fully observe the sacred law, whatever the consequences. Prudential considerations, those that eventually motivate her sister, Ismene, who was earlier quite brave in caring for her father, are cowardly or weak, unmanly. And Antigone is more man than anyone else, for she is a woman. Courage here is not individual, one person sacrificing himself for the sake of another, but rather acting in accord with an ethical commitment defined by a particular situation.[26]

Antigone is a model of courage not only by her acts, but also by her qualities of devotion, loyalty, resilience, and perversion. Those qualities are also characteristic of entrepreneurs, who are, to be sure, usually in rather less mortal and tragic circumstances than is Antigone.

Devotion, Loyalty, Resilience, Perversion

Antigone is sororally devoted to her family, actually to her father/half-brother and then to her brothers. That devotion is in part motivated by eros and love that we might find embarrassing and unseemly: "I'll lie with the one I love and loved by him [Polynices, her brother]" (l. 87). It is also motivated by duty to family, and a finely and perhaps to us curiously wrought ethical sense, so that given a choice of saving a husband or a child or a brother, she would choose to save her brother, for, their parents being dead, there is no way to replace him.

> Never, I tell you,
> if I had been the mother of children
> or if my husband died, exposed and rotting—
> I'd never have taken this ordeal upon myself,
> never defied our people's will. What law,
> you ask, do I satisfy with what I say?
> A husband dead, there might have been another.
> A child by another too, if I had lost the first.
> But mother and father both lost in the halls of Death,
> no brother could ever spring to light again.
>
> (ll. 995-1004)[27]

Polynices is cursed by their father, yet Antigone must bury him. Antigone's devotion makes sure sense in the sacred realm of Greek society, where family and eros (and thanatos) are explicit, where expressions of such devotion are mediated by the gods. For us, such devotion is more problematic. It seems so Oedipal, so atavistic, and so particular, provincial, and traditional. For Creon and for the emerging secularized and rationalized Greek society of the late fifth century, Antigone's choices are politically problematic since they challenge the authority of the state (the polis).

A devotion mediated both by eros and by duty to tradition is the kind of devotion that is needed for entrepreneurial endeavors. Yet these are commitments that the rationalized secular world takes as foolish. To be such an entrepreneur you must live in a culture in which the sacred and the particular—namely, a project that is graced and unique—could possibly make good sense (and not in a managerial corporate culture).

To be loyal to the particular, the parochial, and a specific tradition, as is Antigone, is to be taken by Creon as defiant of the universal and the state. Such resistance is incommensurable, economically irrational, foolhardy, insulting to the order of things. To be so resistant and foolish is to be a woman, "not born to contend with men" as Ismene says (l. 75). For a man to lose to men is one thing, to women another. As Creon puts it:

> I'm not the man, not now: she is the man
> if this victory goes to her and she goes free.
>
> (ll. 541–542)

> While I'm alive,
> no woman is going to lord it over me.
>
> (ll. 592–593)

> Therefore
> we must defend the men who live by law,
> never let some woman triumph over us.
> Better to fall from power, if fall we must,
> at the hands of a man—never be rated
> inferior to a woman, never.
>
> (ll. 756–761)

Creon can be destroyed by a woman, castrated by her pollution. But Antigone, while she might be sentenced to death, never to marry and bear children, is not destroyed at all by Creon, by the universal, by the state. She is not defined against any man. Because she is a woman who ought not count, she is not to be a scapegoat for anything. Her resilience derives from the love and duty, the devotion and loyalty she bears. She cannot be polluted, she cannot be castrated. Her freedom lies in a space that others take as not counting, as insignificant: the particular and the family. That space is an implicit challenge to the larger order, and eventually an explicit challenge that reveals the vulnerability of that order.

The entrepreneur, too, is foolhardy, devoted as he is to his particular project. He is an insult to the prevailing order since his project denies the authority of that order and may even destroy it. Yet the entrepreneur is defined by his project, and not defined against anything else. His loyalty, and his devotion to his project are impermeable to the currently dominant conceptions, for those conceptions do not deign to talk to him in his language. His project might well fail, but that is no triumph of the prevailing order. The project has its own difficulties.

The entrepreneur's freedom is the capacity to lay claim to what others take as insignificant, as not counting, and then to make something of it. And the entrepreneur's making something of it, in his insisting on the entrepreneurial project despite its being, as a matter of course, an insult to the prevailing order, encourages that order to lose some of its hegemony, its counterresistance showing its own weakness, its decline now foreordained. To be resilient, to not be defined by the prevailing order, is to make that order impermanent by its own incapacity to absorb difference and variety and mixture. The successful entrepreneurial venture does not merely displace; rather, by its existence it destroys the conventional order.

Entrepreneurship does happen in modern society, despite that society's universalism and rationality. There is still, it seems, room in that society for the particular and the erotic, for what is not defined by the prevailing puritan order, and despite that order's claims to dominance. Despite Creon's claims and fears, his society could well absorb Antigone's actions, and in fact ought to have, according to the gods. If we define perversion as a mixture of what is mutually forbidden and a dispersal and overturning of hierarchies, then what Antigone knows and what Creon cannot conceive is that the world is perverted.[28] One can, and one must, live with impurity and with systematic violations of the rules—namely, your father Oedipus and your brother Polynices. Domination and necessity are simple facts to be maneuvered around the best you can. Your duties are not defined by abstract rules, but by the particularities of your situation. This is not slavery or a mechanical determinism; it is the only way there could be some interesting freedom at all. While perversion is ever present, it is actually no big deal, nothing that need annihilate you or overturn you. That the world is self-consuming, as I describe in the parable that begins this chapter, is a fact we might live with, but surely not be paralyzed by or try to stop. To be an entrepreneur is to be perverted, to take mixture and dispersal as modes of invention and discovery.

Devotion, loyalty, resilience, and perversion characterize Antigone's courage, a courage that allows her to by the way destroy the more universal claims to authority and dominion that Creon represents. To Antigone, and to the entrepreneur, whatever overturning takes place, whatever creative destruction occurs, is a secondary consequence of pursuing a project that she must take as her own. Antigone is unstoppable because nothing Creon could offer touches her; Oedipus is unstoppable because the prudential considerations offered by others have nothing to do with finding the truth. So, too, entrepreneurs are not to be bought off by prudence and profit, for that is not their currency.

How does Antigone teach us these lessons? I would opine she is no role model for us; her devotion and loyalty (and arrogance and conviction) are too frightening to recommend in a liberal world. But she is exemplary; her courage has a madness to its method that makes it inordinately powerful. As for Augustine, Paul, and Moses, there is something horrifying here, something that takes the oxymoronic (or self-contradictory) notion of creative destruction and makes us aware of its inordinate and frightening power, its tragic dimension. That does not mean we cannot domesticate these exemplars to our rather more prudential modern sensibilities. But domestication comes at the cost of the redemptive power of the tragic.

A Phenomenology of Courage[29]

What we might learn from Antigone is that, when we are courageous, we find that resources depend on our commitment rather than on investment or materials, that failure and error are the occasion for transcendence rather than signs of exhaustion, that devotion is more important than is prudential maximizing, that believing is more important than is skepticism, that power is authoritative rather than sovereign, and that we learn from poignant example rather than from abstract theory.

What I have just said is peculiar for Antigone's Greek world. What I have done in the previous paragraph is to take Antigone's action and describe and contrast it, not with politics as reflected in Creon (and Ismene), but with modern prudential economizing, what might be taught in business or planning school. In this excursus I want to continue in this modern vein, anachronistically adapting what we might learn from Antigone to modern bureaucratic society.[30]

Antigone teaches us that economy, perfection, and prudence have little to do with entrepreneurship. For Antigone, resources are neither limited, nor conserved, nor a matter of an incentive and signaling system. Rather, Antigone is determined. The modern example of such determination that I find most immediate is in sport and athletics, where heart, courage, commitment, and motivation describe doing more than one could have conceived otherwise, delivering more fully than one might have predicted based on the available resources. It is almost always the case that such heart or courage or commitment involves a greater than conceivable level of concentration, a transformation of the conventionally accepted capacities of the fundamentals, and, in the desire to do well and to win, the ability to deliver these performances for remarkably sustained periods.

Playing injured may be a grave mistake, but it is part of this ethos of courage. Sacrifice is rational and for the good of the team. (Antigone's death is for the sake of family.) And if sacrifice is institutionalized (as in modern, but not ancient, society), then victimage rarely leads to death. One comes back from sacrificing one's self and one's body, to go to work again the next day. Chronicity of pain and injury is accepted as part of sport and of war. You learn to live with that pain and the cumulative losses, until you decide it's time to quit.

The reserve that does seem to run out is not the body but the mind, when one "loses it," when one is no longer capable of being present to the task at hand, no longer committed and struggling. Then you, or Ismene, are overwhelmed by fear and anxiety, in effect abandoned. It is possible to recover, to get back into what you are doing, but it is surely harder to do so when you are weakened.

Doing well—deriving more than conceivable from your resources—need not exhaust those resources, although one could go too far. Rather, that achievement of doing well may encourage even greater performance. In this context one never thinks of reproducible events or commodities. Each performance is unique in history, fully representative of history's meaning. Again, one has to keep in mind the question, Why are *we* here? Why are *we* part of this run of greatness?—which of course is the question concerning revelation. Each show is a showing up of Providence and its grace.

For the entrepreneur resources are invented, value is transformed, while the capacity and effort displayed is beyond what anyone could have conceived.[31] Here triumph is beyond explanation. Correspondingly, failure is not damning; it is the occasion for further action. For we may take fortune's gifts and respond with virtue; we may from error and disaster make moves admirable and bountiful. Within the theological and republican traditions, the traditions of sin and vice, there are saving graces and civic virtues, a chance to be blessed and noble. Character is shown by how we wrangle with adversity, and how we accept triumph and praise. Fear and then getting knocked down, the fearful fantasy fulfilled, are the occasion for our being able to show ourselves, revealing our capacities.

If one is prepared and has a properly graduated training, then failure is much less likely to be devastating. (Since Antigone was a little girl and her father made his discovery, she is trained for her role and her fate.) Coming to grips with fear is not so much a matter of steeling oneself, as it is of proper preparation for the experiences of failure, knowing how to make a saving move. Of course, nothing is more powerful than having faced fear and failure, and having worked one's way through it. We learn not to fret, not to focus on what has gone wrong, but to solve the next problem presented to us, and so return to the flow of life.

Here devotion and steadfastness (Antigone) are more important than are brilliance and device. In the realm of sport we are talking about fundamentals and team commitment. Without the capacity to perform the required moves with automaticity and delight and excellence, without the willingness to take on the drudgery that such mastery entails, the chances are for disastrous consequences from momentary failure. Now, losing when overmatched but doing much better than you had thought possible is not a setback. Rather, it is the occasion for further testing of the self. And if you happen to keep winning, commitment will fade unless winning is part of a transcendent authentic goal. Always, we must have a sense of our abiding capacities, and we must honor them by our achievements.

Sacrifice is not something reflective or intellectual, but habitual and active. One knows what to do, and does it. It is what has to be done, by the dictates of the tradition and the demands of being a member. In particular, the members of a team must see themselves in that team's image. Their individual success does not make for team success. Teams require adaptability and resilience, rather than isolated superior performances. As long as command and control are adequate, then teams have very great capacities for substitution and reorganization.

The more general model of devotion is craftwork in which apprenticeship eventually leads to masterly performance that is both automatic and inventive. Of course, without basic skills it is impossible to reliably produce new works. But without devotion and mastery, devotion to and mastery of a tradition, there is no chance to contribute to the tradition and so redeem history through our work.[32] Devotion and steadfastness are not slavery; rather, they are modes of liberation, for they allow you to be competent and effective. Surely, slaves have to exhibit something like devotion and steadfastness, but for slaves those qualities come with resentment and oppression.

Again, Antigone is the model of courage. It is her devotion to her family, and her steadfastness when offered alternatives by Creon, that we revere. Antigone is also the model of loyalty, or rather of the dilemmas of loyalty. Loyalty to her tribe and family is opposed to Creon's loyalty to the state. In the context of a team, loyalty is a matter of being a good member, committed to the team's traditions and to the others you play with. Once we leave the tribal realm for the bureaucratic, then Antigone's problem is most poignant and less clearly resolved. To whom are we devoted?

In Antigone's world, believing matters deeply; dogma beats dialectic. The ironic theme of social science—of the counterintuitive, of the invisible or hiding hand, of the self-fulfilling prophecy—empowers the social scientist. But for the actor in the world, such ironies are disheartening, dispiriting, and ultimately insulting to her actions. It is not that her pride is hurt, for she need not believe she is omnipotent. But it surely helps to feel potent, fertile, effective, and intentional (although irony might make one less righteous). Skepticism makes sense for the philosopher, who will allow any conceivable situation to show up the inadequacies of our received beliefs. But the actor acts in a particular set of situations, and, within that set, received beliefs are empowering, directing, and real.

Believing is also encouraging. Faith is not for the foolhardy, but for the knight.[33] Sacrifice makes sense because commitment gives a larger meaning and a longer range of concern to what is otherwise thought to be waste or inefficiency or foolishness. Here dogma is a coherent exposition, a philosophy (as an athletic coach has a philosophy). It is open to experience, and flexible in its application. But dogma is something coherent and whole, which allows for dialectical argument.

We need courage, revelation, and assent: We need courage to act, or to encourage our natural capacities. Revelation says it could have happened any way, but it happened this way. We need to have the sense of sureness and vision implied by revelation. And in coming to a moment of assent, of commitment, we are capable of confident action. Thinking proves disastrous if it is in its currently popular form of perspectivalism and skepticism. Yet active thinking, say as Hannah Arendt describes, leads to courage and action and the political consideration of others.[34]

Telling stories that feature heroic and courageous actors encourages the listener and gives her a sense of her mission. Those stories set up the archetypal problems, the tasks that have to be taken on. And in these stories, morality, value, and judgment are central subjects of our considerations. The stories are homilies.

Coaches know how to tell these stories, what to point out, how to touch their players so that a player's talent and heart are enlarged and strengthened. Performance and winning are crucial. But we also know when we have been touched, and that poignancy matters enormously. We are then up to winning and to feeling good; we are up to power and authority.

Coaches are authoritative because their guidance is effective and because they defend and support their players. But if sport is a struggle, the players have to believe the coach is going through that struggle too, and has gone through it all before. Authority is earned through testimony and experience.

Here power is properly conceived of as autonomy, vulnerability, devotion, love, and authority. As does Antigone, I distinguish legitimacy from authority, violence from power, and sovereignty from autonomy. The first terms represent formal dominion, while the second represent freedom and assent. I am implicitly arguing for resilience and imagination and command, over strength and control.

Winning is a way of being unique, whatever its consequences for sovereignty or autonomy. Playing a game is a way of being in touch with what you are doing, whatever the agony or the contest it is with others. When you put on your game face (preparing to step out on the field), you are investing yourself with the power to play. Energy devoted to beating others is best found in the playing, not in a goal of annihilation.

We are encouraged, and we learn virtue, by coaching and example. This is surely a matter of erotics (as the Greeks knew),[35] and of learning to see and to pay attention to what matters. Exemplary cases are not simply icons or idols but models we then repeat according to our own interpretation, so that we may be responsible for ourselves. Yet we are within the tradition, a member of the community. So our repetitions are not arbitrary but traditional. We learn to become players, in a game that requires we perform according to rules that allow us to excel and so be free.

Examples are telling. The concrete situations they present to us force us to face the self-deceptions we have been able to finesse by abstraction and fantasy. Such moments of proof show us up. In such a dramatic confrontation, we are forced to learn whether or not we are willing to face our selves. We are hit in the stomach, and so we have gut knowledge. The coach's problem is to set up such telling examples, such situations in which the ball touches us.

Why Rome, Jerusalem, and Athens?

In the third-century CE, in North Africa, the church father Tertullian asked, "What has Athens to do with Jerusalem?"[36] We might well ask, What have Rome, Jerusalem, and Athens to do with Silicon Valley or Pittsburgh? Tertullian was concerned with the development of a Christian identity that would have its own biblical integrity, rather than be assimilated to classical ideas (Roman and Greek), ideas to be intellectually and politically external to that sacred institution of the church.[37] Augustine came to eventually ask more or less this same question, the classical sources and philosophy having failed him, their rationality being no match for the Scriptures' authority and power.

Correspondingly, we ask, what does Antigone and her world have to do with modern rational entrepreneurship? For this ancient Greek culture is very different than our own. In fifth century Athens, Antigone and her story readily echoed back to an even more ancient Greek culture. Surely, we do not live so close to a sacred and mythic world. Yet figures such as Antigone and Oedipus still capture our imaginations, largely because rationalism and universalism[38] have yet to fully replace the sacred and the heroic.

Jerusalem, too, is a foundation for our culture. Augustine, through Paul, represents Jerusalem's episcopal structure; Moses, its congregational. These are not liberal worlds, but worlds in which authority is religiously and covenantally sacred, and action is prophetic. I have argued that entrepreneurs participate actively in that sacred and prophetic mode (a very different one than the Greeks'). What is taken as an atavism still motivates us powerfully. The entrepreneur in many ways embodies that sacred and heroic and prophetic world, and it is because of this embodiment that the entrepreneur is fascinating and problematic for us.[39]

In nineteenth-century German culture rational Athens was contrasted favorably to atavistic Jerusalem, the sunlight of Greece and democracy displacing the darkness of Christianity and authority.[40] But this rhetorical move is surely unfair to Greece's religious and ritual life and to Jerusalem's high Talmudic rationality (or canonical interpretation, as in Augustine). A polemic between Athens and Jerusalem is an ideological artifact (perhaps of anti-Semitism).[41] Both cultures highlight the sacred, the heroic, and the prophetic, namely, the religious and the authoritative. That does not mean that I would want to revere their authoritarian and illiberal qualities. Rather, the sacred, the heroic, and the prophetic, and the authoritarian and the illiberal, are unavoidable features of entrepreneurship.[42]

Greece, and Athens in particular, was a culture of contest (*agon*) rather than commerce.[43] Whether in sport or war, fame and honor went to the winner, shame and slavery to the losers. While winners and losers would, in time, often find themselves in reversed places, there was a qualitative difference between the winner and the losers. Now, it is useful to distinguish such a regime of contest from one in which prudence, rationality, risk taking, and comparative advantage are the natural terms, namely, a regime of competition as in an economy.[44] Contest is about the sacred, the virtuous, action, and aggression; competition is about the mundane, the skillful, the calculating and reflective, and the impersonal objective. To lose in contest is to be degraded, to be polluted by unmanly qualities, to be a woman (recall Creon);[45] to lose in competition is to be someone who happened to come in second.

Contest is the regime of the entrepreneur, competition the regime of the conventional marginalist economic actor. The entrepreneur is making her mark in the world, while the manager wants to become more profitable and penetrate the market a bit further. The successes and failures of the entrepreneur are those of a contestant, as grand and as humiliating.

Sophoclean Athens is on a cusp in Greek civilization, between the Homeric sacred and magical and the Socratic rational. So Antigone is commanded by ancient sacred commitments; yet Oedipus is driven by his capacity to think and to know. There is savagery aplenty here, but it is in the service of a rationality that is about to arise, eventually in its fullest form in Plato.[46] At such a cusp, tradition is reinterpreted through the kind of enormous conflict seen in *Antigone* and the desecration and destruction seen in *Oedipus the King*. Such overturning is precisely what happens in creative destruction. We have seen it when the Hebrews make a covenant among themselves and agree to live by a single God and law. The internal conflict around the Golden Calf and the consequent destruction lead to a new people, the Israelites.

The Protestant ethic and the spirit of capitalism is only one of the many ways of being entrepreneurial, a way that despite its religious theme is remarkably profane and mundane.[47] Entrepreneurship's arenas for action have traditionally been sacred rather than commercial.

Incest, Parricide, and Abandonment: How Transformations Take Place

Entrepreneurs, in creating new combinations of the means of production, rearrange the conventional orderliness of their society, by the way corrupting the traditions and sources of their own productivity. Like Oedipus, entrepreneurs commit incest and parricide, for incest is the mixing of what is conventionally forbidden, and parricide is the murder of your origins[48]—although in justification it should be recalled that Oedipus was cast out from society by his parents for their own good. Such violence leads to a new orderliness and new conventions, those presumably to be overturned in time.[49] Those overturnings may well be annihilating. Or they may be ongoing acts of renewal and destruction, and so tragedy is innovation.[50]

Entrepreneurs interrupt the conventional modes of social transformation and succession by polluting, mixing, and corrupting the genetic and familial lines (those *new* combinations).[51] Yet, like Oedipus, they might well think they are being loyal to their father or their mother and to what they take to be tradition;[52] in fact, they are being even more violent and disrupting than they could imagine or conceive. Entrepreneurs are fully aware of what they are up to, but in the end ignorant of what they are doing, their insight blinding them and that blindness allowing them to act in ways they would find horrifying. To recreate your family and history, as does Oedipus in running away from his (adoptive) parents Merope and Polybus and in bearing children by his birth mother, Jocasta, is an enormous rearrangement of the means of production, one depending fundamentally on misconceptions.[53]

Entrepreneurs reconceive their histories, providing themselves with a new family and history that leads to a different set of conventions and taboos and a different future than they would have had, had they straightforwardly followed the original family's line, as if they could have. In effect, the entrepreneur acts out a family romance ("a childhood fantasy in which the individual believes that his actual parents are not his own and he is really of higher birth").[54] And entrepreneurs, despite the often masculinist identification of their role, are here mythic females, polluting a line by their promiscuity, by their blood, and by their misconceivings.

Oedipus is the model of creative destruction that is entrepreneurship: a model of problem solving that is also structural violation and reorganization; a person buffeted by contingency and errancy; and a castoff (like Moses) who wants to reestablish his own history, and in so doing reestablishes an institution or a people.

Again, all of this mythic doing is done by entrepreneurs in the most everyday ways, as did Augustine, Paul, Moses, mothers, and even Oedipus. To be an entrepreneur is to be this-worldly. But the sacred is present in everyday life, and entrepreneurs cannot help but find themselves with such motives and actions.

Oedipus is a divine foundling.[55] He is cast off, saved, and adopted: bound (as is Isaac) and cast off by Laius and Jocasta because of the prophecy that he would kill his father and marry his mother; saved by the shepherd who out of pity for the little baby could not kill him; and adopted by a father who took him as a long-wished gift ("his [Polybus's] early years without a child made him love you [Oedipus] all the more"),[56] and readopted by a society that once cast him off.[57] Entrepreneurs are such foundlings, for they are cut off from their conventional origins, saved by the seeming weakness and vulnerability of their ideas, harbored and adopted in a foreign land by "better" parents where they can grow safely, and readopted by society as gifts (or providers of gifts) we did not know about until we found them and only then were those gifts seen to be long lost.

Mythically, those who are so wrenched from their pasts then revisit that wrenching upon their original society. Entrepreneurs provide gifts that radically transform the societies that once rejected them and latterly take them in, often leaving behind, sadly and with regret, their harboring adopters (such as Merope and Polybus).

Adoptees understandably worry about incests and parricides.[58] But their not knowing their origins seems to empower them, at least temporarily; their break from their pasts allows them to break traditions. Oedipus's limp, a sign of his having been cast off, his bound infant feet pierced by metal pins, leads him to have a third foot, a staff or cane, which is a phallic sign of his violating power (not to speak of his actual violating inseminations of his mother).[59] Again, adoptees who do not know their birth parents cannot know, and therefore cannot take account of, the meaning and consequences of what they do, and so they explore just what the conventions would have us revere and avoid touching. And so entrepreneurs discover possibilities that others are forbidden to discover, some of which are embraced by society, with consequences yet to be discovered—Thebes took in Oedipus when he solved the riddle of the Sphinx, only to suffer plague in due time. The ironies of Oedipus's knowledge and ignorance, his acting because he is blind and then his own blinding because he has acted, are for the entrepreneur rather more everyday and mundane.[60] Oedipus's having been wrenched is the entrepreneur's role and status. And the entrepreneurial task of mothering a project, an act of devotion and eventual alienation, is perhaps a redemption for having been cast off.

We might ask how entrepreneurs learn to enact these mythic roles. Of course, they are not likely to think of themselves as reenacting Oedipus's role, although they might well have some sort of heroic image of themselves, and then they are inevitably in Sophocles' debt. Rather, the structural issues of disruption and order are recurrent in both the Oedipal and the entrepreneurial realm. The mythical and the practical are, so to speak, working on the same problems. There is no reason to believe they would have to come to the same sort of solutions. But I suspect that the structural issues are rather more powerful in guiding our actions than we might at first believe.

Errancy and Contingency

No entrepreneur would want to be Oedipus. What is tragic in Sophocles becomes ludicrous and embarrassing in more ordinary circumstances. When things go awry in tragedy, they compound into meaningful disaster, they are catastrophic; in ordinary life they are often farce. What the entrepreneur does want, if not a saving grace, is the capacity to buy out or compensate for errors, at least to be able to treat errors as meaningless blips on an otherwise sensible path. But she is not to have what she wants.

Oedipus goes astray as he resolutely goes forward. His fate is a sequence of errancies, each one compounding its successor, yet each act is interpreted at the time as errancy just avoided—what is called Sophoclean irony, as in Oedipus's deliberate demand for the truth. To avoid the oracle's prediction Oedipus's parents have him exposed to the elements on a mountainside; but the shepherd in charge cannot carry out his duty; and it is through the kindness of such strangers that Oedipus survives to fulfill the dreaded oracle.[61]

Now, some entrepreneurial ventures are tragedy turned comedy, a series of mistaken moves that, despite themselves, lead to redemptive triumph. To have known better along the way would have been disastrous.[62] But to hope for such comedy is foolhardy. Here is Oedipus:

> I count myself the son of Chance,
> the great goddess, giver of all good things—
> I'll never see myself disgraced. She is my mother![63]

Rather, how might the entrepreneur avoid playing out the tragic oracular story of failure she has heard many times before? Due care is surely called for. To avoid moves that we are told will doom us would seem prudent, and hence we might take the formulaic advice found in handbooks for the entrepreneur. We might even hope that whatever doom results is merely symbolic and ritual, our having avoided the usual fate by our good sense and prudential action.[64] But this is perhaps not enough.

Jocasta briefly entertains alternative accounts of errancy: a run of errors need not demand another unfortunate turn.[65]

> Fear?
> What should a man fear? It's all chance,
> chance rules our lives. Not a man on earth

> can see a day ahead, groping through the dark.
> Better to live at random [without a plan], best we can.
> And as for this marriage with your mother—
> have no fear. Many a man before you,
> in his dreams, has shared his mother's bed.
> Take such things for shadows, nothing at all—
> Live, Oedipus,
> as if there's no tomorrow!
>
> (ll. 1068–1078)

What is unknowable and a gift of the gods is perhaps incoherent as well. There is for us no fateful story we are fulfilling. Rather, one solves each problem as it comes along. There is perhaps no inevitable irreversible compounding of our choices; it is always possible to return from waywardness to the main road. Everything is possible, nothing fully precluded. What we take as predictively meaningful is merely a dream, a shadowy projection of fantasy onto a reality that is for us altogether meaningless. In modern terms Jocasta is very roughly describing statistical randomness, a "stochastic" process (from the Greek for target, aim, or guess), events being independent of each other much as successive tosses of a fair coin are independent of each other: the outcome of one toss says nothing about the outcome of another.

For entrepreneurs such an account of contingency is problematic. To imagine themselves as randomly walking, their path in effect a diffusive flow (much as gasses diffuse due to the random collisions of their component molecules) rather than a directed project, is almost as demoralizing as to imagine themselves fated by myths and oracles and confounded by their attempts to avoid the consequences of such pronouncements.

Entrepreneurs sense that their actions lie between story and stochasticity. As the Greek choruses often commend, we mortals have to make do, buffeted by meaningful fate and meaningless randomness. The contingency entrepreneurs do face may well be at times tragic, at times stochastic. But their very great skill is to have some sense of when to take contingency as a story they are fated to follow (in their own way, to be sure), and when to take it as meaningless chance they might embrace or avoid, without presuming upon its benevolence or permanence. What Oedipus tries to do, but cannot because in his tragic role he must consistently misread, is to subtly interpret contingency. The ability to read the signs is between divination and prudence, a fine sense of judgment that allows the world its own autonomy, its own capacity to speak to you. It is to pay attention to the details, as they speak in each context, without presuming on their meaning or their meaninglessness.[66] Here again is Robert Irwin, describing his experience at the racetrack: "The thing about the race track is the incredibly wide range of information that has a bearing. If you're going to have a chance there, you have to achieve the discipline necessary for keeping track of all of it. The one thing more than anything else is learning to pay attention...and then *it's like you run your hand over the race*." (There is also much to be said about how entrepreneurs and their society manage loss and error, and I address this in chapter 5.)

For entrepreneurs, and for Oedipus, too, the very great temptation is to see themselves as following a path *or* as acting randomly. They cannot know how a plot will turn out, even if they have a good sense of its structure and constraints. Hence they might pay too much attention to the arbitrariness of choice at each point. They cannot claim to be without plot, without plan and meaning, even if they are acutely aware of what they do not and cannot know. They have to think of themselves as actors with a role in a drama. I call these poles temptations, because to take either of them as the whole story is to limit the entrepreneur's range of consideration; more tragically, it is to substitute formula for judgment. To be driven by inevitabilities or to be thwarted by chance should not discourage the entrepreneur from acting at times strategically, at times following his comparatively arbitrary hunches and animal spirits.

Here temptation is the sin of pride, as if you could know everything (or nothing), when in fact the entrepreneur is somewhere between and must make decisions that are neither fated nor indeterminate. Of course, this is what we do every day, often quite comfortably. The temptation is to think there is someplace else, some other mode of acting, where we might avoid this poignant fact of our humanity.

Moreover, uncertainty is real. We cannot always substitute either traditional myth and oracle or modern probabilistic decision theory for it. There are times when we are truly uncertain, when we haven't got a clue about what to do: we might abstain from choice, or we might ardently follow those animal spirits. To think that this is a matter of oracle or information, when there is none to be had, or of probabilities, when there is no sensible way to estimate them, is to yield to the temptation I have been describing. At these times entrepreneurs might make substantial moves, perhaps prudently and contractually guaranteeing, say by insurance, they can meet their future nominal obligations, no matter what. But those moves are judgments that are about neither discerning the patterns of plot nor weighing of probabilities.[67]

Entrepreneurial ventures often do fail, abjectly so. Triumphalist stories, as in chapters 1 and 2, are not at all the only ones. What was promised turns out to have bound us to errancy. Whether we are entrepreneurs or have gone along with the venture or are merely bystanders, we are misled, disappointed, ruined, humiliated. If we are chastened and educated, what we must not learn is that there is a tragic plot we might now avoid, nor that a prudential regime of probabilities and insurances should have and now will prescribe our actions. To act in response to the world's opportunities is sometimes to be as victimized as Oedipus or as lost as a random walk. Given the variety of attributable causes for a disaster, I am not sure entrepreneurs can learn much, formulaic or procedural, from abject failure—except how to regain their courage (rather than to simply withdraw from the fray). What entrepreneurs do pick up along the way is a finer capacity to evaluate situations, to see their patterns and their unknownness and their uncertainty.

I have been hinting here at modern notions of probability and statistical independence as a tempting way we might account for errancy and triumph. These notions are very different than what the Greeks meant by chance (*tuche*), a story of the gods and the unknowable. Since, however, these modern ways have become canonical in the training of professionals in management or planning, for example, we might attend to them more carefully.

Statistics, Fortune, and History[68]

Contingency is the fact that things turn out surprisingly, that we do not have perfect information, that fortune presents us with opportunities for virtuous action, that pride may well go before the Fall. How do we make our peace with contingency when we are committed to modern rationality as embodied in probability theory and statistics?

In a statistical decision theory, surprise, difficulty, and outcome—just what is contingent—are homogeneous facts, their probabilities combined or their expectations balanced against each other in order to judge whether we are doing the right thing. For fortune, contingency is the occasion for virtuous acts or ignominious failure, as we have seen in the discussion of courage. And, for the historical thinker, surprise, difficulty, and success are cumulative and incommensurable, part of a narrative or a story, which in being written or told is also a judgment about what we might do. (The realm of Oedipus is that of fortune and history, managed by mythic gods.)

Statistics. Probabilistic accounts of contingency, of the fact that we are unsure of what will happen next, are based on two assumptions about the source of contingency: events are (more or less) *independent* of each other, and everything conceivable that is not otherwise forbidden must happen eventually (*plenitude*).

The usual model of independence is coin-tossing of a fair coin, independence being the statement that there is no connection between tosses.[69] Students are admonished that a sequence of heads (on a presumably unbiased coin) does not mean that the next toss will produce a tail, or a head for that matter. Heads and tails are equally likely on each toss. Such an admonition also describes a crucial cultural assumption, the conventional null hypothesis of randomness. Namely, whatever the observed connection between events, it might be that they are actually independent of each other, and any observed connection is a random fluctuation or coincidence (Jocasta's fantasy). If there is a very great deal of information needed to know what will happen next, then the assumption of almost pure random contingency (say, equiprobability of alternatives), and the assumption of independence or almost-independence, is convenient and often the best you can do.[70] Yet the unavoidable ignorance that makes for independence is often intolerable. We want to know (out of curiosity, out of a need to assess credit and blame) just what happened, in detail, in a single event.[71] Neither Augustine, Moses, mothers, nor Oedipus would find this kind of ignorance acceptable.[72]

The second feature of probabilistic accounts is that every sequence of events that is not otherwise forbidden will happen eventually, and often equiprobably. Every possible sequence of, say, ten heads or tails will eventually occur, with no one of them given preference. This assumption has been described as "the plenitude of Nature."[73] Every gradation in Nature, every possibility, has occurred or will occur. Here is the physicist Tullio Regge talking to the writer Primo Levi:

> I, however, would like the universe to contain or eventually contain in its history, which is infinite, every possible object that can be conceived of by the [physical] field equation. A statue of Primo Levi made of Tibetan olive oil cooled to less than two hundred degrees certainly must exist in some part of the universe; it is an extremely improbable object, and it will be necessary to travel a certain number of billions of years in order to find it, but it exists somewhere. The universe is infinite because it must allow for everything that is permitted, because everything that is permitted is obligatory.[74]

Even if events are independent, there is a grander connection: equal heads and tails in the long run. Any given sequence is balanced by a translated sequence: heads for tails, and tails for heads. How long that long run is, and how equal, and just how every possibility is allowed to appear, are matters for careful technical analysis.

In characterizing the source of contingency, plenitude is about as hard to believe as is independence. How could we know that some events or events of a certain kind, otherwise not deliberately forbidden, *must* happen?[75] This is a global accounting, as comprehensive in its own way as the Oedipus story.

Under a regime of independence and plenitude, entrepreneurship becomes a matter of artfully managing a portfolio of risky investments, employing hedges and insurance; and entrepreneurial failure, in bankruptcy, is assimilated to a problem in finance, perhaps no different than a put option in a securities market.

We opt for probabilistic and statistical accounts when we want to avoid facing up to the meaning of actual detailed causal sequences and the responsibilities revealed thereby. Rather than examining a particular problematic situation in idiographic detail, we average over many similar situations and so create greater ignorance and control through statistical inference, again in effect avoiding direct responsibility for particular individuals and events.

Fortune and history. Fortune and redemptive history have provided the traditional accounts of contingency.[76] Events are each unique and even sacred, and they are morally and narratively linked. Whether an event occurs is a matter of grace, fortune, fate, or action.

Lady Fortune presents a person with surprises and challenges and tests.[77] She is perhaps deceptive and wily, the enticer and the seducer, the dangerous tempter. She turns that Wheel of Fortune, sending one to good or evil, blessing or curse. Fortune is a story of chance as opportunity, the chance to show who one is. Fortune presents us with situations that we wrestle with, tame, make our peace with, situations where we might exhibit our virtue. It may be that Lady Fortune even has purposes for us, a series of tests to educate us, a rite of passage, an odyssey.

The deep questions become, Why are we tested, how are we to respond to those challenges, and what is the meaning of such contingency? (Recall that, for probability, contingency is deliberately taken to be meaningless.) The traditional answers concern a person's progress or lack of progress toward greater autonomy, courage, and capacity for invention. Contingency is the opportunity to do good or evil, to rise or fall to the occasion, to prove oneself. Here the game of life is played in society, rather than in a world of abstract events and rational bets, and its consequences are not losses or gains but the kind of person one becomes.[78]

For entrepreneurs, the story of fortune often possesses the ring of truth. Say contingency were dominated by randomness. What we actually encounter are particular surprises, particular challenges, particular crises. (This may be a mistake, but entrepreneurs assume their situation is particular.) And they are taken to demand invention and courage and persistence.

If we assume that the world is rich with meaning and motive, we may develop strategies for "figuring out" those particular cases—that is, seeing them as fitting within patterns or figures or archetyes—and for using that insight to act more effectively.[79] Here redemptive history is a model of contingency. This essay provides a variety of such accounts, which the entrepreneur will fulfill in the matter of course. In our actions we relive and revitalize those patterns and archetypes. Either we do so self-consciously, imitating a role; or, as is more likely, we find ourselves employing such patterns, for those are the only patterns and stories we know. Everyone knows the story, everyone knows that they will take a part in replaying it, and how one then acts (or reenacts) contributes to the outcome. What is contingent is not the outcome, for in this narrative model the outcome must somehow follow the archetypal or original story: it is our fate to repeat it. Rather, what is contingent is just *which* archetypal story is appropriate, just *how* the story is followed (the detailed particulars), and how well we act—effectively, virtuously, fairly—in our roles. Of course, particular actions on our part make an enormous difference, but these differences are well within the archetype.

Such archetypal stories are often the everyday way people figure out what to do, and so make their peace with contingency. "War stories" are retold to novices; archetypes are implicitly invoked by one-line epithets; and various advocates and opponents are blown up larger than life so as to fulfill their heroic destinies.[80]

I call this redemptive history because the stories have endings in which the presumably good triumphs over evil (*or* the other way around); or the prideful learn the difficulties of the world, and so educated they can go out to do battle once more; or the gods are becalmed. And redemptive history is emotionally powerful, a story that engages us sentimentally so that we might be redeemed.

Entrepreneurs' conceptions of contingency deeply influence how they understand their own actions, namely, how they are hopeful and visionary. We may hope for what is close to impossible or surely impossible. We may have a vision of a world that is not at all readily connected to the one we live in now. Hope requires a vision that others can share and find motivating, and a vision requires hope if it is to be fulfilled.

Probabilistically, hope and vision might seem irrational. Were hope taken to be a matter of probabilistic contingency, the relevant probabilities are likely to be low, the expectation values minuscule (unless we are Pascalians who value Heaven infinitely), and the path to the envisioned place is often not even strategically imaginable (so that a decision tree of sequential choices could not be articulated). Usually, we can show there are other, more practical and modest possibilities, corporate rather than entrepreneurial, with more likely outcomes and greater payoffs for the risks we are assuming.

Still, we might argue that hope and vision are perversely rational, even in the probabilistic context, since they encourage people to work harder, to make greater commitments, to mobilize social and natural resources in previously unimagined ways, and to enlarge their range of action beyond what was ever taken as reasonable. (So argued Joseph Schumpeter for the irrational success of the entrepreneur who does not appreciate how risky is the endeavor and so in being too hopeful ends up succeeding.)[81] Thus to be hopeful will actually change the probabilities and payoffs. The hope-free prudent analyst is proven to be defeatist. Hope and vision cause us to revalue the world, reconceiving our situation so that what was once even beyond hope is now within the realm of strategy.

Actual stories of hope and vision are about the challenges to, and transformation of, our collective purposes and central values, eventually leading to the kinds of revolutionary mobilization (successful or not) I have earlier described. Such challenges and transformations are central themes when we consider contingency in terms of fortune and virtue, or in terms of redemptive history and leadership. Here, to be rationally hopeful is to be committed to transcendence and discontinuity. Fortune will provide us with the chance to show virtues we have never needed to exhibit before, or could not conceive of exhibiting. Redemptive history allows for another world, discontinuously or qualitatively different yet in the end connected to this one through actual events, our action, and their narrative accountings.

Hope and vision demand detailed strategies and plans, some of which may be expressed in technical terms. Such plans also depend on leadership and community, how people are led to make a covenant among themselves that allows them to believe they are graced with the possibility of actual hope and vision, as did the Israelites. Rather than being an impractical idea, much of entrepreneurship takes place under such a covenant of hope, vision, and progress. Often it is productive and not at all fanatical and disastrous. Of course, that people possess hope and vision, and a sense of their election, does not mean they are right and good; we are rightly suspicious of triumphant victors telling us they won because they were right.[82]

Pollution and Problem Solving

Entrepreneurs work within arenas where errancy and contingency may be tragic, and where judgment and uncertainty allow room for action and failure. So entrepreneurs transform society through creative destruction, through structural violation: namely, through incest and parricide, through abandonment and adoption, and through errancy that allows for the space between fate and randomness.

Oedipus *is* structural violation. He is a pollution that must be washed away and banished; he is a corruption in the society that destroys its civility.[83] His violations (what I shall call "technology") are insidious and propagating, their original source masked from our knowledge (in the world of the to us arbitrary gods). He fortunately disrupts Theban tradition by his inventiveness,[84] and he is in turn done in by what he at times takes as atavistic tradition, namely, the gods and Teiresias. Jocasta represents that tradition; then she discounts it and dismisses it as being of no account. Such women, as does Antigone, get in the way of the conventional operations of tradition and technology, wherein each representative of tradition is catastrophically disrupted or polluted by its successor. They insist, in the name of the entrepreneur or the disrupter (their husband or son or brother), that tradition, too, is a pollution. Tradition is an atavism that must be resisted for the sake of the gods.

Oedipus knows just what he is doing, if not its significance.[85] Oedipus's technical skill (*techne*) is to solve problems, to interpret riddles, to fit the world together so it makes sense. Much as one might put together a jigsaw puzzle, and only much later note how awful and horrible is the scene it depicts, Oedipus seems to know little of the meaning of the puzzles he solves until the very end:[86]

> No, but I came by, Oedipus the ignorant,
> I stopped the Sphinx! With no help from the birds [of prophecy],
> the flight of my own intelligence hit the mark.
>
> (ll. 451–453)

Then Teiresias asks, "[W]ho *are* your parents? Do you know? All unknowing / you are the scourge of your own flesh and blood" (ll. 473–474), and Oedipus begins to fall apart. For questions and riddles and puzzles have dread-filled consequences, they are not merely formal exercises.

> [*Teiresias:*] Revealed at last, brother and father both
> to the children he embraces, to his mother
> son and husband both—he sowed the loins
> his father sowed, he spilled his father's blood!
>
> (ll. 520–523)

To understand such a puzzle is not only a technical skill; it is an awful judgment as well. Having solved those riddles and problems, Oedipus must then be the sacrifice in order to purify the city, as he has ordered for that corruption. He, like Moses at the end, is the cure for his own technical problem solving, a self-consuming therapeutic.[87]

To be an entrepreneur, as is Oedipus, is to be fully heroic. You cannot so easily take the money and run, for you are an historical figure and cannot escape the consequences of your ingenuity. Entrepreneurs are rarely so melodramatic, self-consuming, and heroic. They are rather more prudent and more accepting of discordance and perversion. But I maintain that what signifies entrepreneurship most poignantly is just this heroic dimension of technology.

We do not know ourselves well enough, or our own enterprises well enough, to know the meaning and consequences of what we make and do and design. We go out and do something, prudently, and then discover consequences we would never have wished for or found acceptable. Of course, that is not the only or main story, for most of the time things turn out roughly as we expected, unsurprising in outline, perhaps interesting in detail. So we surely know something of the meaning of what we do. But what is it that we do not know?[88]

Oedipus does not know himself, and in his gaining knowledge he commits patricide (of Laius, whom he takes to be simply a stranger, itself a problematic notion, given Greek customs about hospitality) and commits incest (with his mother, whom he takes to be his wife). He denies the knowledge offered to him by Teiresias—a blind man, who was for a while a woman. So interplay knowledge, sexuality, and death. Knowledge is a form of violation and pollution and insemination, its consequences deliberately unknown. It must lead us astray.

What we do not know, what we cannot know, are the violations we commit inadvertently and their consequences. We are eventually to know them, to rue the day we committed those violations, then so confident of our rightness. Of course, and this is crucial, our acts can be truly beneficent (as was, for Thebes, Oedipus's solving the riddle of the Sphinx). So we cannot simply say we can separate the beneficent from the violating and ultimately disastrous. Significantly, those violating acts are sometimes the foundation for new orthodoxies, their violent nature relabeled as moments of creation or founding or invention.

Technology is a form of knowledge, and the problem of technology is, What do we do about that knowledge we cannot have, except afterward? Again, technology is violation, just that which resets the boundaries, the taboos, the everyday expectations. How do we live with that violation?

Entrepreneurship's means of action is technological, the introduction of violating modes of organization and polluting devices. We usually think of technologies as devices or systems, not as modes of violation. Yet what is most problematic about what people ordinarily call a technology is that it breaks down the conventional and traditional modes of life. It may do so innocently, under our own guidance. A new mode of production (as in agriculture) reveals the conventional relationships we no longer find tenable. To do *x* we find there is an implicit set *y* that comes along with it, and those *y*s are of pervasive consequence. We cannot simply plug in a technology and expect it to have only local effects. Technologies violate the taboos, yet in those violations, in those technologies being set in place, the culture is transformed, the taboos rearranged.[89]

Whatever technologies do, they are insidious. At first we misunderstand those violations that make for technology. Yet they are influential despite or because of our mistaken assessments. Initially, Christianity was adopted for its perhaps superior healing powers, and only later did it become that catholic and exclusive religion that denies the integrity of the beliefs it claims to replace.[90] Initially, quantum mechanics was a machinery that could calculate atomic properties. Only later does the physicist appreciate the worldview she seems to have inherited and affirmed.[91]

We adopt a mode of belief or action because it has practical consequences we find attractive, and only later do we find that we are engaged in a different way of looking at the world, a way that denies what we had always taken for granted. More generally, violations are at first seen as practical and of limited extent, rarely as revolutionary and exclusionary of the past. They often remain that way. But some of the time, violations turn out to attack the central tenets or crucial points of what appeared to be a coherent system, and that system eventually yields to those violations.[92] If technology is insidious, that insidiousness is something we can learn to attend to.[93]

What we want is to be righteous and saved. All the literature on salvation requires that we listen and hear the call of the truth, participate in the nature of things. And then we might be inventive or courageous or ignominious. But we have to hear what is being said, for that is not at all like what we expect, what we think we already know—although of course we already know what we shall hear, but we are not yet ready to hear it.

Entrepreneurs transcend the conventions through the particularity of their projects (here, Antigone's family). Devotion, loyalty, resilience, and perversion enable that particularity to survive, inseminate, and thrive if it can, so it too might achieve dominion. Technology is the name we give to our incests, to those crossings and violations we do not recognize and that may force us to reorganize our society. Technology is something we cannot fully know; even our self-knowledge builds in our own eventual violation. In practice, we may not be much destroyed by such violation, even if it seems self-consuming; tradition and convention are remarkably hearty and robust. But sometimes they are not.

How do we redeem the violations and incests? It is characteristic of modern liberal society to pecuniarily compensate those it sacrifices, and to manage its way around catastrophe. We are therapeutic rather than creedal, to use Phillip Rieff's terms.[94] How might we achieve redemption and closure?

5

RESTORING THE VEIL OF ORDER
Redemption and Design for Oedipus, Prospero, and Their Daughters

The Mythic and the Tragic. Redemption, Healing, Jubilee and Bankruptcy, The Politics of Bankruptcy and Entrepreneurship, Fluctuations. Memory and Philanthropy, Letting Go, Sacralization.

Once we launch an enterprise and if we are lucky, the enterprise is an unfinished business. It is on its way. So Augustine and Paul, Moses, mothers, and Oedipus are on their ways: creatively molding a disrupted order, the original disruption being sometimes a consequence of their own acts. Entrepreneurs jump into a rift, widen it, and so have room for what was otherwise inconceivable. In the matter of course, enterprises come to be incorporated, seen as whole and inevitable and routinized, or they fail and are allowed to disappear, or they are absorbed into other enterprises. What was once a pollution now fits in: whether as purified and redeemed through sacrifice; or as domesticated (what was once considered an outrageous perversion now is part of a variety of heterogeneous possibilities); or as the dominant order (its maturity in effect denying its awkward, callow, bastard origins).[1] How do we place a veil of order on the bacchanalian revel that is history and development and truth, thereby healing rifts, letting go, and making for closure (namely, that "owl of Minerva" Hegel refers to in *The Phenomenology of Spirit*). Just how do entrepreneurial endeavors become part of the heavy stuffed furniture of society? Put differently, if tragedy is an account of our being subject to the gods' wrath, how might such accounts allow us to leave the theater to get on with life's ordinary, mundane tasks?

The Mythic and the Tragic

A tragic, redemptive, mythic vision has informed our discussion. We are after the Fall (to use the Hebrews' rather than the Greeks' version), now subject to errancy, imperfection, unresolvedness, and rationality. Our world is more interesting, too. Having been sent out of the Garden, however, do we literally live in the profane way that keeps us under the dominion of the sacred?—as contrasted to modern scientific and probabilistic conceptions of the meaninglessness of order and error. It seems that we do live by myths, according to the critic George Steiner.

> It is a defining trait of western culture after Jerusalem and after Athens that in it men and women re-enact, more or less consciously, the major gestures, the exemplary symbolic motions, set before them by antique imaginings and formulations. Our realities, as it were, mime the canonic possibilities first expressed in classical art and feeling....[Consider] an episode in Nazi-occupied Riga. Caught trying to sprinkle earth on the publicly exposed body of her executed brother, a young girl, entirely unpolitical in her sentiments, is asked why. She answers: "He was my brother. For me that is sufficient." In December 1943, the Germans descended on the village of Kalavrita in the Peloponnesus. They rounded up all the males and did them to death. Against explicit orders, in peril of their own lives, the women of the village broke out of the school in which they had been imprisoned and went *en masse* to lament and to bury the slain.[2]

To be sure, I find myself in an embarrassing position. I have throughout this essay tried to justify in various ways the presence of the mythic structures in our everyday lives—without actually believing they would be acted out so literally and deliberately. Steiner's point is that the tragic is embedded in our language, so it is unavoidably repeated in our lives. We might also say that the mythic is one of God's modes of everyday appearance in our world. In any case, even in so ordinary and everyday an activity as commercial or manufacturing entrepreneurship, the story is fully mythic and fully everyday, fully sacred and fully profane, fully structural and fully particular. It is a perversion.

Whether it be confession, epic, clinical case study, or conventional tragedy, I have been discussing works in which imperfection is pervasive and errancy is a recurrent temptation.[3] From at least one religious point of view, this choice of works is realistic. For we live on this earth, an imperfect and sinful, postlapsarian world. The entrepreneur's, and the protagonist's and the playwright's, task then becomes making from this rent world something that holds together and has its own integrity and resilience, always subject to recurrent assault by centrifugal forces and internal conflict. Given what we now know about what happened after the Garden, this designing for temptation or designing for imperfection was God's task in The Creation and it is the physicist's task in describing the early universe.

Tragedy allows us to touch the awful, to recognize it, to become familiar with what we might otherwise be tempted to deny. Entrepreneurship rends the world; its creative destruction is awful, hard to recognize for what it is (rather than be celebrated or condemned), readily romanticized rather than seen as an actual process. Entrepreneurship is violent and savage, the antithesis of civilization, yet entrepreneurship is fully present in civilization. And tragedy is the classic means of dealing with this presence of savagery in civilized life. What makes tragedy work, and what allows in the end for entrepreneurship, are rituals of forgiveness, redemption, repentance, and reconciliation characteristic of contest or *agon*. In a tragic world, and in an entrepreneurial one, the protagonist and the entrepreneur do not control violence and destruction through some form of prudence and self-control.[4] They enact violence and destruction. Ritual is redemptive here.

Tragedy names what is ordinarily unspeakable: incest, parricide, curse. Entrepreneurship, too, is remarkably unspeakable, since it is so economically irrational, so unfitting the usual prudential balancings we are supposed to engage in. Entrepreneurial acts may come to be seen as beneficial and even familiar; but, close up, they are frightening and alien. To think of entrepreneurship in tragic terms is to allow for "reliving and undoing, through aesthetic participation, of archaic evil."[5] This is a hyperbolic way of speaking. But one of my purposes here is to take what is usually not spoken of, or what is spoken of in denigrating terms (for example, "It is irrational to act this way"), and to make it sensible within structures with which we are familiar but ordinarily do not think apply to this mundane practical arena.[6] These descriptions, drawn as they are from the centers and sources of our culture, are likely to elicit from the practicing entrepreneur a remark to the effect, "That's about right, you've got it."

We might think of the entrepreneur as a colonist, taking over what is seen as virgin or abandoned land, and repatriating it in her own name.[7] That is just what the entrepreneur's endeavor is supposed to do, although of course to the latest of the putative aboriginals, or to the predecessor entrepreneur, that virgin land is very much occupied by ongoing peoples and institutions (which successors might say are inefficient or old-fashioned or transient). Augustine, Moses and the Israelites, Oedipus, and Prospero are colonists for the sake of civilization, taking back in their names the North African church, the Promised Land, Thebes, and the Island—along the way putting down and perhaps even destroying the Donatists, the Canaanites and the Hittites and the other peoples, Thebes itself, and Caliban. Presumably none of these antagonists were there first either. Creative destruction is not nice. A justification for creative destruction in terms of progress, or a claim that the colonists are right, is in the end self-defeating and in the near term reeks of pride.

Tragic descriptions neither romanticize the destroyed and lost past, nor justify and celebrate its successors. They show that colonialism is not just a story of victimization of the weak by the powerful or a story of the triumph of civilization over the savages.[8] Rather, entrepreneurship taken as colonization is a story of the redemptive sacrifice of the transformative figure[9] (the entrepreneur), a tragicomedy that provides forgiveness for injury and repentance for wrongs, reconciliation through the harmonies of fruitfulness (as in material progress, liberty, or marriage), and the honors of memorialization.[10] Tragedy is how we make our peace with the presence of savagery in civilization.

None of this excuses the destructions or idolizes the creations.[11] Tragedy, no matter how ethical, is redemptive, not moralizing. Pride is a necessary and deeply problematic human quality, as it is in these sacred traditions.

Redemption–forgiveness, repentance, reconciliation, purification, memorialization–is not exculpatory. Redemption is structural and ritual, allowing us to close a disruptive, catastrophic rift. Redemption does paper over harms wrought by the entrepreneur; it also papers over the entrepreneur's failures. Redemption is societal, compensating losers to some extent, freeing failures so they might try again, terminating ongoing sequences of retribution. Thereby redemption allows a society to address problems anew and not be so haunted by atavisms. Sacred ceremonies, whether in godly or courtlike places, do this redemptive work, putting an end to sequences and cycles of action, rewriting history so that there is a caesura for the moment. Here think of Oedipus being received by the gods at Colonus, or of Prospero's courtlike judgments and punishments.[12]

Redemption

Insofar as society as a whole benefits from creative destruction, we might expect it to develop institutions for closure and redemption that would in effect encourage entrepreneurship. If entrepreneurial harms and failures were to be forever unexcused, say in torts and debtors' prison, it is likely that potential entrepreneurs would be strongly discouraged by the retributions they would risk.

Healing, philanthropy, and judgment are three modes of redemption. As for healing, through sacrifice, forgiveness and jubilee and bankruptcy, and historical memorialization, we may heal rifts and wounds. Through deliberately allowing for a next generation's fructiferousness, we let go the cycle of retribution.[13] And by placing a veil of order on that past, by telling new stories and by judging things anew, so there is a re-creation, we revalue the world so that we may act inventively once more.

Healing

Oedipus works enormous good in Thebes, fathers a new kingly generation, and in time comes to see himself as the curse or pollution on his adopted homeland. Against his wishes, he is exiled by Creon with the tacit assent of Oedipus's sons Eteocles and Polynices. Blind and wandering, with Antigone's guidance and the oracles' reports brought by Ismene, he eventually finds a place of redemption in Colonus, outside of Athens. He is now a prize to be won, for his presence (dead or alive) assures victory in war. He vengefully rejects the Theban entreaties of Creon. He curses both his sons for having abandoned him, for having failed to succor him in his need, and so spurns the desperate entreaties of Polynices. Eventually, he is called to the gods, blesses Athens rather than his native Thebes, says goodbye to his doomed daughters, and so is redeemed.[14]

The entrepreneur is to be sacrificed. He is the scapegoat (in Greek, the *pharmakos*),[15] absorbing the costs of his society's transgressions. As presented in Sophocles, those costs are dreadful and enormous. Oedipus misleads, ruins, and chastens his family: his mother-wife, his brother-sons and sister-daughters, and Thebes itself. Yet in the end Oedipus regains his power and dignity, here speaking to the chorus at Colonus:

> Don't reject me as you look into the horror
> of my face, these sockets raked and blind.
> I come as someone sacred, filled
> with piety and power, bearing a great gift
> for all your people.[16]

But he also curses his sons to kill each other and leaves daughters who cared for him to be barren and abandoned. Addressing Antigone and Ismene:

> Such disgrace, and you must bear it all!
> Who will marry you then? Not a man on earth.
> Your doom is clear; you'll wither away to nothing,
> single, without a child.[17]

Thebes and Creon, as we saw in *Antigone,* are condemned as well.

The dramatic power of the Oedipus story is perhaps inarguable. But no one could commend its mode of redemption, given that train of awful consequences. That violence might remind us of the Mosaic sacrifice of the murmurers, which again we find hard to accept whatever its justification.

About two thousand years after the first playing of *Oedipus at Colonus,* Shakespeare's *Tempest* presented another account of redemption as forgiveness, repentance, and reconciliation. While there are deep tragic elements in the play, for it is an account of the deceptions of authority, of vengeance, and of regeneration, *The Tempest* is usually taken as a comedy or romance.[18]

The duke of Milan, Prospero, and his three-year-old daughter, Miranda, are exiled to an island by his usurping brother, Antonio (Prospero had given to him the task of governing while Prospero pursued the study of the liberal arts). Although the island is occupied by the aborigine Caliban and the sprite Ariel, Prospero employs his magic to take it over. He also employs his magic a dozen years later to shipwreck on the island Antonio and an aristocratic party from Naples. Through a series of tribulations and tests, symbolic sacrifices, and humiliations—all arranged by Prospero and carried out by Ariel (in effect the agent of reconciliation and redemption)[19]—the treacherous and ludicrous are shown the evil of their ways (although Antonio does not fully repent); a husband, Ferdinand the son of the king of Naples, is found for Miranda; and Prospero gives up his magic and returns with the rest of the party to Italy, thus freeing Ariel and giving the island back to Caliban; and, finally, a reconciliatory marriage is to ensue.[20] The cycle of usurpation is brought to a close, albeit in a highly artificial and designed way; for it is the deliberate artifice of Prospero that does all the work, the repentant almost mechanically responding to the lessons taught to them by their trials.

Such redemption is morally unsatisfying. Do the redeemed really mean what they are saying? And does it matter? If Oedipus is mythic, Prospero is fantastic. "What a splendid king you'd make of a desert island—you and you alone," as Haemon refers to Creon's rule (*Antigone,* ll. 826-827). Prospero describes his doings:

> My high charms work,
> And these, mine enemies, are all knit up
> In their distractions. They now are in my power;
> And in these fits I leave them. (3.3.88–91)

This is a remarkably efficient magic, for in the end not only is there redemption of sorts but actual life can go on, many of its problems having been resolved (such as letting go of your daughter and finding her an appropriate marriage partner).[21] And so Prospero says to the audience:

> Now my charms are all o'erthrown,
> And what strength I have's mine own,
> Which is most faint. Now 'tis true,

> I must be here confined by you [the audience],
> Or sent to Naples. Let me not,
> Since I have my dukedom got,
> And pardoned the deceiver [Antonio], dwell
> In this bare island by your spell,
> But release me from my bands. (5.1.319-327)[22]

Prospero's is too neat a story, perhaps too much a comedy.

Of course, it is not so neat an ending. The fraternal conflicts between Prospero and Antonio are too profound to be reconciled by the mechanical means of magic and marriage (say, compared to Sophoclean tragic means).[23] There is much unfinished court business to be played out back in Italy. And that is what we might hope for. At least for us, if not for Sophocles, redemption should lead to new tasks; it cannot be transfiguration and death.

There is a middle ground between Oedipus's awful tragedy and Prospero's remarkably neat and innocent resolution. Redemption might be a matter of compensation rather than blame, such as is now enshrined in modern theories of law and economics.[24] Problems of rights are not sacred, for they can be settled by means of pecuniary compensation. Creative destruction can thus become blessed, freed of ancient hauntings; and those who lose can be made more whole again. The relevant passages come from the Hebrew Bible, here God speaking to Moses, and Moses to the Israelites.

> When men quarrel and one strikes the other with stone or fist, and he does not die but has to take to his bed—if he then gets up and walks outdoors upon his staff, the assailant shall go unpunished, except that he must pay for his idleness and his cure. (Exodus 21:18–19)

> Do not deal basely with [or, Do not go about as a talebearer among] your countrymen. Do not profit by the blood of your fellow: I am the Lord. (Leviticus 19:16)

> If you see your fellow's ox or sheep gone astray, do not ignore it, you must take it back to your fellow. If your fellow does not live near you or you do not know who he is, you shall bring it home and it shall remain with you until your fellow claims it; then you shall give it back to him. (Deuteronomy 22:1–2)[25]

In sum, compensation is required and is sufficient; we cannot ignore the needs of our neighbors; and debts are always to be repaid. In this commercial world the facts of obligation are marked by the facts of compensation. Here, Hebrew Scriptures are not moralistic but are concerned for community and well-being. One cannot walk away from one's obligations in this world of the reasonably honest person subjected to temptation.

Now it might be argued that paying one's dues does not offer redemption. The sacred requires more than mundane acknowledgment. Compensation still leaves us bereft of the healing that is the foundation of community. The counterargument is that compensation as such is not meant to heal, not meant to enter into the realm of Oedipus or Prospero. Rather, healing takes place on the symbolic level, the act of payment being symbolic as well as pecuniary. And pecuniary compensation does a great deal of good, good that is worth doing. Even more significant, there is no contradiction among compensation and healing and redemption in this Israelitic realm. Technically, redemption actually is a matter of buying back or paying back.

The redemptions entrepreneurs might want, or the redemptions that might be expected of entrepreneurs, are of varied sorts, none precluding the others. While we, nowadays, perhaps too sharply separate the commercial from the sacred realm, historically they have been intimately linked. Commercial and sacred redemption arc not polar opposites. This will be seen most poignantly when we discuss biblical jubilee and commercial bankruptcy.

I should note one recurrent theme. Whatever the mode of redemption and forgiveness, it might be argued that to forgive people, to let them off the hook so to speak, will only encourage greater sinfulness and profligacy and, even worse, it will actually harm those who are forgiven. They will become further alienated from the center of society. So, for example, economists argue that easier bankruptcy (namely, bankruptcy more easily declared by the debtor) ends up hurting debtors, since in response credit becomes less available to them.[26] Yet the empirical literature finds that the incentives work in much more complex ways, mediated by social situations often out of the control of the debtor. For example, entrepreneurs and single mothers often become bankrupt because of their lack of backup and the inherent riskiness of some ventures.[27] Redemption and forgiveness serve larger societal goals, such as encouraging invention, growth, and experimentation. Forgiveness promotes community and enterprise. The lack of forgiveness proves to be socially paralyzing.

Jubilee and Bankruptcy

Biblical jubilee is the meeting ground of sacred redemption, forgiveness for errancy, and commercial compensation. It is described in Leviticus 25:1–2, 10, 25–28.

> The Lord spoke to Moses on Mount Sinai: Speak to the Israelite people and say to them:...you shall hallow the fiftieth year [(7×7) + 1]. You shall proclaim release [liberty] throughout the land for all its inhabitants. It shall be a jubilee [referring to a ram's horn, *yobel*] for you: each of you shall return to his holding [land]...If your kinsman is in straits and has to sell part of his holding, his nearest redeemer [literally, "next of kin"] shall come and re-

> deem what his kinsman has sold....If he lacks sufficient means to recover it, what he sold shall remain with the purchaser until the jubilee; in the jubilee year it shall be released, and he shall return to his holding.

Jubilee is sacred. It is God who speaks of a numerologically marked fifty, the redeemer is connected to you by blood; and the land is owned by God. But jubilee is also commercial. The details of computing the exact rents given in Leviticus evidence mundane principles of accounting and pricing: "In buying from your neighbor, you shall deduct only for the number of years since the jubilee; and in selling to you, he shall charge you only for the remaining crop years" (Leviticus 25:15). Jubilee serves the larger interests of Israelite society, in effect providing social compensation for individual error and bad fortune, so holding society together through solidaristic gifts. And such a compensation is provided under a sacred provision.

Modern notions of bankruptcy draw from the traditions of jubilee, and serve similar social purposes. If imperfection serves the interests of growth and innovation, and that is the message of the Fall in that Edenic garden, then how is society to encourage the right kinds of imperfection? For the Greeks, the gods encourage that imperfection, good and bad; in the Shakespearean world, there is sinfulness and greed, guided by an artful hand, here Prospero's. In modern societies, market structures and the chance to accumulate wealth are used to encourage venturesomeness and invention. What is needed as well is a way of limiting the harm to those who venture and lose. Hence the gods take in Oedipus, Prospero arranges for forgiveness, and bankruptcy codes free one from the threat of debtors' prison.

Formally perfect markets will not allow for fruitful imperfection. Those markets have to be in disequilibrium and to be unbalanced to allow for windfalls (and catastrophe) rather than just marginal change.[28] They have to be inseminated or polluted with incorrect information to encourage the entrepreneur to venture and work harder than she would have were she discouraged by better information.[29]

Moreover, the discipline and ethos provided to market capitalism by the conventional commercial culture may not be present in a more speculative entrepreneurial culture. In fact, it is just this distinction between a culturally disciplined market and a speculative entrepreneurial one that historically has been at issue. In the seventeenth and eighteenth centuries such a market discipline was contrasted unfavorably with a discipline based on virtue and land itself, epitomized in the landed gentry, in part because market and speculation were conflated. Corruption due to unreal property, such as in options and credit instruments, a matter of what was called Court and City, was contrasted unfavorably to virtue and Country (again, of landed property), a conflict between commercial wealth and landed aristocracy.[30]

Speculation and lack of rational discipline, as such, are traditionally condemned. To recall the quote from Max Weber in the preface, "To the English Puritans...that Jewish capitalism [involving 'speculative promotions, and the construction and financial projects of princes'] was speculative pariah-capitalism, while the Puritan [capitalism] was bourgeois organization of labour."[31] As for discipline, "Capitalism cannot make use of the labour of those who practice the doctrine of undisciplined *liberum arbitrium,* any more than it can make use of the business man who seems absolutely unscrupulous in his dealings with others, as we can learn from [Benjamin] Franklin."[32]

If bankruptcy is to be seen as a legitimate institution, we must come to believe that within the speculative realm we can distinguish the cases of vice and corruption from those of honorable bad fortune, or, alternatively, give up practically on such a distinction.[33] Throughout the nineteenth century in England, for example, economic transformation brought in its train widespread reverses as well as advance. In politics and in the novel, an important question arose, Should the gentlemanly ethic of repaying one's debts to the last penny, often permanently destroying the debtor and his family, be allowed to lead to enormous societal disruption and instability?[34] Conversely, is corporate limited liability too destructive of just that responsible social fabric that made for the savings that fueled this economic transformation, however great limited liability's capacity to raise entrepreneurial capital? If we believe there is honorable bad fortune then we might justify, in the interest of the state, our abandoning a narrow individualist moralism, taking bankruptcy now as a necessary institution.[35]

Ironically, bankruptcy has of late become an explicit matter of a firm's financial policy, say, to avoid large liability judgments, the debtor's power to protect himself fully rationalized. The nineteenth-century moral question of distinguishing corruption from bad fortune is perhaps out of order; the question is now a practical one of financial and business policy, on the part of the firm and the state.

There is a culture of speculation based on strategic planning and on seemingly arbitrary animal spirits, and on compensatory institutions such as bankruptcy (taken as a matter of legal, moral, or financial judgment). (Again, this is not a culture of probabilistic risk, for which the model is financial investment theory.) In particular, U.S. bankruptcy law is now distinctively generous, allowing reconstruction of the firm rather than its immediate liquidation, as well as the abolition or discharge of a wide variety of debt, in each case not permanently penalizing or stigmatizing the failed speculator.[36] In this manner the culture allows for speculative ventures and potentially imprudent decisions; their untoward consequences are taken as justifiably unanticipatable losses.[37] The speculator or entrepreneur is made morally whole again and is not marked by imprisonment or the like.

The meaning and implications of large losses can be shifted from the worlds of morality and law to the worlds of Providence and fortune. No matter whether the disasters actually seem to be deserved, are truly providential, or are merely a matter of luck, procedural recourse justifies the outcome (that is, puts it in place) and frees the speculator from what are now taken as accidents of history. This analysis may be applied to large positive returns, so correspondingly making a fortune subject to confiscation, since ownership is no longer a matter of individual effort but rather of state provision of property rights and the like.

Put differently, it may be unclear whether a particular bankruptcy is a consequence of corruption or of mistaken vision. Between commercial errancy and sacred Providence or fortune there is much room for what might appear to be false dealing, misrepresentation, and reverses—all of which still might be regarded as honest hope disappointed—without ever presuming either that the bankrupt is a financial wizard and scoundrel or that Providence and fortune are fair.[38]

Speculators may view their efforts as visionary. I take this to mean that they see their projects as unique and sacred, not subject to the forces of market and finance. To the economist, they are playing Russian roulette. To their minds they are engaged in the sacred act of making something out of nothing, sometimes called creation. In such a regime, only a collective or divine effort succeeds, and in either case belief in and commitment to the vision is crucial to its being realized. Here think of Moses getting the Israelites to march in the desert. Such belief can easily be mistaken, the vision itself being deliberate deception by the speculator, as many of the Israelites thought and murmured about Moses' vision. But sometimes speculators get awfully close to that Promised Land, even if they do not enter it.

The Politics of Bankruptcy and Entrepreneurship

Uncertainty encourages entrepreneurial endeavor in that it allows lots of room for action, especially for those who possess information niches. They have knowledge of what others take as the unknowable, so they may act with assurance while others are unlikely to act at all. But uncertainty will also slow entrepreneurial activity, insofar as a consequent failure is damning. More generally, a culture that encourages ventures but does not too heavily penalize mistakes will have greater innovation and growth. If that venturing is done in a decentralized fashion, as in markets, a greater variety of opportunities will be explored—again, if the penalties for failure are also suitably restricted in their extent.[39] Insofar as they restrict penalties, limited liability corporations, bankruptcy and insolvency law, and social insurance against catastrophic losses (for example, the side effects of vaccines) are what might be called political modes of producing entrepreneurs. I use "political" here because such governmental provisions might be developed out of a concern for liberty and justice rather than from an economic and pecuniary motive, especially in a nation founded by debtors.

So the U.S. Constitution gives Congress the power "to establish uniform laws on the Subject of Bankruptcy throughout the United States." The history of such laws is fitful, at least until the twentieth century.[40] But, in general, it came to be recognized that it was better that people be working rather than be in debtors' prison, the latter a fate of many a prominent and good citizen in the early years of the Republic—the most famous case being that of Robert Morris, who helped finance the Revolution but later, as a consequence of real estate speculation, spent three years in Prune Street Jail in Philadelphia. He was freed by the Bankrupt Act of 1800.[41]

The national-interest argument was articulated by Henry Clay (1840).

> The right of the State (Nation) to the use of the unimpaired faculties of its citizens as producers, as consumers, and as defenders of the Commonwealth, is paramount to any rights or relations which can be created between citizen and citizen [contract]....I maintain that the public right of the State (Nation) in all the faculties of its members, moral and physical, is paramount to any supposed rights which appertain to a private creditor. This is the great principle which lies at the bottom of all bankrupt laws.[42]

Bankruptcy laws not only provide for greater productivity but also are a safety valve for the rigors of free market economies.[43] Jail, indentured servitude, and slavery seem too harsh a penalty for failure in commerce and the marketplace. Moreover, such penalties would be socially disruptive, perhaps revolutionarily so. In any case, discussions of bankruptcy in the context of U.S. history emphasize how an entrepreneurial culture is fostered if one can have high rates of innovation and failure, and some form of limited liability. Again, the American culture is distinctive both in fostering risk taking and in the comparative leniency of its bankruptcy laws. The relationship of debtor and creditor is highly individualistic in the United States, with each transaction considered alone and on its merits, with little desire to regulate creditors systematically. Hence, the need for bankruptcy to modulate the effect of untoward contracts.

Business failure can even be a stimulus to innovation, especially of those financial and contractual devices needed for business reorganization.[44] Dissolution may be societally and politically unacceptable, as in railroads, and so risk-bearing, losses, and property rights are altered so that the trains roll on. Big industries may not be subject to the same sort of bankruptcy regimes as very small ones, but the possibility of failure is still a source of entrepreneurial invention, but now in terms of the financial instruments employed. Similarly, tax laws that encourage debt and so make bankruptcy more likely can have positive consequences for innovation and entrepreneurship.

The possibility of failure, for small businesses, is often taken in the United States as a desideratum for entrepreneurship. Since personal monies and assets usually sponsor small businesses, this willingness to put up one's own assets is taken as a signal of commitment to the business and of the quality of the inside information the entrepreneur possesses. And that commitment and information increases the likelihood of success.[45] Small startup businesses have comparatively high failure rates. But we might naturally expect this, since a large business is more likely to have a stable base, precisely because it has survived the rigors of being small: the smaller businesses absorb the search and error costs in finding what "should" be a large business.[46]

Fluctuations

Losses might be defined as a matter of fate: the entrepreneur followed a particular path that inevitably leads to failure, no matter what is done. Such narrative and tragic accounts are perhaps appealing to our sense of righteousness, and they are often recognizably true to life. But they might well discourage the entrepreneur and so discourage innovation and risk taking in society. In the last several hundred years, loss has come to be thought of as untoward fluctuation, namely, as a random event, and so we might be insured against loss by buying marine or life insurance or by purchasing an option or hedge in a securities market.[47] Good (or bad) management can shift the probability distribution of such fluctuations, or can even take particular random downside events and manage them to low, or higher, loss. Here loss is not inevitable. Rather, loss is unavoidable fluctuation, perhaps because of imperfect information and an uncontrolled environment, and an accumulation of such untoward fluctuations. While gains are technically mirrors of losses—here, both being random fluctuations—and may be treated as such, politically and morally they are outside the realm of failure and so receive much less attention. Confiscation of windfalls as a parallel to bankruptcy is rarely effective politics.[48]

If we can further encourage people to embrace risk, say, by a policy of lowering the interest rate, we may encourage the sponsoring of entrepreneurial endeavors, in hopes of the long-term gains more than balancing the bankruptcies, although the distributive consequences may be socially disruptive. Insofar as loss can be limited by bankruptcy relief, entrepreneurship may be further encouraged. Also, from the point of view of the entrepreneur, issuing debt (as against equity) indicates seriousness of purpose and confidence in one's venture.

Technically,[49] the now conventional account of such probabilistic losses is expressed in terms of risk: the variance, σ^2, of a stochastic process (say, the randomly changing price of a security), at market equilibrium that risk varying as the rate of return on an investment.[50] In this equilibrium regime, expected return (and so in effect risk) is fully incorporated into price, and uncertainty is fully accounted for by statistical variance.[51] Moreover, the uncertainty and high variance or risk of entrepreneurial ventures means that there is a comparatively high minimum expected rate of return to overcome, a hurdle price, if people are to enter into such endeavors—not only because of uncertainty, but also because entrance here is in effect an irreversible decision, a qualitative shift to a new regime of endeavor.[52]

Put differently, and treating society as a firm and borrowing from the literature on corporate finance:[53]

> For instance, the effect of changes in the market rate of interest on the overall cost of capital is the same as the effect of a change in the price of butter on the price of whole milk.[54] Similarly, just as the relation between the prices of skim milk and butter fat influences the kind of cows that will be reared, so the relation between i [the yield on a security] and r [the interest rate, the cost of debt] influences the kind of ventures that will be undertaken. If people like butter we shall have Guernseys; if they are willing to pay a high price for safety, this will encourage ventures which promise smaller but less uncertain streams per dollar of physical assets. (Modigliani and Miller[55])

If we can by public policy alter the consequences of people's tastes, we may encourage comparatively fewer Guernseys, namely, fewer conventional safe investments, and consequently comparatively more entrepreneurial endeavors. The policy issues are subtle. We want to provide encouragement for the socially desired number of entrepreneurs.

> For suppose that a large fraction of the population habitually dines in restaurants which are required by law to serve only cream in lieu of milk (entrust their savings to institutional investors who can only buy bonds). To be sure the price of butter fat will then tend to be higher in relation to that of skimmed milk than in the absence of such restrictions (the rate of interest will tend to be lower), and this will benefit people who eat at home and who like skim milk (who manage their own portfolio and are able and willing to take risk).[56]

Now consider the point of view of the individual entrepreneur. She can issue debt or equity. By the arguments of Modigliani and Miller the value of the firm will be unaffected (or "invariant").[57] Any cheap debt she takes on is balanced by the greater cost of equity. Work subsequent to Modigliani and Miller's suggests there is noninvariance. The entrepreneur might choose to issue equity to share risk, and debt to maximize her payoff and her incentive. Outsiders might not be neutral between debt and equity in assessing an entrepreneurial endeavor—the choice of issuing debt (vs. equity) being a signal of entrepreneurial seriousness and a bond against not doing one's best as an entrepreneur.[58]

Entrepreneurs take the unknown and the uncertain and convert it into manageable and limited risk: "A [real estate] developer's fundamental role in city building is to accept risk that no one else will. Developers' success depends on their ability to unbundle huge risks into manageable proportions that can be allotted among various participants."[59] Modern bankruptcy practices, portfolio analysis, and financial instruments (such as options) remove speculative endeavor from the realm of law, the state, and political economy, and place it into the realm of markets.

Uncertain endeavors are characterized by unknowable variation and change. Under the modern regime of probability that variation is modeled as a process of random fluctuation, what is called risk. Moreover, the mechanisms that are the source of variation and change, whatever those mechanisms be, are now epitomized as random fluctuation. And random fluctuation—noise—is now the only operative dynamical mechanism in the endeavor. Uncertainty has become noise. Insofar as such an endeavor may be said to learn or absorb information, that information is absorbed through that same mechanism, namely, as shocks to a random process, shocks indistinguishable from random fluctuations. We have gone from a story of fate to an account deliberately stripped of meaning, deliberately absent of inside information, specialized craft, and knowledge of an industry and a firm.

Trading in some noisy market is the way the entrepreneur gets both her random shocks and her knowledge.[60] In this realm the entrepreneur has to be wary of purported information that might be a reasonably likely coincidence or random fluctuation. And the entrepreneur has to learn to go for broke at times, for prudential spreading of risk may preclude any possibility of success.[61]

Bankruptcy serves to limit as well as to paper over and so heal tragic loss. In its modern form, bankruptcy converts an uncertain and moral world into one subject to risk and probabilistic fluctuation. These are saving graces. But they do not justify a unique historical project, as an entrepreneur is likely to view her entrepreneurial endeavor. Nor do such graces justify the kind of attention to detail needed if the entrepreneur is to have a leg up on chance.

Memory and Philanthropy

Ritual sacrifice and legal and pecuniary jubilee offer redemption to those who are left by the wayside or destroyed. Sacrifice and jubilee justify destructions and losses accumulated along the way, putting them in their meaningful places. Sacrifice and a notion of progress justify those who are destroyed by the entrepreneurial endeavor; jubilee and bankruptcy justify those who fail in their endeavors.

Those who are triumphant and succeed, however, still need redemption so that their place is secured, at least in history and in God's eyes. For they are merely stewards of their success. They, too, shall be triumphed over and succeeded. Such is a gospel of wealth, as in Andrew Carnegie's writings,[62] and much of it is already suggested in Leviticus 25:23-25: "But the land must not be sold beyond reclaim, for the land is Mine; you are but strangers resident with Me. Throughout the land that you hold, you must provide for the redemption of the land. If your kinsman is in straits and has to sell part of his holding, his nearest redeemer [next of kin] shall come and redeem what his kinsman has sold." So we are stewards of our wealth, not perpetual owners. Our successes are gifts, no matter how we believe we have earned them.[63] And so our obligation is one of serial reciprocity, namely, of "passing on" that gift we have received. We let go of the material signs of our triumph in order to become memorialized in the community, in order to become literally historical. That is what passing it on will do. Redemption through such memory is philanthropy.[64] This is, to be sure, a remarkable act of redemption, especially for those in the grips of the market, in which carrying out each transaction effectively erases memory and history—namely, we have what we call private property. To be redeemed, to have paid back, is here outside the realm of such markets, for here exchange is a matter of gift, not purchase, and property is stewardship.[65]

Redemption through memory might seem fairly straightforward nowadays, what with the possibility of establishing a charitable philanthropy under modern tax codes. But to part with wealth, even through intimate and celebrated means, the entrepreneur perhaps heading the board of her foundation, is rather more difficult, the demands of redemption being actually quite stringent. Those demands are a matter of giving up control, letting go and passing on, and so acknowledging one's stewardly role, no mean task for most entrepreneurs. The problem is exemplified in how difficult it is for Oedipus and for Prospero to give their daughters to another male in marriage, even if the stewardship and serial reciprocity of one's children has always been a way that families cement relationships among each other and so create society.

Letting Go

There is no mother to bring up Antigone and Ismene, for of course Jocasta killed herself; and Miranda's mother is only present as witness to Prospero's paternity of Miranda:

> Thy mother was a piece of virtue, and
> She said thou [Miranda] wast my daughter; and thy father
> Was Duke of Milan, and his only heir
> And princess no worse issued. (1.2.56–59)

So it is their fathers, who are close to them, who will bring them up, readying them to be married off. That upbringing is marked by devotion and incest. For the fathers, there is a very great temptation to consume just what might redeem them, rather than to let go. The daughters are in effect agents of their fathers' needs, which are for both redemption and companionship. Does the entrepreneur use up and condemn his wealth, or does he let it go?[66]

Oedipus tragically uses up his wealth. He needs his daughters to survive, his sons having abandoned him:

> Oh thank god for you!
> My two girls, dear sisters, young as you are,
> as far as the life within you lends you power
> I have my daily bread, safe-conduct through the land
> and all the lovely kindnesses of kinship.
> But your two brothers turn their backs
> on their own father, for throne, for scepter.
>
> (*Colonus,* ll. 497–503)

Antigone travels with her father and deals directly with his pollution, Ismene deals with the sacred and the oracular.

> [*Oedipus:*] Antigone, from the time she left her childhood behind
> and came into full strength, has volunteered for grief,
> wandering with me, leading the old misery, hungry,
> feet cut through the bristling woods...
> . . . .
> And you, child [Ismene],
> in the early days, all unknown to Thebes
> you left the city, brought your father the oracles,
> any prophecy said to touch his life.
> You were my faithful guard, you took that part
> when I was an exile from the land.
>
> (ll. 376–379, 384–389)

They are doomed not to marry.

> Such disgrace and you must bear it all!
> Who will marry you then? Not a man on earth.
> Your doom is clear: you'll wither away to nothing,
> single, without a child.
>
> (*Oedipus the King,* ll. 1642–1645)

Yet, according to Creon, she is still quite marriageable (here referring to Antigone): "And at her ripe age unmarried, look, a prize / for the first rough hand" (*Colonus,* ll. 853-854).

The relationship of Oedipus to Antigone and Ismene is close:

> I've got my dear ones now. Now,
> even if I should die, I'm not destroyed, not utterly,
> not with the two of you beside me. Come, little ones,
> here, press hard! I'll wrap my arms around you,
> closer, tighter—father together with his children!
>
> (ll. 1259–1263)

And his children are of course his virgin half-sisters: "they're men, not women, look, when it comes / to shouldering my burdens" (ll. 1548–1549). Antigone and Ismene are bound to their father-brother, and so not available to any other man. They redeem their father, but they are then condemned, as we see in *Antigone*.

Prospero is no less bound to his daughter, Miranda, fully in charge of her since she was three.

> Have I, thy schoolmaster, made thee more profit
> Than other princes can that have more time
> For vainer hours, and tutors not so careful. (1.2.172–174)

No women to be sure have been involved in Miranda's education.

> [*Miranda:*] I do not know
> One of my sex, no woman's face remember,
> Save from my glass, mine own; nor have I seen

> More that I may call men than you, good friend [Ferdinand],
> And my dear father. (3.1.48–52)

Caliban does not count, and he actually tried to take advantage of Miranda. Prospero is obsessed that eros be properly controlled by marriage, namely, by his paternal (and regal) rights.

> Look thou [Ferdinand] be true; do not give dalliance
> Too much the rein. The strongest oaths are straw
> To th' fire i' th' blood. Be more abstemious,
> Or else good night your vow. (4.1.51–54)

Prospero will give up his daughter if her marriage is under his command. And then he might well let go. He no longer needs his youthful and male powers if she is married: "I'll break my staff…I'll drown my book [of magic]" (5.1.54, 57). Ferdinand too is under Prospero's command, for his father, Alonso, is not available to contest these proceedings: "I chose her when I could not ask my father / For his advice—nor [by Prospero's doing!] thought I had one" (5.1.190–191).[67] This is a comedy of sorts, after all; and Prospero can "pass it on," albeit he believes under his own control.

It seems that when there is no wife around, nor a motherly replacement, then for the bereft husband and father, and for his daughter, the demands of devotion and the possibilities of incest are enormous. While it is sometimes presumed to be the case that a woman needs a man to be complete, here it is clear that these men need women—their daughters, no less—if they are to exercise the powers they once exercised in their ventures. To let go, to memorialize, to give up control, is an enormous act of grace on their parts, and it appears to us moderns as morally necessary, committed as we are to autonomy and individuation.[68] But for Oedipus it is impossible; he would not otherwise survive. For Prospero it must be done on his own terms; yet it is done and that counts for a very great deal. To be a steward and to pass it on, to treat your wealth as a gift that demands reciprocity—letting go rather than hoarding ("I made it; I own it; it's mine")—is just that redemptive act that in philanthropy or marriage restores to community what has been rent and destroyed.

Sacralization

Married, Ferdinand and Miranda, to be king and queen of Naples and Milan, will face all the actual complexities of Italy and their own complexities, rather than the artfully contrived ones of the island. For Prospero, to give up magical control is to give the world its own autonomy, to rely no longer on sacred art but on ordinary statecraft. Prospero must give up his magical books if he is to have grandchildren and so eventually to die himself, that is, to be part of history and humanity. Similarly, Augustine studies philosophy, but that proves ultimately unsatisfying, and he comes into himself when he is called to the church and must rule and judge as bishop of Hippo. Theology blooms under the demands of defending the church and adjudicating conflicts in his bishopric. From concrete experience comes wisdom and knowledge. We do not understand, we cannot understand, the surprises and subtleties embedded within our principles until they are actually realized and so come into conflict with each other.

What was once contingent yet something we controlled is now necessary, having its own autonomy: the island and philosophy, respectively, become Italy and the church. And that is just what happens to successful entrepreneurial endeavors. Through virtue we have met challenges, through covenant we have bound ourselves to the enterprise. What once might have seemed play to others and even to ourselves is now serious business. Marriage and incorporation are sacraments, taking what was arbitrary and making it revealed and determinate.

The liberating act here is judgment.[69] Judgment is taking the part of the other, seeing things in general, and so learning to value the world in a way that participates in one of its authentic possibilities. From the point of view of the entrepreneur, that participation is evident in a natural new combination of the means of production, one that others acknowledge and go along with. It is a success. The project allows the entrepreneur to provide a persuasive demonstration that brings others along, so that they join the enterprise, which then meets even wider needs. So we have an account of leadership and marketing.

Judgment is leadership. To take the world in a particular concrete way is to appreciate its necessities or transcendental conditions. It is to discover one of the world's possibilities, that is, what was once seen as a closed tradition is still alive, fruitful, and open to surprise. The dumb world speaks to you. Put differently and oxymoronically, entrepreneurs are in the business of manufacturing the transcendent: what was put together contingently now seems necessary and beyond what any person could have enforced on society.[70] The entrepreneurial endeavor is established and actual and inevitable. No wonder the entrepreneurial role might be sacred. And so entrepreneurs' greatest temptation is to be God. Such a god, such an entrepreneur, is a great designer.

An accounting of our temptations will not eliminate or avoid them, but it can be a vindication of God's justice in permitting error and evil in the world. Such an account is called a theodicy, here a justification for entrepreneurship's creative destructions.

A temptation lures us to evil and puts us to a test. The primary temptation is the sin of pride, our desire to be God, to control and to perfect the world. Perhaps the most insidious of the prideful temptations is for complete knowledge of the world.[71] It is perhaps a human virtue to hope for a single design for the world, but expecting that we could know that design is the sin of pride. The world might well be designed, perhaps by God. Need it be designed in accord with our conceptual powers (or vice versa), so that we could understand it? That would be most wondrous, a design suited to our intellect. Kant argued that we assume that the world is designed, and designed for our conceptual powers, so as to organize our inquiries into the nature of the world. Such an "ideal of pure reason" regulates our thought about nature. He describes how we are tempted to see that ideal as something we know to be true, how we are confused by that temptation, yet how we are encouraged to do great work under its sway. Whether or not the world actually is designed, or by whom, or what that might prove, we are in the grips of a dialectical temptation that might encourage the entrepreneur to do more than seems rational, and so succeed (or fail) nonetheless.

The diabolical does not destroy us most of the time; we can recover from our bouts with it; we get along nicely and uneventfully. Bankrupts and misalliances are in effect absorbed. Pollutions and degeneracies are everywhere present. The world's potholes, quicksand, whirlpools, and craters attract us. But we have learned to walk or swim gingerly around them, and when we are caught, we seem not to fall in all the way. We are almost always "on rope," as they say in the circus. We have a sense of closure and order and a sense of graceful failure.

The great and admired cities and enterprises are often a product of mercantile greed, royal ambition, speculative rapaciousness, and unregenerate slavery. Modern designers and entrepreneurs are not God. They almost always work in teams, or at least have to face the consequences of collaboration and negotiation.[72] Often chance and effects of combination dominate fortune and intention. Kant's God as Architect has to bargain away the dream in order to get something built. Yet, and this is crucial, we are still entranced by an order that is decipherable by us.

It is almost surely the case that not everything fits and is in the right place, that not everything happens for a reason. There are leftovers and free riders. Still, the world is marginally adequate and orderly enough for us. And so, on that margin, entrepreneurs have work to do.

Epilogue

In *The Man Nobody Knows* (1925), the distinguished advertising man Bruce Barton, son of a minister, provides "A Discovery of the Real Jesus": Jesus built an organization; he was a forceful executive; he was masculine, strong, and an outdoors man; he was sociable. Jesus was as well a fine speaker who knew how to reach out to others; he was an advertising man, announcing the news in a simple, brief, and sincere form. Jesus was the founder of modern business, where service to the customer comes first. Weber would have been pleased to hear that "[a]ll work is worship; all useful service [is] prayer" (p. 180).

Sacred figures and texts have always been the occasion for practical homily, not only because they are sacred but because they represent in the most complex form our possibilities for being human. In a recent book, *Achilles in Vietnam: Combat Trauma and the Undoing of Character* (1994), Jonathan Shay shows how the Achilles of the *Iliad* has much to teach us about the consequences of betrayal and contempt in grief and dishonor. And so we might understand the experience of combat veterans of the Vietnam War. It is just in this profound manner that we need to understand the entrepreneur.

Entrepreneurial Vocations is meant to be a justification of the actual experience and calling of entrepreneurs, displaying (and allowing us to identify with) the creative and tragic dimensions of that work. Whether the entrepreneurial task be that of building, leading, nurturing, destroying, or redeeming, these sacred figures show us the way. And so we might recognize ourselves and our actions, not only as economic and managerial, but as transcendent and entrepreneurial. Those who preach and teach these texts and stories, who have always seen them in light of their meaning for us, will I suspect be not much surprised by what they have learned here. Yet those texts and stories are renewed in each era by their application to the tasks of the time.

We become our understanding of ourselves. Insofar as that understanding is more deeply informed by the fullest range of human experience, we have the chance to enact our visions. What we learn from Moses and

Augustine, from mothers, and from Oedipus, Antigone, and Prospero is just how we might be human.

Appendix

Teaching and Self-Study Guide

Entrepreneurial Vocations derives from my teaching students in professional schools over the last twenty-five years, as well as from the comments of experienced practitioners. (See the articles I have written on "The Critique of Poor Reason: Using Literature to Teach [Policy] Analysts" and "What Does Jerusalem Have To Do With Athens: Roles for the Humanities in Planning.") It may be useful to have some guidance in how the book and its sources might be employed in the classroom and in self-study. One of the problems that students with less experience have is seeing how these models apply to their own endeavors. What is especially nice is to listen to more mature students say how the stories we study describe "exactly" what they have experienced. The other problem lies in the sources, some of which are not easy reading. I have listed several films and a vocal performance that might be used instead. Also, Gloria Naylor's *Linden Hills* and Jonathan Shay's *Achilles in Vietnam* are very readable and convey many of the issues I discuss in a more contemporary form. Finally, some students (especially those who have not been involved with the rearing of children) will find chapter 3 a bit strange. Experienced mothers and fathers will testify to its aptness. In any case, I have on occasion throughout the text discussed some of the problems of taking these models to heart.

I should note that the book can be used in ways very differently than I describe below. For courses that read any of the Great Books, the relevant chapter allows the teacher and the students to take on the materials in a new way. For courses in homiletics, each chapter may suggest modes of preaching that are close to the listeners' experience yet faithful to the original words and stories. And for courses in strategy, entrepreneurship, or business ethics the books offer case-study material to enhance the more conventional case studies used in such courses in schools of business and management.

As for the classroom, the course-catalog description of the course I originally taught reads: "Entrepreneurship as understood in the sacred realm, with applications to the more conventional areas of business, public action, and planning and development. Main figures discussed include Moses, Paul and Augustine, Oedipus and Antigone, Prospero, and mothers."

The Syllabus

This course explores what it means to be an entrepreneur: how to think of yourself in terms of models and ideal figures; your moral stance in the world; the justification for the extraordinary returns and losses some entrepreneurs receive; the social role of entrepreneurs; how entrepreneurs make decisions, their personal character, and the nature of invention and creativity (what I shall call design). I want to give you the intellectual and spiritual wherewithal to be an effective, admired, and creative actor in the world. I believe this kind of education is for the long run, the stuff that you will look back on with gratitude—since it is the kind of material that has traditionally made a big difference according to the testimonials of the great entrepreneurial actors in business, art, religion, government, and the military. In research on what those actors found most important in their development, they always speak of experiences that are between the conventional niches, and that feel whole and authentic.

You know everything I am going to teach you. Everything. My job is to enable you to realize what you know, to use that knowledge, and to appreciate the traditions you naturally participate in. Your experience and reflection, enhanced by the reading, is just what you need to fully participate in class. I hope to give you a rich enough language so that you can understand your own actions and feelings, and so be more capable and effective. In many ways my role is much like the athletic or music coach, who sees past your current hangups and offers both a larger vision and exercises that will help you achieve it.

There are perhaps three main themes to the course: ways of thinking about entrepreneurship as *decision making;* as *character* and ethics, ethos, and leadership; and as *design* and judgment.

As for decision making, the crucial issues concern matters of risk and uncertainty, disequilibrium and preemptive moves, how something arises out of nothing, and big decisions. Here I am a Schumpeterian, concerned with "that kind of change arising within the system which so displaces its equilibrium point that the new one cannot be reached from the old one by infinitesimal steps. Add successively as many mail coaches as you please, you will never get a railway thereby." It is change that requires "new combinations of the means of production." I shall introduce a variety of models that account for discontinuity and invention.

As for character, and ethics and ethos and leadership, my main concern is to justify virtuous behavior. Namely, I want to talk about courage, integrity, commitment, and solidarity—drawing from a very wide range of models, whether they be the founding father of a nation or the mother and her child. I believe one of the fundamental issues is the nature of contingency in entrepreneurial activity, whether it be statistical or a matter of fortune and hope. I am less concerned here with behavioral accounts of entrepreneurs, than with encouraging students morally. By the way, the testimonials I receive always come in the following form, often a few months or years later—"I wasn't always sure what was going on in class, but now I see, and this is one of the most useful courses I ever took."

Finally, in discussing design and judgment, I want you to come to understand that judgment is a claim on others' allegiances (and not simply an objective evaluation), and that design is a commitment to a wholeness and order that is generous yet comprehensive. When I talk about problem solving, I use the example of how to deal with a crying baby in the middle of the night to ask the question, What does it mean that the last thing that you do is what works? This standard of test is rather different than what is portrayed as scientific method, yet is the dominant idea in most enterprise.

This course is very practical, but it does not have the character of nuts and bolts. Put differently, something like seven or eight of my teachers have received the Nobel Prize in physics. What I learned from them was not mainly how to do physics problems—rather it was how to think and how to go about living a committed serious life. That's what I try to do with my own students.

Reading
P. Brown, *Augustine of Hippo*
M. H. Krieger, *Marginalism and Discontinuity*
G. Naylor, *Linden Hills*
R. Pirsig, *Zen and the Art of Motorcycle Maintenance*
Shakespeare, *The Tempest*
Sophocles, *The Three Theban Plays (Oedipus the King, Oedipus at Colonus, Antigone)*
M. Walzer, *Exodus and Revolution*

One might add or substitute:
J. Shay, *Achilles in Vietnam*
Augustine, *Confessions* (parts of first ten books, Chadwick translation)
J. C. Beker, *Paul, The Apostle*
D. Winnicott, *Playing and Reality*
Gospel at Colonus (tape or CD, Nonesuch)
The Tempest (videotape, Random House "children's" version)

Prospero's Books (videotape; Director, Peter Greenaway)
Forbidden Planet (videotape)

The reading is meant to provide you with a richer set of examples and ideas, something that is more than just the lecture or your experience. Rarely is the reading didactic (as in a conventional textbook) or material for analysis (as in literature courses). Often, before we discuss it, there may be no obvious connection between the lecture and the reading. Again, I will try to explain what is going on ahead of time.

Schedule

1. Naylor, *Linden Hills* (or Shay, *Achilles in Vietnam*); M. H. Krieger, "Corruption and the Culture of Real Estate Development," *Business and Professional Ethics Journal* 13 (Fall 1994): 19–32.

Naylor's novel uses real estate development to pose many larger questions that will inform our discussion this semester. It may be useful for some of you to think of Dante's Inferno, with its circles of Hell. Besides the issues of substance, we will ask how a story poses questions for us—namely, how our experience becomes ethically problematic—in practical terms.

2. Brown, *Augustine of Hippo* chapter 10 on Augustine's conversion and on conversionary decision making, chapter 14 on the pulpit call and on being "called" to a vocation; part 3 (especially chapter 19 to the end), and chapters 28–31 on establishing influence and dealing with heresies and competitors; *Entrepreneurial Vocations,* chapter 1.

The great economist Joseph Schumpeter described entrepreneurship as involving new combinations of the means of production. We want to discuss just what it is that entrepreneurs do, and what it is that they do that is different from other actors. How is this related to the entrepreneur's political and social and economic environment? As our example, we'll discuss St. Augustine, arguably the most influential of the Church fathers, who in his conversion to Christianity provides the Western model of making a big decision, and who as bishop of Hippo (in North Africa) exerted extraordinary influence and power in a manner that can only be described as entrepreneurial. This is a rather unconventional example, especially for those used to models of entrepreneurs as Silicon Valley icons. But, historically, the great entrepreneurs have lain in the realm of religion and the military.

What kinds of decision did Augustine make, what does it mean to be called to a vocation or to be elected, and why is domination of your ideas or product not equivalent to absolute conviction about everything?

3. Walzer, *Exodus and Revolution; Entrepreneurial Vocations,* chapter 2.

Entrepreneurs who cannot gain the commitment of others to the entrepreneurs' projects are doomed to fail. Why are we committed to each other? Here is a story of the Founder and the Covenant, the Mother and the Infant, and the various stories of liberalism concerning matters of contract or market. How does commitment lead to action?

Leadership is a real quality. It is not the same as management. We'll discuss Moses and the Israelites in the desert, the relationship of leaders to followers, to get a feel for what is at stake here. Authentic leadership is intimately related to integrity.

4. Pirsig, *Zen and the Art of Motorcycle Maintenance,* part 3 (on "Quality"); *Entrepreneurial Vocations,* chapter 3.

Values are located in our actual actions and behavior and objects and institutions, and in our sentiments and arguments about those actions and things. Seemingly fixed values are transcended by behavior, and so there are violations and sin. A second theme is the nature of quality and judgment, and the fact that quality is often not reducible to criteria, but rather is a matter of "participation," an object being the occasion for quality to happen. As for judgment, it is almost never a matter of "my personal opinion," since you want others to agree with you and so you offer reasons and guidance so that they might see things as you do.

In examining how creative people actually work on problems, I use a poignant example—dealing with a crying baby in the middle of the night. What happens when it is the "last thing you do" that works?, and how is this different from conventional experimental design (but reminds one of double-blind medical experiments in which once a treatment is seen to be effective for many, the experiment is discontinued and all receive the treatment). One of the most influential ways of solving problems is to adapt a solution to a previous problem—often through historical analogy. How do we do this without being foolish?

5. Sophocles, *Oedipus the King, Oedipus at Colonus; Entrepreneurial Vocations,* chapter 5.

A crucial feature of technology is its insidiousness, the fact that we cannot know how it will turn out. Conversely, how are we to make our peace with tradition in fields that claim to be innovative and reconstructive? For tradition provides all the possible avenues for action as well as the current orthodoxy. The play of technology's violations (entrepreneurship!) with tradition's domesticating tendencies. I discuss the costs of entrepreneurship, the costs of "creative destruction," and who should bear them. I discuss along the way the new mercantilism of A. D. Chandler, A. Amsden, and M. Porter.

You will read the Oedipus trilogy, for it provides the archetypal example of how contingency plays out in insidious ways, and how we make our peace with the ways it turns out.

6. Sophocles, *Antigone; Entrepreneurial Vocations,* chapter 4.

Ruthlessness and cunning may well be required in many human endeavors. But what is most remarkable is how often matters of character and courage are rather more central. This is largely because we live in a community of others whom we must respect if we are to survive (for they can otherwise crush us, literally or in litigation). Leadership and integrity seem to characterize many of the great entrepreneurs (here we'll watch Moses lead the Israelites).

We want to examine the meaning of courage and character in actual practice; of virtue, fortune, and errancy; and the meaning of the hero, whether it be the mother in childbirth or Odysseus. What is the role of failure and of dogma? Perhaps the most exemplary courageous figure in literature is Antigone, who stands up to the state for the honor of her family.

Compassion is the joining of issues at the right time, taking into account human need and necessity, knowing when to invoke global values and when to be parochial and local. Compassion is the capacity to meet both need and rationality, both human necessity and efficiency.

7. Shakespeare, *The Tempest*

How does design make for things we take as whole and good? Topics in design: the tradition of arguing for the existence of God from the perceived design of the universe; its relationship to the search for a single design in entrepreneurial activities; the nature of such a temptation and its relationship to current cosmological ideas; error and perfection.

We'll read *The Tempest* because the relationship of the messiness of the real world (vs. some ideal) is addressed there. Why must you deal with actual nonsense rather than re-create a cleaner, better world? Why is the messy world also likely to be the most creative and fruitful?

Writing Projects

There are three writing projects in the course: a biographical study, an application of the ideas in this course to a situation you have already encountered in another course, and a life plan.

1. Life plan. An autobiographical essay that sets out your present life in terms of your experience and future goals, considering formative influences, current values, future aspirations. You want to write a document that will prove useful five and ten years down the road, giving yourself some perspective on where you come from and how you are changed by experience and reflection. Entrepreneurs have often written such documents, especially early in their careers. Length: As long as you need.

2. Application essay. Entrepreneurship is not only a matter of an actor, but often is reflected in the structure of organizations and governments. Drawing from your other courses, find a situation that might be characterized as entrepreneurial, but that seems to have no motivating actor. Apply the ideas of the course to making sense of this situation. Length: 4–6 pages.

3. Biographical study. Over the semester we read several stories about individuals (Augustine, Moses) who might be described as entrepreneurs. I want you to choose such a figure from a realm that interests you, find an authoritative biography or two and read it, and then analyze that figure's action in terms of the course's concepts. It may be useful for two or three of you to take on a very significant figure, perhaps reading different sources, writing your papers more or less independently, and then commenting on the other persons' interpretations and accountings. Length: 6–12 pages.

Notes

Preface:

[1] P. Selznick, *Leadership in Administration* (New York: Harper and Row, 1957), speaks of the establishment of institutions (vs. organizations).

[2] This is a more general cosmological and theological question. See R. Dales, *Medieval Discussions of the Eternity of the World* (Leiden: E. J. Brill, 1990).

[3] J. G. A. Pocock, *The Machiavellian Moment* (Princeton: Princeton University Press, 1975).

[4] M. Weber, in *The Protestant Ethic and the Spirit of Capitalism* (1904–1905, 1920), tr. T. Parsons (New York: Scribner's, 1958), is acutely aware of the methodological subtleties of his claims, for example pp. 90–92.

[5] Weber, *Protestant Ethic,* p. 271. On "pariah," see p. 190 n. 73.

[6] Note that Weber's is a differential explanation; namely, why capitalism and to some extent Western science and art blossomed under these regimes, rather than in Catholic regimes, for example. See the whole issue of *Science in Context* 3 (Spring 1989), on the Weber-Merton thesis.

[7] Correspondingly, I am not disturbed if religious actors act entrepreneurially, since I take entrepreneurship to be sacred and missionary, concerned with matters ecclesial, the establishment of institutions, rather than taking it to be competitive and contractual. I can imagine a very different perspective, as in an essay by M. Marty, "Clergy Ethics in America."

[8] M. Weber, in "Science as a Vocation," in *From Max Weber,* ed. H. H. Gerth and C. W. Mills (New York: Galaxy, 1958), pp. 154–155, suggests that intellectuals might employ religion to "furnish their souls with, so to speak, guaranteed genuine antiques." I hope, of course, that this is not going on here. The heralded disenchantment of the world is not quite so thorough as we might like to believe. The fact that this Christian tradition has a strong anti-Jewish thread is rather more significant for me.

[9] As a Jew of the sort I am, I know little about existence or belief; I know about practice and commitment. Similarly, as a physicist of the sort I was trained to be, I cannot get interested in the existence of electrons or belief in them; again, I know about practice and commitment. I expect the world to make some sense; that there really is just one story to be told, however varied and misfit its manifestations (a monotheism of sorts); that what is called the sacred is real. I am a scientist by training, so I do not confuse reality with the material, or existence, or belief. Reality is about what you do and where you are going, as I argue implicitly in *Doing Physics* (Bloomington: Indiana University Press, 1992).

[10] W. J. Baumol, "Entrepreneurship in Economic Theory," *American Economic Review* 58 (1968): 64–71; H. Barreto, *The Entrepreneur in Microeconomic Theory* (London: Routledge, 1989); but cf., M. Casson, *The Entrepreneur* (New York: Barnes and Noble, 1982). Institutional accounts of entrepreneurship take judgment and treat it as a cognitive activity. W. J. Baumol, *Entrepreneurship, Management, and the Structure of Payoffs* (Cambridge, MA: MIT Press, 1993), chapters 1–3, follows up on Baumol's article. Bau-

mol, following the work of Nathan Rosenberg, emphasizes the importance of small continuous changes—besides the Schumpeterian bacchanalian revel.

See also M. Schneider, P. Teske, and M. Mintrom, *Public Entrepreneurs* (Princeton: Princeton University Press, 1995) for a view of entrepreneurship from the point of view of political science and institutions rather than conventional economics.

[11] See, for example, J. Timmons, *New Venture Creation* (Homewood, IL: Irwin, 1990); or, exceptionally, P. Drucker, *Innovation and Entrepreneurship* (New York: Harper and Row, 1985). See also C. A. Kent, D. L. Sexton, and K. H. Vesper, eds., *Encyclopedia of Entrepreneurship* (Englewood Cliffs, NJ: Prentice Hall, 1982). There are many undergraduate texts that despite their claimed differences are remarkably similar in how they divide up the tasks of the entrepreneur and the guidance they offer.

[12] J. M. Burns, *Leadership* (New York: Harper and Row, 1978); A. Wildavsky, *The Nursing Father* (University: University of Alabama Press, 1984).

[13] H. Livesay, "Entrepreneurial Dominance in Businesses Large and Small, Past and Present," *Business History Review* 63 (1989): 1–21; H. Livesay, "Entrepreneurial History," in Kent, Sexton, and Vesper, *Encyclopedia of Entrepreneurship;* N. Rosenberg and L. E. Birdzell, Jr., "Science, Technology, and the Western Miracle," *Scientific American* 263 (November 1990): 42–54.

[14] A. O. Hirschman, *Development Projects Observed* (Washington, DC: Brookings Institution, 1967).

[15] Here I am thinking of the annual Babson College conferences on entrepreneurship.

[16] In this paragraph I have quoted various phrases from Schumpeter, without using quotation marks, for which see J. Schumpeter, *The Theory of Economic Development* (Cambridge, MA: Harvard University Press, 1934), pp. 83, 85; J. Schumpeter, *Capitalism, Socialism, and Democracy* (New York: Harper and Row, 1950), p. 93. See also chapter 5 on Schumpeter in J. Elster, *Explaining Technical Change* (Cambridge: Cambridge University Press, 1983).

[17] See Casson, *Entrepreneur*. Note that here I do not allow for sheer speculative urges (what Keynes called "animal spirits"). Moreover, while in historical retrospect we might see discontinuity, in actual lived experience there may be only marginal incremental changes.

[18] A. O. Hirschman, in *The Strategy of Economic Development* (New Haven: Yale University Press, 1958), pp. 16–17, puts it nicely:

> Following Schumpeter's lead, economists and historians alike have hitherto considered the innovating entrepreneur primarily as a strong individualist. His leadership, his willingness to assume risk, his breaking through old patterns of finance, production, and distribution were emphasized and almost made him look like a rebel against society. To stake success on a process or product that has not been tried out before no doubt takes courage, imagination, and a certain willingness to defy the old order, and did so particularly in the tradition-minded European societies during the first stages of the Industrial Revolution. In any event, these qualities were then the most spectacular aspect of entrepreneurship—so much so that the other necessary component was practically overlooked.
>
> This other component involves the ability to engineer agreement among all interested parties, such as the inventor of the process, the partners, the capitalists, the suppliers of parts and services, the distributors, etc., etc.; the ability—so important in underdeveloped countries today—to enlist cooperation of official agencies in such matters as customs duties, permits, exchange control regulations, etc.; the ability to bring and hold together an able staff, to delegate authority, to inspire loyalty, to han-

> dle successfully relations with labor and the public, and a host of other managerial talents....To keep a proper balance between the equally vital "cooperative" and "creative" components of entrepreneurship is obviously a difficult task.

[19]See Pocock, *Machiavellian Moment,* on the republican tradition. As for the rise of capitalism and republicanism, see A. O. Hirschman, *The Passions and the Interests* (Princeton: Princeton University Press, 1977).

[20] Oedipus is perhaps not so surprised as he allows when he finally understands explicitly what Teiresias is telling him (S. Fraiberg, "Two Modern Incest Heroes," in *Selected Writings of Selma Fraiberg,* ed. L. Fraiberg [Columbus: Ohio State University Press, 1987]).

[21] Here I draw from Schumpeter and Hirschman.

[22] I want to provide a "mutative interpretation," an account that might allow an entrepreneur to see herself in a richer light. Sherry Turkle suggested this phrase of James Strachey.

[23] Here I have paraphrased pp. 9–13 of D. Buttrick, *Homiletic* (Philadelphia: Fortress, 1987).

[24] Weber, *Protestant Ethic,* pp. 28–29, is lovely on matters of trespassing on other fields, and the fact that such synoptic work is often mistakenly taken as having a deeper, more wide-ranging intuition than specialist work.

[25] M. H. Krieger, "Criticism, Conversion, and Confession," in *Advice and Planning* (Philadelphia: Temple University Press, 1981), discusses the Bay Area Rapid Transit System, which has recurrently been shown to be uneconomic—as if pecuniary concerns were meant to explain why it was built or to justify its operations.

Chapter 1:

I have followed Peter Brown's *Augustine of Hippo* (Berkeley: University of California Press, 1967), supplemented by R. A. Markus's *Saeculum: History and Society in the Theology of St. Augustine* (Cambridge: Cambridge University Press, 1970) and his *End of Ancient Christianity* (Cambridge: Cambridge University Press, 1990). As for Paul, I have employed the work of J. C. Beker and of A. Segal. On prophecy, I have drawn from Abraham Heschel, N. O. Brown, and J. B. Soloveitchik. Much of what I say in this chapter has been shaped by lectures on Dante by John Freccero I heard in the mid-1970s at the University of Minnesota.

Augustine should not be taken as a unique figure, although he is surely an outstanding one. As Peter Brown makes clear (in *Power and Persuasion in Late Antiquity: Towards a Christian Empire* [Madison: University of Wisconsin Press, 1992]), the combination of political maneuvering and authoritative rhetorical talent, so characteristic of Augustine, was a preeminent mode through which Christian figures, such as Ambrose (339–397, bishop of Milan, and Augustine's teacher), gained wider legitimacy in the Roman Empire.

I should make a more general remark about the scholarship I employ. I make extensive use of a few secondary works, which are in their own way canonical. To experts what I say about a particular author should be more or less unexceptionable, although to be sure there are alternative canonical interpretations (for which see note 2 below). What should be of interest, and hopefully worthy of argument, is not the interpretation I offer (which is fairly standard), but the meaning of that interpretation for theories of professional practice. This is a book in applied homiletics, so to speak, for which see D. Buttrick, *Homiletic* (Philadelphia: Fortress, 1987).

[1] We might take this as evidence of the hero's extremism, and of course in a narrative we might expect that a reversal would take place, the hero now recruited into the life of war and pollution.

[2] See Brown, *Augustine of Hippo*; Augustine, *Confessions*, tr. H. Chadwick (Oxford: Oxford University Press, 1991); S. Weinberg, "The Cosmological Constant Problem," *Reviews of Modern Physics* 61 (1989): 1–23.

Note how much my discussion depends on Brown and Markus. I am much more concerned here with employing a single reasonable interpretation than whether it is the only one. It serves my analytical purposes; other interpretations might well challenge them. In this sense this chapter is not so much about Augustine, but about one conception of him as it informs a conception of entrepreneurship. That another interpretation would inform a different, even conflicting, conception of entrepreneurship does not much concern me. What is crucial in the end is whether a conception proves realistic and effective for entrepreneurs.

[3] See M. H. Krieger, "Criticism, Conversion, and Confession," in *Advice and Planning* (Philadelphia: Temple University Press, 1981), pp. 103–139; and M. H. Krieger, *Marginalism and Discontinuity* (New York: Russell Sage Foundation, 1989), chapter 1, for much more detail on the structure of big decisions.

[4] Hindsight allows Augustine to be confident of the reliability of his method of decision.

[5] Current writing on entrepreneurial invention or the sociology of science, for example, emphasizes that almost always there are multiples rather than singletons, to use Robert Merton's terms of art, for which see his *Sociology of Science* (Chicago: University of Chicago Press, 1973).

[6] Krieger, "Criticism, Conversion, and Confession."

[7] P. Davidson, "Is Probability Theory Relevant for Uncertainty?" *Journal of Economic Perspectives* 5 (1991): 129–143.

[8] H. Arendt, *The Human Condition* (Chicago: University of Chicago Press, 1958), on storytelling.

[9] On foolishness, see J. March, *Decisions and Organizations* (Oxford: Basil Blackwell, 1988).

[10] Brown, *Augustine of Hippo,* p. 138.

[11] Given Augustine's great rhetorical gifts, one can never be sure that this is not a setup, or at least related to us in the most affecting fashion. I keep imagining Augustine cooperating in this scene from the beginning.

[12] See H. Barreto, *The Entrepreneur in Microeconomic Theory* (London: Routledge, 1989).

[13] Here I am thinking of Max Weber's use of Schiller's term *Entzauberung*. I use the term *command* to indicate that we do not obtain control over those myths.

[14] It is true that historians produce among themselves rather different interpretations in their works, and those differences are not readily reconciled. But it is also true that they will agree on much of what actually occurred, and there are professional canons about how one should handle documentary sources and about the character of truth in history (one of the achievements of nineteenth-century historiography), despite all the recent arguments.

[15] Mark Casson also uses "judgment" to describe the distinctive capacities of the entrepreneur, in *The Entrepreneur* (New York: Barnes and Noble, 1982). Judgment, for him, is that idiosyncratic seeing of new possibilities that others could not conceive of. My use surely includes this, but it is drawn from Kant in the *Critique of Judgment*. See also

Krieger, "Criticism, Conversion, and Confession."

[16] Of course, these questions about predictability, rightness, and application are the archetypal questions of a form of social science. They are not, I would maintain, the archetypal questions of much of natural science, as it is actually done, where the main question is to make sense of what is going on. What is most interesting, and this says a great deal about the history of professional education, is how that form of social science came to be dominant in the professional schools and how its distance from practice has been explained away.

[17] Obviously, this description, which is in the victors' terms, is *not* derived from the Gnostic or Donatist or Pelagian point of view, a not insignificant bias.

[18] My use of religious language here is motivated by its power of description and justification: it makes sense of and encourages entrepreneurial action. There is perhaps a structural reason why this language is likely to be powerful. Entrepreneurship is that realm in which "more" takes place than can be accounted for in terms of management science or prudential considerations. Insofar as religion is that meeting ground of the sacred and the profane, theological language also includes more than can be accounted for in everyday terms. (If religion were only about the sacred, we, in our ordinary lives, would have no access to it. It would be noumenal, to use Kant's way of putting such issues on the side.)

[19] See chapter 19 of Brown, *Augustine of Hippo,* for much of what follows. There is some argument about exactly whom the Donatists are named after.

[20] Brown, *Augustine of Hippo,* p. 217.

[21] E. Pagels, *The Gnostic Gospels* (New York: Random House, 1979). Here we surely have an echo of pejorative Christian characterizations of Judaism, say by Paul much earlier, or eventual Catholic characterizations of the early Gnostic churches, ones in which purity, sacredness, secretness, and personal commitment are crucial.

[22] See Markus, *End of Ancient Christianity,* chapter 1, on conversion, and on tolerance for what is taken as atavistic native or pagan ritual.

[23] See R. MacMullen, *Christianizing the Roman Empire* (New Haven: Yale University Press, 1984), as well as Markus, *Ancient Christianity,* chapter 1, on the extent of the conversion of pagans who retain some of their pagan rituals. Markus believes that MacMullen is all too lenient. See also Markus, *Saeculum.*

[24] The argument of Markus, *Saeculum,* turns on the distinction between the eschatological and the sociological.

[25] See Markus, *Saeculum,* pp. 138, 142, on discipline; Brown, *Augustine of Hippo,* chapter 21. From a liberal point of view, that authority is taken as not so reducible is a tragedy, a justification for murder.

[26] A similar story can be told about the Pelagians. See Brown, *Augustine of Hippo,* chapters 29, 32.

[27] Of course, the historian will point out that this is the Roman Empire, and it is anachronistic to ask for liberal values and actions. How does Augustine act within this larger context? we might ask.

[28] We might argue that this is "internalization of the aggressor," for which see chapter 5. In Penelope Leach's writing we find an alternative vision, much informed by Winnicott. See chapter 3.

[29] Much as Schumpeter's description of entrepreneurship as creative destruction is perhaps ambivalent about the losers (are they deserving? or merely sacrificed to the future?), so this description of entrepreneurship as illiberal is problematic.

[30] Here I paraphrase Markus, *End of Ancient Christianity,* p. 214.

[31] Markus, *Ancient Christianity,* chapter 11, on the Desert and the City. Markus describes how the saeculum, which once allowed for the meeting of the secular and the sa-

cred, yielded to asceticism and the decline of secular culture.

[32] We have a world and a church without classical culture, one in which Augustine would be bereft.

[33] Brown, *Augustine of Hippo,* pp. 323–324.

[34] Here I follow Brown, *Augustine of Hippo,* chapters 26, 27.

[35] There is much technical discussion among economists about how to distinguish such profit from rent or interest or return on investment.

[36] See R. Dales, *Medieval Discussions of the Eternity of the World* (Leiden: E. J. Brill, 1990), on the problem of eternity being a challenge to Creation or other such marked moments.

[37] These distinctions come from Andrew Carnegie, "The Gospel of Wealth," in *The Andrew Carnegie Reader,* ed. J. F. Wall (Pittsburgh: University of Pittsburgh Press, 1992), but I take them more immediately from the writing of Robert Payton.

[38] The logic is not technical, heuristic, political, managerial, or analytical.

[39] As a physicist by training, I do not professedly believe in mass or whatever or even in differential equations. My problem is to make sense of what naturally occurs.

[40] Paul plays a dominant role in books 7 and 8 of the *Confessions,* and in book 8 the actual conversion is related. As for Paul's conversion, see A. Segal, *Paul the Convert: The Apostolate and Apostasy of Saul the Pharisee* (New Haven: Yale University Press, 1990). I have deliberately chosen both a Christian source (J. C. Beker, *Paul the Apostle: The Triumph of God in Life and Thought* [Philadelphia: Fortress, 1984] and *The Triumph of God* [Minneapolis: Fortress, 1990]) and a Jewish source (Segal)—compare their titles, one emphasizing apostleship, the other conversion. Correspondingly, imagine a Manichaean source on Augustine.

[41] In Beker's terms, particularity is called "contingency," as against the "coherence" we might expect to appreciate when revelation is truly revealed at redemption.

[42] N. Frye, *The Great Code* (New York: Harcourt Brace Jovanovich, 1982), provides the phrase "myth redeems history." Here I have played on the distinction between the actual and the possible.

[43] Here I paraphrase T. Leavitt, in R. P. Bagozzi, *Principles of Marketing Management* (Chicago: SRA, 1986), p. 30.

[44] J. G. A. Pocock (*The Machiavellian Moment* [Princeton: Princeton University Press, 1975], p. 34) calls Augustine an antiapocalyptic because of his commitment to an everyday worldly institution. Compared to the Donatists, his commitment is surely more everyday. But, from Paul's point of view, that commitment is the correct way of being apocalyptic. One ought not abandon the world.

[45] A. Segal, *Rebecca's Children: Judaism and Christianity in the Ancient World* (Cambridge: Harvard University Press, 1986), pp. 179–181.

[46] Of course, this is a commonplace, as are my earlier remarks about marketing and strategy. We learn from Paul how to exemplify such a commonplace, what it would mean in practice.

[47] Segal, *Paul the Convert,* p. 194.

[48] Segal, *Paul the Convert,* p. 216.

[49] See Beker, *Paul the Apostle,* pp. 11–12, for a wonderful quote on apostleship from Kierkegaard. It also shows that Kierkegaard does not appreciate the need for contingency and particularity in the apostle's task.

[50] See Frye, *Great Code*.

[51] Believing that creativity exhibited in great work explains the production of great work is a dialectical illusion, mistaking cause for outcome, as Kant would have put it in the *Critique of Judgment* in his discussion of genius.

[52] Hence my use of "influenced" above, as in "flow through."

[53] See L. Weschler, *Seeing Is Forgetting the Name of the Thing One Sees* (Berkeley: University of California Press, 1982), on Robert Irwin's use of the term "in response."

[54] M. H. Krieger, "What Planners Do," in *Advice and Planning,* pp. 191–198, leaves out the notion of a covenant. I am too individual and universalistic, as is Kierkegaard. I need to be concerned more with matters of community, as I am in the "Advice" essay in that book, and of particularity.

[55] As for the way that Moses would understand, I am less sure. In chapter 2 I am less concerned with Moses' relationship to God in his prophetic role, more concerned with his relationship to the Israelites and the relationships among the Israelites themselves. Given that the Hebrew prophets are historically very ancient, we might fairly ask if Paul and Augustine are to be taken as prophets. In Jewish terms they are surely too late to be prophets. In Christian terms they act much like prophets, both in terms of revelation and their response, at the moment of conversion and throughout their subsequent lives. But they do not recurrently receive revelation, as did the ancient prophets. After their revelation, their conversionary moments, they are resolutely bound to this-worldly problems.

[56] I provide a description of entrepreneurship rather than an explanation. As Heschel argues in his great work on the prophets, without a phenomenology explanation has no work to do. Phenomenology sets the questions that explanation might well take on.

[57] J. B. Soloveitchik, "The Lonely Man of Faith," in *Studies in Judaica,* ed. L. D. Stitskin (New York: Ktav, 1974), pp. 69-133. I have deliberately not discussed the prophet's ecstasy and agony. For more on all of this, see A. Heschel, *The Prophets* (New York: Harper and Row, 1969). For the entrepreneur these are surely signs that something extraordinary is going on. Here I concentrate on the structure of prophecy, not its experience.

[58] See N. O. Brown, *Apocalypse and/or Metamorphosis* (Berkeley: University of California Press, 1991).

[59] There is much disagreement within religious and theological thought about what is needed to be ready to hear God's message and to be in God's presence. One need not be righteous, so it seems. Similarly, we do not know how one can be ready to hear the call of creativity, except that it seems likely that one cannot be focused on that hearing.

I make no claim to just what corresponds to God in the realm of creativity (and it could well be God); rather, the claim is that the phenomenologies are similar.

[60] Brown, *Augustine of Hippo,* p. 53.

[61] As for the Gnostic Elijah, Moses instantiates this role insofar as he is a scapegoat.

[62] Brown, *Apocalypse and/or Metamorphosis,* chapter 5. We might say that rabbinic Judaism also performs such institutionalization. The rabbinic hierarchy is to be sure rather weaker than the priestly one that preceded it.

[63] The moral dilemmas might be finessed by economics and statistics, a nineteenth-century legacy. They are employed in contemporary corporate contexts to do ethical work. On statistics, see T. Porter, *The Rise of Statistical Thinking* (Princeton: Princeton University Press, 1986); on mathematization of economics, see M. Schabas, *A World Ruled by Number* (Princeton: Princeton University Press, 1990). Adam Smith was as much concerned with matters of morality as those of economy, for a proper morality made for a working economy. See J. Q. Wilson, "Adam Smith and Business Ethics," *California Management Review* 32 (Fall 1989): 59-72. As for statistics and social policy, see I. Hacking, *The Taming of Chance* (Cambridge: Cambridge University Press, 1990).

[64] These features are always present in religion. Analogy, language, and allegory are to be taken seriously. "Resurrection language is eschatological language that is intelligible only within an apocalyptic world of thought where it is at home" (Beker, *Triumph of God,* p. 66). "Whenever apocalyptic categories are demoted or degraded as if they are purely culturally determined or an obsolete survival, Paul's resurrection theology is

transmuted into something else" (p. 90). Heschel (*Prophets*) makes similar remarks in his discussion of prophecy.

Practically, we know a good deal about what entrepreneurs do, but that is often taken as craft not readily subject to analytic attention.

[65] If religious traditions provide accurate renditions of entrepreneurship, then conventional management science categories are likely to deny us access to what is crucial to becoming entrepreneurs.

[66] E. Pagels, *Adam, Eve, and the Serpent* (New York: Random House, 1988). More generally, an ad hominem argument connects actual experience with theology taken as phenomenology. Given Augustine's very great passions (compared to the more modest ones of, say, Augustine's antagonist Julian of Eclanum), it is not surprising that Augustine believes external authority is needed to keep them in check.

[67] Brown, *Augustine of Hippo,* pp. 236–237.

[68] The entrepreneur needs help, help from a "buddy"—otherwise there will be no success. I suspect that is the purpose of male games of hierarchical or episcopal domination.

[69] On sacrifice and mortification see K. Burke, *The Rhetoric of Religion* (Berkeley: University of California Press, 1970), a study of Augustine.

Chapter 2:

My discussion of Moses and the Israelites is rather less elegiac and personal in tone, rather more theological and systematic in method, than my discussion of Augustine and Paul. Where the first chapter demonstrates that religious language might speak directly to entrepreneurial practice, here I hope I to be both more theological and more practical.

About Moses one must go to the Hebrew Scriptures, but I have also followed the legends according to L. Ginzberg's *Legends of the Bible* (Philadelphia: Jewish Publication Society, 1975). The problems I discuss here were first made clear to me by M. Walzer, *Exodus and Revolution* (New York: Basic Books, 1985), and manifestly I remain indebted to his reading. A. Wildavsky, in *The Nursing Father* (University: University of Alabama Press, 1984), presses rather more explicitly the implications of the Moses story for political leadership. Compared to the scholarly and hermeneutic efforts of Walzer and Wildavsky, who ground their arguments rather thoroughly and scrupulously in the details of the text, my efforts in this chapter are best seen as homiletic, driven by the lessons I wish to draw.

The work of René Girard is crucial to all discussion of sacrifice and scapegoat. And Freud, in *Moses and Monotheism* (1939; reprint, New York: Vintage, 1959), suggests we might think of Moses as the overestimated father who is then humbled, something of a family romance.

[1] E. Said, in "Walzer's *Exodus and Revolution:* A Canaanite Reading," *Grand Street* 5 (Winter 1986): 86-106, argues that this triumphalist vision characterizes the Israelites in their relationship to the Canaanites. He emphasizes the sectarian character of the Israelites' story, the one they tell themselves, and so its limits (especially for others). For my purposes, however, it is just the Israelitic story—with all the potential problems Said adumbrates—that characterizes entrepreneurship. For a reply to Said by Walzer, and Said's reply, see "An Exchange," *Grand Street 8* (Summer 1986): 246–259.

[2] Rabbinic Judaism might also be subject to this attack. But I think it is fair to say that the Talmudic oral law is systematically and deliberately rather more bound to the written Torah than is Augustine, in his bishopric role as judge, bound to the New Testament.

[3] As for Jesus, what I say in the text concerning the earlier end of the age of prophecy is the moderate Jewish position, and more generally the stand on future prophet-claimants

to be messiah (no matter how subtle their claim). On popular conceptions of Jesus as a leader or model entrepreneur, see L. P. Ribuffo, "Jesus Christ as Business Statesman: Bruce Barton and the Selling of Corporate Capitalism," *American Quarterly* 33 (1981): 206–231; Jay Haley, *The Power Tactics of Jesus Christ, and Other Essays* (New York: Grossman, 1969). Barton's book was entitled *The Man Nobody Knows* (Jesus) and it appeared in 1925–1926.

[4] In our discussion in the first chapter we claimed that Augustine's entrepreneurship was in creating an institution, one whose qualities in terms of entrepreneurship are not specified. It need not be an entrepreneurial organization.

[5] M. Walzer, *Exodus and Revolution* (New York: Basic Books, 1985).

[6] As oral literature, the lists and repetitions serve rhythmic and mnemotechnical purposes, and there is in fact much pleasure to be heard in their being sung and related and heard. The details matter theologically because we are telling *this* story; they matter rhetorically because in the telling we are listening and we will hear—paying pleasurable attention as well—*this* story only if we hear it with all of its details intact. More generally, scriptural commentary, whether by means of casuistry, homily, or hermeneutic, depends on the exact details of the text.

As for rhythm, here is Christopher Smart in *Jubilate Agno* (1760), ll. 731–732:

> For the Lord commanded Moses concerning the cats at the
> departure of the Children of Israel from Egypt.
> For every family had one cat at least in the bag.

[7] But compare S. Brams, *Biblical Games: A Strategic Analysis of Stories in the Old Testament* (Cambridge: MIT Press, 1980), or A. Wildavsky, *The Nursing Father: Moses as a Political Leader* (University, Alabama: University of Alabama Press, 1984), for such abstractions. Brams shows how actions in the Old Testament are game-theoretically rational, once we impute not unreasonable motives to those actors. Wildavsky is again concerned to show the rationality of Moses' actions, once we fully appreciate his particular historical contexts.

[8] This is just how orthodoxy assails reform. Reform's power is to insist that it takes the *whole* text seriously.

[9] The Israelites have a special task, but salvation is not restricted to them.

[10] Of course, that state power might be rather more modest or under the command of its citizens, as in a contract tradition. But that is not at issue here.

[11] Now it might be argued that to read the story of David in the Bible and then to see parallels in your own life, were you named David, is going too far. But here the issues are not philosophical ones about generalization and lawlikeness. In this realm of storytelling and meaning, the problems are about coherence and order and purpose. And in finding coherence and order and purpose in reading such a story, one is to become motivated and encouraged.

Abstract and formal social-scientific accounts as in economics are in general explanatory but they are not motivating. They might be true, but be unresponsive to our needs. (See S. Krieger, *Social Science and the Self* (New Brunswick: Rutgers University Press, 1991), for an alternative kind of accounting that aims to be motivating.) Such explanations are perhaps too smart by half, since the kinds of breaks and tensions that motivate the entrepreneur are explained away (using notions such as transaction costs, or institutional change and cognitive reordering). They do not accord enough with experience, as it is actually experienced (nor are they meant to) to affect how people think of themselves—especially in this realm of entrepreneurial action (as contrasted to the corporate one in which changes are in general marginal and prudential rather than discontinuous and conversionary). The advice one might give an entrepreneur derived from marginalist and prudential scientific explanations (as in much of economics) is likely not to address the entrepreneur's needs, those of character and courage and of conceptualizing him- or herself as taking on such a role.

[12] See the appendix on Jewish scrupulosity rituals, and release therefrom, in J. Rapoport, *The Boy Who Could Not Stop Washing* (New York: NAL, 1990).

[13] See also the beginning of chapter 5. And, M. H. Krieger, *Advice and Planning* (Philadelphia: Temple University Press, 1981). The issue here is not at all freedom of the will vs. determinism (in which we would follow patterned stories as automatons or as pseudo-autonomous actors).

[14] I have referred to "story" rather than "archetype" because stories are specific and detailed and concrete, and driven by our sentimental involvements. Archetypal narratives and figures are formal and analytic abstractions, ones which we might appreciate reflectively but which are not meant for sentimental involvement. We are motivated by stories, not by archetypes. Even if stories might well be analyzable archetypally or formally, in *all* of their detail let us say, they work for us as stories, in the end, *as* stories. (This would be a Proppian or formalist analysis, but one presumably encompassing *all* the details.) To be educated in the formal analysis of situations may make us more acute appreciators and observers, but the humanistic problem is to take on that story, to recover it from analysis and to live with it. Put differently, analysis then demands courage if we are to act.

[15] I have come to understand this point from formative conversations with Steve Porter.

[16] The vital question is not how to follow a story, but how to follow it in your own way so that you are not merely going through the motions. (Much of what I say here is a reworking of M. Heidegger in *Being and Time* (1926), the use of "authenticity" being just the first major debt.) Now, some of the time going through the motions is more than enough to achieve what we want. But entrepreneurial situations are by their natures such that they are failed by standard operating procedure and mechanical action. Here, the question is, How are you to follow a story by its own lights for your own mission?

What is surely demanded is an attention to exact detail and an interpretation of the details. The issue is not scrupulosity, as if a single failed move need lead to disaster or defilement. Rather, stories become our own, they have been authentically integrated into ourselves, by how we take them in their particularity. They are not even formulas, which once memorized are fully known, although we know the meaning of formulas and archetypes only through their exemplifications. The infinite productivity of art and literature depends on the work of art being appropriated by us *as a work*, not in its formal structure, not in its epitome or outline. I believe this is true for the natural sciences, too. What may look like formal abstract mathematics and technology and formulae, is in fact just the site where the details and contexts—the modes of application, as they actually are realized—matter enormously. To change the context or the detail is to offer the chance for an entirely different appropriation or understanding or meaning. And we cannot delineate ahead of time which are the most crucial facts, which are secondary or irrelevant. The color of the room may matter enormously, the particular mathematical notation (even if formally equivalent to another one) may matter enormously—to us, in our doing. To a clinician, and this includes practicing physicists as well as, say, psychotherapists or internists, to change a detail may well be to change the whole story that is being told. Not always, but sometimes, and often enough so that clinicians really must be there, on the scene, to know what is going on.

We, in our lives, follow along the line of a story not only because we have told ourselves that story, but also because the story's logic or causal structure is not unlike how the world actually does work. And that is in part why the story has become part of our tradition, and also why the story changes as our world changes. We do not need to explicitly review the story, or check it out at each point, to follow it. Yet, again, that structure is in no sense interestingly determinate. That logic is sufficiently open so that along the way we might make prudential decisions, say, drawn from theories of rational choice and economy. Yet, while prudence is all well and good, actually we are driven by structure and motive and by the integrity of our roles. And, of course, we must fill in the details given our own particular situations, if the story is to be our story.

We find ourselves following a story, following it in a way that is our own, finding the tradition rich but also demanding that we make our peace with it. The great stories are in effect already-there for us, whether or not we have read them. They are in our language and grammar. We could not be the persons we become without having absorbed them, however distantly, as we grow and mature. (See also the appendix on Teaching and Self-Study.)

[17] Just because we are concerned with story and how it is followed, we are less concerned with scholarly historical accounts, which are driven by the demands of document and proof, or with canonical texts, again driven by matters of authenticity and authority. While one might be concerned with the historicity of Moses and with the Hebrew Bible as such, what I am even more concerned with is the life of that story. So, for example, I am driven here by Louis Ginzberg's *Legends of the Bible* (Philadelphia: Jewish Publication Society, 1975), perhaps more than the Masoretic text of the Hebrew Bible. And in the same vein, in the first chapter I am more concerned with a biography of Augustine and with modern theological accounts of Paul, rather than with their own testimonials. Of course, this would violate scholarly canons were I not centrally concerned with the life of stories (rather than with history or authentic texts).

[18] Here I closely paraphrase Walzer, *Exodus and Revolution,* pp. 149, who refers to W. D. Davies, *The Territorial Dimension of Judaism* (Berkeley: University of California Press, 1982).

[19] Walzer, *Exodus and Revolution*. For purposes of argument, compare with Said, "Walzer's *Exodus and Revolution,*" on occupying others' lands, the nature of riparian rights, and more generally stewardship and who was there "first."

If you do not believe you are in Egypt, if you take your tasks as conventional and justified, if the Promised Land is a pipe dream (at least compared to the reality and rewards of where you are now), then your problem is not wilderness and marching. You live in a tame world where people march together as a matter of course, perhaps in a rather pedestrian yet still satisfying way. And then you might be interested in how you might make your organization "more entrepreneurial."

[20] For example, if early adopters of an entrepreneurial invention find it intrinsically satisfying and effective, the value associated with that invention becomes concretely realized and manifest in such a way that later adopters can more readily appreciate it. Value is created and affirmed in the use of the invention, and commitment comes from those experiences of value creation. Early Christian converts found Christianity to be practically effective and so were committed to the sect, and only later was that effectiveness abstracted into doctrinal commitments. R. MacMullen, *Christianizing the Roman Empire* (New Haven: Yale University Press, 1984); but, cf., on MacMullen, R. A. Markus, *The End of Ancient Christianity* (Cambridge: Cambridge University Press, 1990), ch. 1, pp. 6–9. Markus argues for examining how contemporary people saw the distinction between the convert and the nonconvert, rather than using anachronistic criteria. See p. 161 n. 23.

Of course, it is no mean task to make those inventions (of new combinations of the means of production) and to set up those initial situations in which value is created and affirmed. And so the entrepreneur perhaps deserves the protagonist or heroic role. But actual commitment comes from those moments when value is created, when invention is real and actual and "works" for others. I do not mean to suggest that mere working is enough to gain commitment, for that invention's value needs to be a focus of people's need and attention. And sometimes it simply is. At others, there are long waits and lots of entrepreneurial effort focused on creating a market before the creation of value could ensure commitment. Working is not so obvious then.

[21] This is taken from Pat Riley, speaking as coach of the Los Angeles Lakers basketball team.

[22] For example, Wildavsky, *Nursing Father,* analyzes these tasks of leadership, situating them in the particular contexts of the Israelites along their way.

One of the dilemmas of the contractual relationships that bind athletes to their teams is that the coach's authority transcends contract, in fact has nothing to do with it, in his coaching role with team members. This role and relationship is altogether more serious than something that can be mediated by lawyers paid by the hour or the like.

[23] R. M. Green, *Religion and Moral Reason* (New York: Oxford University Press, 1988), pp. 87–90.

[24] M. Hodgson, *The Venture of Islam* (Chicago: University of Chicago Press, 1974), vol. 1, p. 80, in discussing Islam, suggests that such a community requires a creative act (revelation and response, "acceptance" of the truth); group commitment thereto (institutionalization, allegiance); and cumulative interaction within the group (debate, dialogue, dialectic).

[25] As we shall see in our discussion of motherhood, we must believe that we are on the way before we can conceive of bonding.

[26] Recall that in *The Divine Comedy,* Dante begins with. "In the middle of the journey of our life" (albeit Dante is referring to his age of 35, one-half of the Biblical three score and ten).

[27] C. van Allsburg, *Two Bad Ants* (Boston: Houghton Mifflin, 1988), p. 15.

[28] I emphasize these aspects, to distinguish this story from the story of conversion of chapter 1. Surely, Augustine is unhappy before his conversion, he is unsatisfied with the answers he has. He is rather more unsatisfied than are the Israelites, he is less oppressed, and he moves more out of an insight than from the pressure of external circumstances. See, for example, T. Kuhn, *Black-Body Theory and the Quantum Discontinuity* (New York: Oxford University Press, 1978), on Planck—who is like Augustine but who is driven by a formal device, the physical significance of which is appreciated much later. Kuhn's account, in *The Structure of Scientific Revolutions* (Chicago: University of Chicago Press, 1970), of problem-shifts in a field depends, as does the story of the Israelites, in part on the dying off of a generation, a community phenomenon. But Kuhn gives less attention to the problems of backsliding and marching.

[29] While we might think that an individual, say a hero, is drawn and driven by an insight or an idea or a moment of inspiration—and that is just how in the first chapter I describe Augustine as a driven entrepreneur, coming to his moment in that Milan garden, eventually pursuing its meaning as bishop of Hippo—such a story is probably not the case for a group. As we would find in Augustine's Catholic Church, and as we find most powerfully in the story of the Israelites, a group of not so heroic individuals is to be driven by external forces, often violent ones. And it is driven in a ragtag way, not whole and together. To analogize a group's delays and resistances to an individual's denial and ambivalence does not capture the diversity of the members' commitments or their capacity to form subgroups that may be vanguards or laggards or "murmurers." While we might think of scientific or ecclesiastic revolutions as, in the end, a matter of generational succession, "old" ideas dying off with old scientists, even prophylactic sacrifice of murmurers (the killing of three thousand of those who idolized the Golden Calf) is only the beginning for the Israelites.

[30] Here, feelings are sentiments within an archetypal or formal structure. See, H. Plessner, *Laughter and Crying* (Evanston: Northwestern University Press, 1970).

[31] Of course, the oppression is only eventually taken to be undeniable, rather than bearable and necessary.

[32] That the people are not yet a coherent group indicates that one cannot apply the personal and individual and corporate notions of the first chapter. That we might describe such moving using corporate notions is perhaps an expression of a hope that they might become coherent. But the actual phenomenology of marching is rather more like an orderly rout.

[33] See chapter 1, at note 33, on *peregrini* in Augustine.

[34] Here I speak patent ahistorical nonsense (unless history is efficient, an interesting form of synoptic rationality). I am thinking of physicists' use of optimization principles, as in the principle of least action, to convert history into efficiency. They are useful for physics in part because a wide range of details are deliberately not to count in the physicists' context.

[35] John Bennett, Jr., has pointed out to me how in clinical work a detail may change the whole interpretation. Clinicians believe this sensitivity is intrinsic to an interpretation, each detail being necessary, the story sensitively dependent on all of the details in their mutual coherence.

[36] In each historical case, we can point to proximate causes. But there are distal causes that may be influential; their temporal order may be significant; or it may be just that things got bad enough, say random fluctuations that went over the line of reversibility. See W. Brian Arthur's work (for example, "Positive Feedbacks in the Economy," *Scientific American* 262 (February 1990): 92–95), in which these processes are characterized as nonoptimal and nonergodic (sensitively dependent on initial conditions).

[37] There is a large empirical literature in politics and psychology on leadership and motivation, often centered on what kinds of leadership are most effective, in which circumstances, and on what gets people to move and how. The problem of commitment cannot be solved (either for empirical prediction or for pedagogy and training of leaders) by invoking "leadership," mainly because the actual dynamics of binding are the tasks of solidarity, a problem of a very different sort. For my claim here, and elsewhere, is not that one can explain how and when people march in terms of the entrepreneur's qualities in relation to his people. The entrepreneur's substantive promise or idea, the land of milk and honey, is crucial.

[38] Professional education is both a training in skills and an inculcation into a culture. If form and ritual are not resolutely committed to the profession, they are likely to be disenchanting. Reformism need not be the problem, as long as the essential tenets of the profession are reaffirmed; there is then merely an argument about just which are the essential tenets. But if those tenets are seen to be torn, then form and ritual are formal and ritualistic rather than binding and committing. What is given up is the possibility of learning to be an *X*. For to learn the various skills without an organizing vision is very much to become a robot without a personality. Perhaps this is a useful position, but it is not a position that calls forth the best from actual persons. For they hear no calling. Put differently, conventional analytic explanations often explain away why any reasonable person would be committed to any particular mission. What we want instead is a form of analysis that leads to an encouraging pedagogy, one that makes it possible for a student to hear a calling in the best sense.

I should note that I am not here justifying the conventional ideology of any profession. Rather, I am claiming that there must be at least an ideology that is seen as coherent and justified, one drawing from the tradition and participating in ultimate value.

[39] It would be virtually impossible to recruit many young persons to a life in scientific research if they were given stark statistics about the unlikelihood of Nobel Prize work, if they were told the details of the politics of science, if they knew just how long they would

be treated as novices, or if they knew that being smart, a seemingly transcendent characteristic, is important only to the degree that one is wily and entrepreneurial. So I recall my own training in science as unskeptical and transcendent (and several of my teachers received a Nobel Prize in physics), and so the literature that studies the training of scientists points out. Form and ritual are given the transcendent power to lead one to election into the fraternity (and it is not a sorority); doubters and skeptics are labeled as not good scientists. The systematic study of the actual doing of science is quite problematic in this sense, since it disenchants the world of science and so would discourage its initiands were they to believe such studies applied to them.

[40] On such "liminal" moments, see A. van Gennep, *Rites of Passage* (London: Routledge and Paul, 1960); V. Turner, *The Ritual Process* (Chicago: Aldine, 1969).

[41] By the way, to be a scapegoat is a formal or structural fact, not a fact about one's sense of oneself or a requirement that one be pitied or martyred. More generally, my description here is structural, saying something like: If there is to be binding, the following must be present, and this is how they must work together. But it is only in the detailed working out of these structural requirements that we understand their meaning.

So I go from concrete, particular, detailed stories (Moses, or a story of more conventional entrepreneurship) to a structural account and then back again to those detailed stories, to see them in a different analytical light. The seemingly idiosyncratic details of the entrepreneur's own story are now seen as structurally necessary (even if the details are unpredictable in their detail).

[42] See, for example, Walzer, *Exodus and Revolution*. We need not decide which violence is justified. All are to be contained as history, if there is to be legitimacy in the present.

Judith Shklar, in "The Liberalism of Fear" (in N. Rosenblum, ed., *Liberalism and the Moral Life* (Cambridge, Mass.: Harvard University Press, 1989)) reminds us of how dangerous is such violence, how much it is likely to be out of control, how ultimately unjustified it may well be. That it might happen as part of a structure of transformation does not at all justify it.

[43] This discussion is influenced by the work of René Girard on the scapegoat.

[44] Walzer, *Exodus and Revolution,* p. 53.

[45] Now we might imagine, quite sensibly, that changes are marginal, that the process is evolutionary, that the transformation does not require an entrepreneur at all, at least of the sort I describe. See M. H. Krieger, *Marginalism and Discontinuity* (New York: Russell Sage Foundation, 1989).

[46] Note that Moses is *not* compassionate, and only when God would doom the Israelites can Moses allow them their failures. Also, Talmud comes well after Moses.

[47] Here I follow M. Ignatieff, *The Needs of Strangers* (New York: Viking, 1985).

[48] I owe much of this section to work of Walter Zisette, Jr., including passages from a paper of his.

[49] Of course, disruption is just what analytical methods are supposed to do, and so again my argument might well be seen as illiberal, hostile to analytical method.

[50] Here I am following Marcel Mauss, *The Gift* (New York: Norton, 1967).

[51] There is much scholarly literature on the exact nature of such covenants and the differences among those covenants in the Bible, for there is a sequence of them, as well as about their more ordinary analogs or origins in the ancient political realm (which readily conflated the political and the sacred). There are also distinctions to be drawn about the nature of this absolute commitment; promise and obligation are open to interpretation. The voluntaristic character of covenants (If you do *X,* then...) seems to imply the capacity to get out of the covenant if *X* is not done. But it turns out that the failure of *X* allows only for redemptive acts. There is no way out. The narrative is unending under the pro-

tection of this covenantal commitment.

[52] If we could buy our way out, then, as we shall see in chapter 5, entrepreneurial endeavor would be abandoned for investments whose payoff is more in accord with the risks involved.

[53] Correspondingly, contracts are subject to breach and malfeasance.

[54] What makes, say, an economic interpretation of the U.S. Constitution so problematic is that that founding then loses its uncorruptedness. And so, as Pocock argues, there is the possibility of a jeremiad concerning the perilousness of virtue in the actual world. J. G. A. Pocock, *The Machiavellian Moment* (Princeton: Princeton University Press, 1975), in his last chapters especially, discusses property and the republican tradition.

[55] Conversely, the idea's authority is not a matter of the cumulation of our individual gifts (or votes or market power), nor does authority come from some outside certifying agent.

[56] The most natural of responses to these questions is that, if we are searching for one right answer among many wrong ones, then such searches are sure to be difficult. What we call sacrifice and suffering are mere events that we would find untoward but otherwise possess no meaning for us if we thought naturalistically or in evolutionary terms, when there is no teleology. What else are sandstorms and flood? Or, since the world is mostly desert and wilderness, what else should we expect but a difficult time? A sacralizing word like *sacrifice* or a personal word like *suffering* are perhaps appropriate crutches for describing our experience were we ignorant of these objective facts about the desert's omnipresence.

To actual entrepreneurs these natural answers represent the pride of natural science, rather than anything like an adequate moral and experiential account of the world, an account that might be useful for improving their own practice and thought. Those natural answers, in their attempt to disenchant the world, are profoundly demoralizing. And they are wrong.

[57] Walzer, *Exodus and Revolution,* p. 53. I imagine that we could learn without wandering in the wilderness, but the evidence is not comforting.

[58] It is a convention of modern thought that faith is stultifying. It would seem this is a misreading of history. In any case, one need not insist that all faith is empowering to find that faith is often encouraging.

[59] The lessons cannot be learned through an analytic technology, not even by playacting or doing problem sets or case studies. We can learn a great deal from these latter methods, but the schooling of the soul is a rather different task.

[60] Along the way we learn how to solve technical problems, but we surely did not need to go through the desert for that.

[61] Here Augustine took his lesson on discipline. Walzer, *Exodus and Revolution,* p. 62.

[62] I should again note that I am not an advocate of sacrifice. Rather, I am trying to describe what sacrifice does. Note that sacrifice is a matter of exchange, of the sacrificial victim for a benefit. On the other hand, the scapegoat is meant to be the condensation point for pollution.

[63] Put differently, a more gentle world would be insufficiently interesting for entrepreneurship. But it might be useful for capitalism, as A. O. Hirschman argues in *The Passions and the Interests* (Princeton: Princeton University Press, 1977).

[64] For example, G. Scholem, *Sabbatai Sevi* (Princeton: Princeton University Press, 1973).

[65] Here I am thinking of Robert Irwin's usage of "acting in response" [to a call] as described in L. Weschler, *Seeing Is Forgetting* (Berkeley: University of California Press, 1982).

[66] Walzer, *Exodus and Revolution,* chapter 4, points out that without some milk and honey *now* people cannot so readily maintain their commitment to the promise.

[67] For example, *Mission Impossible* or *The A-Team* or *Knight Rider*.

[68] Anti-Judaism (rather than anti-Semitism) finds it hard to believe the Hebrew Bible's accounts of the Israelites' resistance, perhaps attributing their resistance to a dramatic device of saying "no" enough times to have power over the asker. This strikes me as being too smart by half. The killing and suffering the Israelites endure *are* humiliating.

[69] Here is Margaret Atwood on Northrop Frye: "[S]ince one of his major themes was the way in which plots resemble other plots—whether they are to be found in fairy tales, epic poems or soap operas—there was nothing he refused to consider. He knew also that the way in which we understand ourselves is less through theory than through story. In the life of any individual, as in the lives of communities and nations, stories are primary." "Northrup Frye Remembered," *Michigan Quarterly Review* 30 (Fall 1991): 647–649, at p. 648.

[70] Hirschman, *The Passions and the Interests;* N. Rosenblum, ed., *Liberalism and the Moral Life* (Cambridge: Harvard University Press, 1989).

We might account for the entrepreneur by employing notions of imperfect economic markets and risk-taking, as is done in some of the social science literature. See H. Barreto, *The Entrepreneur in Microeconomic Theory* (London: Routledge, 1989), on I. Kirzner's work.

[71] As Walzer puts it:

> —first, that wherever you live, it is probably Egypt;
> —second, that there is a better place, a world more attractive, a promised land;
> —and third, that "the way to the land is through the wilderness." There is no way to get from here to there except by joining together and marching.
> (*Exodus and Revolution,* p. 149)

[72] I leave open the question whether the Torah, all of it, was given on Mount Sinai (and hence its proleptic quality) or was given later through the prophets.

Chapter 3:

I have used a small number of sources to ground the models I shall be describing, namely, the work of the child psychologist Selma Fraiberg and that of the pediatrician and psychiatrist D. W. Winnicott. They strike me as the closest to actual experience. For Fraiberg, her *Selected Writings,* ed. L Fraiberg (Columbus: Ohio State University Press, 1987) will do nicely, and for Winnicott I like best what he has written for mothers (*The Child, the Family, and the Outside World* [Baltimore: Penguin, 1964] and *Babies and Their Mothers* [Reading, MA: Addison-Wesley, 1987]) as well as *Playing and Reality* (1971; reprint, London: Routledge, 1989), a rather more technical book that concentrates on transitional phenomena. Fraiberg and Winnicott are devoted to children and their mothers and fathers. The moral demands of clinical practice insist upon themselves, even in the scientific realm. Fraiberg is quite eloquent about the necessity for the clinical eye (*Selected Writings,* pp. 96–98), not because she is romantic about clinical work but because she would not have learned what she did about blind children and their needs if she had not been forced to pay attention to every detail. I think the descriptions in P. Leach, *Children First* (New York: Knopf, 1994), are terrific.

I should note that I formulated this chapter well before I knew of Daniel Stern's *Interpersonal World of the Infant* (New York: Basic Books, 1985). Otherwise, I might have been able to use his model and insights more systematically. Stern emphasizes in a poignant way the infant's autonomy since birth; in his view, the growth of self is the issue.

Another powerful resource is the work of Stanley Greenspan in his description of adaptive responses to sensory regulation difficulties and in his account of "closing circles" of action, endowing meaning to what a child does.

[1] I shall use "autonomous" and "authentic" to capture the fact that we are involved with others, that growth leads to independence that allows for appropriate dependence, that growth allows for the otherness of others' desires and needs and so the ownness of your desires and needs.

[2] Fraiberg, *Selected Writings,* p. 85.

[3] Fraiberg, *Selected Writings,* pp. 100–101.

[4] Here I am following the insights of John Bennett, Jr., in his comments on this chapter. See also chapter 1 on prophecy as an account of creativity, where the prophet is transformed by his prophetic mission, much as here the mother is transformed by the infant and so is creative.

[5] Stern, *Interpersonal World of the Infant.* Stern's careful staging awaits as careful a phenomenological analysis in the entrepreneurial realm. So my use of "attunement" cannot be so detailed and meaningful as it is for Stern.

[6] I explicitly argued that the entrepreneurial idea seemed to function much as God does.

[7] Not as a "nursing father carrying an ungrateful people on his bosom," following Aaron Wildavsky's discussion in *The Nursing Father: Moses as a Political Leader* (University: University of Alabama Press, 1984). The actual text reads, in a translation of the Masoretic text: "Did I [Moses] conceive all this people, did I bear them, that You should say to me, 'Carry them in your bosom as a nurse carries an infant [suckling child],' to the land You have promised on oath to their fathers?" (Numbers 11:12; *Tanakh,* p. 225) Moses is designated Israel's wet nurse. The *Kings James Version* reads: "Carry them in thy bosom, as a nursing father beareth the sucking child."

[8] Of course, suckling can be mythologized, either as bliss or as greed.

[9] The entrepreneur might be analogized to the mother, the entrepreneurial idea to the child. The idea must become autonomous and so be independent of the entrepreneur, that is, it becomes institutionalized. And so it is present or responsive in a complex not-so-forgiving world.

In actual infant development, an infant's growing autonomy with respect to mother becomes the model of autonomy in the larger world, a process the child repeats again and again and so masters. The infant's bonding to mother and then to the world is again a model, now of how an entrepreneurial endeavor becomes entrenched in the world, for the people who work on it and for those who buy into it. So the entrepreneurial endeavor becomes autonomous and authentic, on its own and in the world.

[10] There are no fathers in this chapter, in part because fathers have played such a small role in theory about infanthood. Winnicott acknowledges the importance of the father's support for the mother, and current research indicates the variety of behavioral styles introduced by the father. See, for example, R. L. Tyson, "The Roots of Psychopathology and Our Theories of Development," *Journal of the American Academy of Child Psychiatry* 25 (1986): 12–22.

Mothers presumably need not be women. Men do mother as well. But there is a large literature on why women do most of the mothering, for which see N. Chodorow, *The Reproduction of Mothering* (Berkeley: University of California Press, 1978), and D. Dinnerstein, *The Mermaid and the Minotaur* (New York: Harper and Row, 1976). Although I have used "she" when referring to mothers, my experience indicates that mothering can be done by males.

[11] P. Leach, *Your Baby and Child* (New York: Knopf, 1979).

[12] A. Rich, *Of Woman Born* (New York: Norton, 1986), p. 23.

[13] Here I am thinking of J. J. Gibson's ecological psychology of perception, where all the information is out there in the environment waiting to be "picked up" directly. The mother and the infant are out there for each other, telling each other everything directly (J. J. Gibson, *The Senses Considered as Perceptual Systems* [Boston: Houghton Mifflin, 1966]).

I am arguing against a conception that treats the self as observable only through behavioral evidence.

[14] D. W. Winnicott, "The Ordinary Devoted Mother," in *Babies and Their Mothers*, pp. 6–8. See also, Winnicott, *The Child, the Family,* which I think is even more direct.

[15] Winnicott, "Ordinary Devoted Mother," p. 9. To be sure, this curious form of a "factor" is rather more complex than we usually think of factors. Moreover, babies too may fail, incapable of eliciting from their mothers what the babies need.

[16] Augustine, *Confessions,* tr. H. Chadwick (Oxford: Oxford University Press, 1991), ch. 1, § 7–11.

[17] "Cicero (*De finibus* 5.55) remarks on the value placed by philosophers on infant behavior as a guide to the understanding of human nature" (Chadwick's note, *Confessions,* p. 9 n. 10).

[18] I have chosen to compare two male writers to avoid too obvious inferences about whether women are more likely to be responsive to the world of mothering than men are. (Of course, some women and men do not define themselves in terms of their being potential or even actual parents, biological or otherwise.) Experience is the great teacher only if one has the courage to remember, and that courage is perhaps rare. See Fraiberg, *Selected Writings,* pp. 130–135, on "identification with the aggressor."

[19] This resistance is described by the critic Northrop Frye: "[The teacher] is someone who attempts to re-create the subject in the student's mind, and his strategy in doing this is first of all to get the student to recognize what he already potentially knows, which includes breaking up the powers of repression in his mind that keep him from knowing what he knows. That is why it is the teacher, rather than the student, who asks most of the questions" (*The Great Code* [New York: Harcourt Brace Jovanovich, 1982], p. xv).

[20] Contrastively, and more conventionally, it is not a language of demand, choice, decoding, incentives, probabilistic fluctuation, and rule and algorithm.

[21] This section was given as a talk at a conference on motherhood sponsored by the Department of Occupation Therapy, University of Southern California, 28 April 1989. A somewhat modified version appears in the proceedings of that conference: R. Zemke and F. Clark, *Occupational Science* (Philadelphia: F. A. Davis, 1996).

[22] This list of baby's capacities is drawn from Winnicott, as in *The Child, the Family.*

[23] S. I. Greenspan (*The Development of the Ego* [Madison, CT: International Universities Press, 1989]) speaks of giving meaning to what is done by the child, even if the child's acts would otherwise seem to be without intention or to be random, so "closing circles" of action.

[24] See S. Cavell, "The Avoidance of Love: A Reading of *King Lear,*" in *Disowning Knowledge* (Cambridge: Cambridge University Press, 1987). This bonding is not at all mechanical and gluelike, but rather demands our response if we are to define ourselves as human beings.

[25] The first quote comes from the advice given on the emergency placard on airplanes, and the second comes from Leach, *Your Baby and Child.*

[26] V. Hearne, *Adam's Task* (New York: Vintage, 1986).

[27] It would seem authority and membership are not a matter of incentives and economic markets. Incentives rarely work in these circumstances because what is desired by

both mother and child is membership, not compliance. For an opposed viewpoint (which makes no claim about this particular situation), see J. Buchanan, "The Constitution of Economic Policy," *Science* 236 (12 June 1987): 1433–1436.

[28] And so it would make no sense to speak of "quality time" (when one is supposed to be fully focused on the child, it would seem in mutually pleasurable activities—as contrasted to time when one is either not present or busy with other matters).

[29] See, for example, J. Cole and H. Zuckerman, "Marriage, Motherhood, and Research Performance in Science," *Scientific American* 256 (February 1987): 119–125, which suggests that scientists who become mothers do not show it in their scientific productivity. Other, formerly necessary tasks are dropped.

[30] The historian's narrative conception perhaps seems closest to these notions. Since in narrative conceptions we have a sense of time that counts (rather than all time counting equally), we might find ourselves talking about "quality time" again.

[31] Rich, *Of Woman Born*. On need, see M. Ignatieff, *The Needs of Strangers* (New York: Viking, 1985).

[32] Of course, males may be these mothers.

[33] Stern, *Interpersonal World of the Infant,* provides a poignant description of the early development of the self through a series of qualitatively different stages, denominated by the social capacities of the infant.

[34] All the usual philosophic talk about frameworks and relativism and cultural specificity is in practice defeated by the actuality of the stages. The transformations and changes are dramatic and fully present. These phenomenological facts might be said to be about the patterns of human interaction, and so be demystified. But they are experienced as existential facts, not as an analyzed pattern.

[35] My purpose here is to defend against arguments that treat entrepreneurial endeavors as having a 50% probability of being failures in five years. Probabilistic risk is not the issue; devotion is. First, I want to defend against notions of method or procedure or business plan that are said to be necessary to success, not because such plans may not be helpful but because they encourage one to not pay continuing close attention to the particular details of the enterprise and rather to concentrate on some objective abstract method. Second, I want to defend against the strategy that claims to be "realistic" and uses various scientific methods, such as test markets, to increase the odds of success—not because such a strategy will not help (it should, and it does), but because the reality of markets is only relevant if the product is launched. To ask too skeptically about market or product before launch is to prevent the growth that might ensure success.

[36] I have added "like" here to indicate that nowadays autism represents an organic disease unrelated to blindness at birth, not a situationally induced disease.

[37] S. Fraiberg, *Insights from the Blind* (New York: Basic Books, 1977), p. 13.

[38] See also, on adaptive solutions for children with pervasive development disorders, S. I. Greenspan, "Reconsidering the Diagnosis and Treatment of Very Young Children with Autistic Spectrum or Pervasive Development Disorders," *Zero to Three* 13 (October-November 1992): 1–9.

[39] Fraiberg, *Insights from the Blind,* pp. 160–161.

[40] See Greenspan, "Reconsidering the Diagnosis," on how parents' "closing circles" of otherwise unconnected behavior by the child leads to meaningfulness of the world for the child.

[41] I take it that pleasure has an intrinsic motivating power for us—an unoriginal claim.

[42] As Kierkegaard puts it, how does Abraham live with the contradiction (namely, "beyond the ethical")?

[43] Winnicott, *Playing and Reality*.

[44] D. W. Winnicott, "The Capacity to Be Alone," in *The Maturational Process and*

the Facilitating Environment (New York: International Universities Press, 1965), p. 30.

[45] This phenomenology describes what entrepreneurs do, what I believe entrepreneurs recognize themselves as doing. But I am making only a structural analogy, not a reductionist claim that entrepreneurship is psychological or psychoanalytic. Similarly, when I speak of pleasure, I am not referring to a claim that enterprises experience pleasure (or that entrepreneurs do). Rather, the self-sustaining, motivating character of pleasure, for both infants and their mothers, is structurally analogized in an entrepreneurial endeavor to a motivating, self-sustaining form of management. As for a "going concern," that Winnicott uses a commercial analogy (where, etymologically, *concern* is "to mix or mingle together") does not say that infants are enterprises; rather, they exhibit structural features of some such enterprises, just the ones I have been emphasizing here, and which I claim entrepreneurs know. In this sense Winnicott has in mind a rather less corporate, rather more swashbuckling entrepreneurial notion of a going concern.

[46] By the way, before we demonize mothers, we might also want to keep in mind that all of us will mistake and miss, be unable to hold, and be preoccupied.

[47] I take it that modern business education, even in its current revisions, is methodical, systematic, scientific, objective, exoteric. One might "master" business, as business administration or management. Enormous social good arises from such programs, both in terms of better enterprises and fairer social and cultural systems. Put sociologically, achievement of a certain sort replaces ascription (race, class, family tie); the downside is that the solidarity associated with ascription must be reinvented, also perhaps a good thing. I have no need here to deny the power of method, when it proves powerful.

I have, to be sure, no easy answer to how the considerations provided in this book are to be integrated readily into any of the usual core courses in management or entrepreneurial education, since those courses were designed to exclude them. Such courses are always seen as providing analytical methods or exemplary cases. The actor is to be justifiably and publicly rational. But to talk like a mother is to be ridiculed by one's classmates.

For more on all of this, see M. H. Krieger, "Broadening Professional Education," *Liberal Education* 76 (March-April 1990): 6–10.

[48] Or as Stern might argue in *The Interpersonal World of the Infant,* the infant has been going off on her own from the beginning.

[49] I am thinking here of Greek tragedy, not so much for its unhappy consequences, as for its sense of fate and fortune. See, for example, M. Nussbaum, *The Fragility of Goodness* (Cambridge: Cambridge University Press, 1986). One might argue that each time is a first time, the next step forged from where we are now and what we appreciate of what we are supposed to do. Or we might argue that we follow formulaic patterns, going by the book, much of the time.

[50] Hearne, *Adam's Task.*

[51] I have deliberately mixed these masculinist (*vir*tue, for example), Christian, and republican terms with the female gender, to see how well they might be recovered from their parochial origins. See H. Pitkin, *Fortune Is a Woman* (Berkeley: University of California Press, 1984).

[52] As stories, pathologies are interesting tragic failures that horrify us as they educate us. In case studies we learn about them in novelistic accounts that read as obscene and voyeuristic. And so we might be taught to develop an ethos of mothering. Analytically, we might develop a nosology of disease, largely an account of abandonment and invasion, when transitional space is impossible and the enterprise is destroyed by demands it could not then possibly meet. Of course, ethos and nosology are only secondary to being that devoted mother.

[53] Stern, in *Interpersonal World of the Infant,* provides a set of stages that read much more neutral, much less moralizing and charged than these, less about sacrifice and more

about developing talents.

[54] Fraiberg, *Insights from the Blind,* p. 15

[55] On "gumption traps," see R. Pirsig, *Zen and the Art of Motorcycle Maintenance* (New York: Morrow, 1974), pp. 305–318.

[56] Things might have gone that particular way in any case, as in any conversation or interaction. But that is just one more fact that adds ambiguity to conversation. Or we note that that skeptical claim has nothing to do with our actual situation. It is a philosophic and scientific observation in the middle of our intimately taking care of baby. Or we note that the subtlety of conversation precludes such a dumb interpretation. By the way, it might be that things would have gone on *this* way independent of what I did, but that is just a fact, not a skeptical revealing that destroys meaning and interaction.

[57] Hearne, *Adam's Task.*

[58] Differential equations and Markov chains are characterized by the fact that what we did just now is also historical, in that it is a cumulation of the past doings, fully epitomized in what we did just before we did what we did just now.

[59] I owe to Carol Nagy Jacklin a series of wonderful discussions on null hypotheses, as well as the phrase "life is a contaminated experiment."

[60] L. Weschler, *Seeing Is Forgetting the Name of the Thing One Sees* (Berkeley: University of California Press, 1982), pp. 140–141.

[61] As we shall see in chapters 4 and 5, contingency can be domesticated if we treat it as probabilistic, a formulation perhaps more useful for finance than for entrepreneurship.

The entrepreneurial world is too complex to allow us to believe we solve problems. See M. H. Krieger, *Advice and Planning* (Philadelphia: Temple University Press, 1981), chapter 1. We work on problems, we define them, we make problems go away. But rarely can one solve problems, as supposedly does the engineer; in fact, this is a misconception of engineering. Considerations of failure modes, cost-quality interchanges, and practical implementation make engineering a more unsettled process than is usually portrayed. See H. Petroski, *To Engineer Is Human* (New York: St. Martin's, 1985).

[62] Stern, *Interpersonal World of the Infant.*

[63] T. Leavitt in R. P. Bagozzi, *Principles of Marketing Management* (Chicago: SRA, 1986).

[64] There is, to be sure, an internalized father, grandmother, and uncle, too.

[65] Fraiberg, *Selected Writings,* p. 135.

Chapter 4:

I have found C. Segal, *Tragedy and Civilization: An Interpretation of Sophocles* (Cambridge: Harvard University Press, 1981), and A. W. Gouldner, *Enter Plato: Classical Greece and the Origin of Social Theory* (New York: Basic Books, 1965), very helpful. I have used Robert Fagles's accessible translations in Sophocles, *The Three Theban Plays* (New York: Penguin, 1984).

[1] J. Schumpeter, *Capitalism, Socialism, and Democracy* (New York: Harper and Row, 1950), p. 83.

[2] See A. O. Hirschman, *Development Projects Observed* (Washington, DC: Brookings Institution, 1967), on "the hiding hand" in economic development, which allows the entrepreneur to act because he is ignorant of the consequences of his action. See also J. Elster, *Explaining Technical Change* (Cambridge: Cambridge University Press, 1983), chapter 5, on Schumpeter and Hirschman.

[3] My account here is motivated by the Oedipus story (in detail) and by L. Winner, *Autonomous Technology* (Cambridge: MIT Press, 1977); W. B. Arthur, "Positive Feed-

backs in the Economy," *Scientific American* 262 (February 1990): 92–95; W. B. Arthur, "Competing Technologies, Increasing Returns, and Lock-in by Historical Events," *Economic Journal* 99 (1989): 116–131.

This description is abstract and moralistic, historical yet mythic and structural. Here I am thinking literally of formal structuralist analysis, as in Segal, *Tragedy and Civilization.*

[4] As for savagery, see Segal, *Tragedy and Civilization,* who also refers to René Girard's work.

[5] In chapter 3 we were concerned with the entrepreneur as mother, entrepreneurship as a process of separation; here the entrepreneur wrenches tradition, the project a wrenched child.

[6] From Segal, *Tragedy and Civilization,* p. 46. If one focused on the self of the child, then wrenching would be a less central consideration.

[7] See R. Girard, *Violence and the Sacred* (Baltimore: Johns Hopkins University Press, 1977), and *The Scapegoat* (Baltimore: Johns Hopkins University Press, 1986). A *pharmakos* ("a cure or a medicine," in my text, and so a *pharmakon*) is "a person often already condemned to death sacrificed in ancient Greece as a means of purification or atonement for a city or a community" (*Webster's Third New International Dictionary*).

[8] I take this subhead from Segal's title (*Tragedy and Civilization*).

[9] The story paraphrases Bernard Knox's summary in Sophocles, *Three Theban Plays*, pp. 27–29. My quotations in the text come from Fagles's translation.

[10] See Sophocles, *Oedipus the King,* tr. S. Berg and D. Clay (New York: Oxford University Press, 1978), p. 97.

[11] Segal, *Tragedy and Civilization,* pp. 46–47.

[12] "Sophocles did not share Aeschylus' belief in a Zeus who worked through the suffering of mankind to bring order out of chaos, justice out of violence, reconciliation out of strife. There was little in the age he lived in to support such a conception. As a youth he had danced in the celebration for the victory of Salamis, a victory of the Greeks united against Persia, but in his manhood he saw the dissolution of that unity, the growing hostility between Athens and Sparta which moved inexorably towards the disastrous war in which he was to pass the last years of his life. The Olympian gods in Sophoclean drama are enigmatic, masked figures whose will humanity can for the most part only guess at, and only identify with justice by a kind of heroic, defiant faith" (B. M. W. Knox, *The Heroic Temper* [Berkeley: University of California Press, 1966], pp. 53–54).

[13] S. Fraiberg, "Two Modern Incest Heroes," in *Selected Writings of Selma Fraiberg,* ed. L. Fraiberg (Columbus: Ohio State University Press, 1987), pp. 659–673.

[14] My claim here, to repeat, is not psychological, not psychoanalytic, not psychohistorical. Rather, it is that tragedy provides the phenomenology of entrepreneurship.

Put differently, "Supposing truth is a woman" (as Nietzsche asked in the first sentence in *Beyond Good and Evil* [New York: Vintage, 1966]): by convention wily, devious, insidious, inventive, and transforming. Entrepreneurs, if they are male, discover *that* truth through their relationship with mother, their initially taking that relationship as simply a matter of separation and growing up, so being driven to reinvent the world by the need to master that incomprehensible loss. For autonomy is rather more about fully inheriting a tradition of insidious forces than about being "on your own." (The relationship of mother to daughter is rather different, since daughters are in many ways explicit repetitions of their mothers. Manifestly, were we to be consistently concerned here with a model of mothers and their daughters, exclusively, we might theorize differently about entrepreneurship.)

[15] As claimed by M. Nussbaum, *The Fragility of Goodness* (Cambridge: Cambridge University Press, 1986).

[16] See Gouldner, *Enter Plato,* on pederastic homoeroticism and the force of contest in Greek society. A. O. Hirschman, *The Passions and the Interests* (Princeton: Princeton University Press, 1977), rephrases the issue for two thousand years later as one between the murderous passions and the moneymaking interests.

[17] See S. Traweek, *Beamtimes and Lifetimes* (Cambridge: Harvard University Press, 1988), on the training of young scientists, who are deliberately not told the whole truth by their seniors.

[18] G. Steiner, *Antigones* (Oxford: Clarendon Press, 1986). Antigone appears to be exemplary, especially when compared to Ismene and Creon. But Ismene surely shows much daring and courage in *Oedipus at Colonus,* keeping her exiled father in touch with the oracles, traveling large distances by herself. As for Creon, he appears rather more modest in *Oedipus the King* (l. 657), not power-hungry. He finds himself threatened, and so he becomes self-righteous.

Antigone is not "about" courage, for works of art are not successfully understood by such a simple denomination.

[19] *Oedipus the King,* ll. 1642–1645.

[20] See Steiner, *Antigones*.

[21] See, for example, Segal, *Tragedy and Civilization*. Structural accounts of ritual do allow for the particulars of each story or ritual enactment. The claim here is that those particulars are definitive, the structure being something discerned afterward. It could not be prescriptive.

Pollution is surely a motive. But most of the time we live with it quite comfortably, ignoring its dirt so we can get on with what we are up to. Women, for example, do live with blood. Masculinistly, they have been viewed as polluted, and so they are said to have no problem living with blood. It is rather more interesting to find just when such pollutions are ultimately problematic rather than merely practical problems. What is curious are the rare times when we find we cannot live with pollution, when we are compulsively scrupulous.

[22] See R. Scodel, *Sophocles* (Boston: Twayne, 1984), pp. 65–66.

[23] Nussbaum, *Fragility of Goodness,* argues that Antigone and Creon have each gone too far. This is in part the point of view of prudential fourth-century Greeks, where Antigone is taken to be foolish. Recall that in *Oedipus at Colonus* Ismene is quite courageous, not so obviously a foil for Antigone.

[24] "To those who face him, friends and enemies alike, the hero seems unreasonable almost to the point of madness, suicidally bold, impervious to argument, intransigent, angry; an impossible person whom only time can cure. But to the hero himself the opinion of others is irrelevant. His loyalty to his conception of himself, and the necessity to perform the action that conception imposes, prevail over all other considerations" (Knox, *Heroic Temper,* p. 28). See also chapter 1 of Knox on how the Sophoclean hero is defined by his focus on his task.

The arbitrageur or the innovating entrepreneur who perceives an opportunity also does what others perceive as foolish. He might be justified by the outcomes of his action, not by the obligations he has incurred.

[25] Antigone as *agonistai,* or contestant, is driven more by her project than by a desire to contest another, more by epitaph than by agony.

[26] As for courage, I am thinking of the annual awards announced in the newspapers. See also D. N. Walton, *Courage* (Berkeley: University of California Press, 1986). Antigone's is a commitment that Kierkegaard would say is beyond the ethical (but one might compare Kierkegaard's with Hegel's discussion of *Sittlichkeit* and family).

[27] B. M. W. Knox (in Sophocles, *Three Theban Plays,* p. 46) points out how problematic this passage has been in the interpretation of *Antigone*. The source of this piece of

reasoning is Herodotus's *Histories*.

[28] For more on perversion as I understand it, see "Economy, Perversion, and Fetishes," in M. H. Krieger, *Marginalism and Discontinuity* (New York: Russell Sage Foundation, 1989), chapter 5.

[29] This section is an edited version of M. H. Krieger, "Courage and Character in Planning," *Journal of Planning Education and Research* 7 (1988): 191–194. I am grateful for the insights of John Gaber, Pat Hanley, Jeff Heilman, Cliff Strong, and Walter Zisette, Jr. Twenty years ago, Harvey Sarles first made me aware of these issues in the bodily arts.

[30] This adaptation will surely be a stretch, the more we know of ancient Greece. But such a stretch is in many ways the history of modern thought, wrenching from ancient societies (of Rome, Israel, and Greece) notions fully embedded in their culture and then making those notions do work for us.

[31] Money and payoff are not relevant, despite Creon's constant refrain about the corruptions being offered to his troops.

[32] As I discussed in chapter 3, the good-enough mother is devoted, present for her baby, creating a world for him as she gives meaning to his needs.

[33] Here I have Kierkegaard of *Fear and Trembling* in mind.

[34] Hannah Arendt, *The Life of the Mind,* volume 1, *Thinking* (New York: Harcourt Brace Jovanovich, 1978).

[35] See Gouldner, *Enter Plato;* D. Halperin, *One Hundred Years of Homosexuality* (New York: Routledge, 1990).

[36] For further references, see M. H. Krieger, "What Does Jerusalem Have to Do with Athens," *Journal of Planning Education and Research* 14 (1995): 217–221.

[37] R. A. Markus, *The End of Ancient Christianity* (Cambridge: Cambridge University Press, 1990), p. 27.

[38] The rationalism and universalism represented by Plato, let us say, for which see Gouldner, *Enter Plato*.

[39] Augustine, Paul, Moses, and Antigone are not persons I would want to comfortably hang around with. They are authoritarian and intolerant. I suspect that entrepreneurs (in contrast to corporate leaders) are also often not persons one would want to hang around with.

[40] See H. S. Harris, *Hegel's Development* (Oxford: Clarendon Press, 1972), a study on the early Hegel.

[41] For more on this polemic, see M. Bernal, *Black Athena* (New Brunswick: Rutgers University Press, 1987).

[42] Similarly, motherhood is as I have described it sacred, heroic, and prophetic (rather than mechanical and biological), and authoritative and illiberal. In these senses it provides us with exemplary situations characteristic of entrepreneurship.

[43] Here I follow Gouldner, *Enter Plato,* chapters 2, 3. I have over the years learned a great deal about such contest from Walter Ong and his work.

According to M. I. Finley, *The Ancient Economy* (Berkeley: University of California Press, 1985), Greece was not commercially entrepreneurial. Patterns were set, traditions followed, to be upset by war, conquest, and famine rather than by commercial endeavor and economies of comparative advantage. I should note that Finley's argument seems to be a subject of some controversy.

[44] Competition is here used in a technical sense of a certain kind of market, rather than athletic competition as in a footrace. Evolutionary nature is no more competitive than are economies in this sense, for rarely is the competition directly one on one.

[45] Gouldner, *Enter Plato,* suggests that relationships between males were strained by this fact, and that strain was reflected in the particular form of homosexuality practiced in ancient Greece.

[46] Hence, Gouldner's book is entitled *Enter Plato,* referring to that point in Greece's (Athens's) history.

[47] Weber argued and approved this as necessary. On the Weber-Merton thesis, see *Science in Context* 3 (Spring 1989), an issue titled "After Merton: Protestant and Catholic Science in Seventeenth-Century Europe."

[48] Parricide includes the murder of the mother or the father.

[49] See M. Sahlins, *Islands of History* (Chicago: University of Chicago Press, 1985), for an account of how violations lead to new taboos and orderliness.

[50] A deep question is whether that series of overturnings is unending, propagating forever, or is eventually cured or redeemed (as it is in Sophocles). Or we might well live with such overturnings but not be destroyed by them, what I have called perversion—denying both eternal recurrence and redemption. Such perversion is altogether less dramatically satisfying but is rather more practical than are its polar alternatives. See Krieger, "Economy, Perversion, and Fetishes."

[51] Technically, sex is mixture of different elements. There are allowed mixtures, seminal lines so to speak, inseminating and preserving the genetic stock. Here we are concerned with forbidden mixtures.

I have not addressed here the issues in classical studies concerning matriarchy and *Mutterrecht* (as in the *Oresteia*), for which see S. Goldhill, *Reading Greek Tragedy* (Cambridge: Cambridge University Press, 1990), pp. 51–56.

[52] Oedipus swears loyalty to Laius (*Oedipus the King,* l. 301), whom Oedipus takes not to be his father, as if Laius were his father (which of course Laius is).

[53] Imagine being loyal to your father by sleeping with your mother. Imagine the age difference. Imagine hiding from yourself the hidden desire as a hidden desire. The interesting question is how the Greeks viewed it (perhaps taking into account the age differences required for permitted homosexuality), and in what sense we might say that Oedipus knew what he was doing when he married Jocasta (for which see Fraiberg, "Two Modern Incest Heroes").

[54] *Webster's Third New International Dictionary.*

[55] "Like other divine foundlings—Romulus, Cyrus, Ion—Oedipus is the child of the god and the beast at the same time....But Oedipus' tragedy is the foundling story in reverse. When he discovers where and who he is, it is to lose, not gain, a throne, to move not from the wild to the palace, but vice versa. Sophocles uses these folktale motifs not to assert the divinity of the hero but to explore the paradox of the 'godlike' king's bestiality" (Segal, *Tragedy and Civilization,* pp. 223–224).

[56] *Oedipus the King,* ll. 1122–1123.

[57] In *Oedipus at Colonus* the Thebans wanted him back once more to save their nation, after having cast him out again at the end of *Oedipus the King*.

[58] Sophocles' writing about adoptees and their need to know the truth is heartrendingly true for adoptees who do not know who were their birth parents. On these warranted worries, see J. Boswell, *The Kindness of Strangers* (New York: Vintage, 1990).

[59] See Segal, *Tragedy and Civilization,* pp. 207–217.

[60] Of course, that role is not at all ironic as it is carried out (as it was not at all ironic for Oedipus).

[61] I refer to Boswell, *Kindness of Strangers*. Or, *Snow White.*

[62] A. O. Hirschman's principle of the hiding hand (*Development Projects Observed*) is a modest version of this principle of the virtue of ignorance. Schumpeter argues similarly, that a fully informed entrepreneur would never take certain risks, although he might well succeed nonetheless—so ignorance leads to (irrational) risktaking that works out well some of the time.

[63] *Oedipus the King,* ll. 1188–1190.

[64] See Scodel, *Sophocles,* pp. 65–66.

[65] See Nussbaum, *Fragility of Goodness*.

[66] I realize that this description, which I take to be a true-to-life phenomenology, might be read as mystical. So we might ask, When are mystical accounts true to life?

It would be interesting to ask how entrepreneurs are trained to read these signs, what kinds of formative experiences give them this sensitivity. My suspicion is that what is most crucial is the capacity to allow the world to speak to you in its own way, in other words, not to presume upon fate or chance, not to presume upon story or randomness. So speaks the distinguished biologist Barbara McClintock of her scientific method, in E. F. Keller, *A Feeling for the Organism* (San Francisco: Freeman, 1983).

[67] Here I have followed P. Davidson, "Is Probability Theory Relevant for Uncertainty?" *Journal of Economic Perspectives* 5 (1991): 129–143, where he attributes to Keynes the term "animal spirits." See also, M. Casson, *The Entrepreneur* (New York: Barnes and Noble, 1982), for a description of entrepreneurship in which judgment plays a central role.

[68] This section is an edited version of M. H. Krieger, "Contingency in Planning," *Journal of Planning Education and Research* 10 (1991): 157–161.

[69] M. Kac, *Statistical Independence in Probability, Analysis and Number Theory* (Providence: Mathematical Association of America, 1959); W. Kruskal, "Miracles and Statistics," *Journal of the American Statistical Association* 83 (1988): 929–940.

[70] Such an assumption of independence applies to actual coin tossing. A coin toss is governed by deterministic classical mechanics, and one should be able to predict what will happen. But so much information is needed, and the outcome is so sensitive to how you do the initial tossing, that in effect one has independence or randomness. (This is what is called "chaos.") When we "randomize" an experiment, we again create an artificial independence, washing out inadvertent influences, making the conventional null hypothesis plausible. Such strong contingency is attractive as a background, for then we may hope to isolate specific deliberate influences—whether they be crooked gambling devices or superior fertilizers—using statistical techniques rather than by taking the world apart.

In general, noise and independence are the counterintuitive assumption. In everyday life we often assume just the reverse, that connections are sure, that causal sequences are well known, that we can turn knobs and know the effect (in driving, in ordinary conversation). How else could we be effective actors in the world? No wonder independence is hard to believe, and hard to take seriously. Unless one thinks probabilistically and statistically, runs in coin tossing of a presumably fair coin are not initially taken as signs of independence but rather as signs of systematic bias or of knowable information. Data mining is a very great temptation. See, for example, F. M. Fisher, "Statisticians, Econometricians, and Adversary Proceedings," *Journal of the American Statistical Association* 81 (1986): 277–286. Of course, if you have good reason to suspect an unfair coin, then you are in a different situation.

[71] The development of statistics and much of social theory in the nineteenth century might be seen as an effort to justify that ignorance and provide a way of managing it. Hence the discovery of social laws that would allow us to affect means or variances, but not any single event. On statistical thinking in the nineteenth century, see T. Porter, *The Rise of Statistical Thinking* (Princeton: Princeton University Press, 1986).

[72] Advocates of risk analysis might argue that we have an atavistic, totemic urge for direct causation. What we need is a statistical conception of the balances of life. In sum, is statistical averaging a way of avoiding true knowledge, or is it a way of avoiding misleading icons and idols?

[73] A. Lovejoy, *The Great Chain of Being* (Cambridge: Harvard University Press, 1936).

[74] P. Levi and T. Regge, *Dialogo* (Princeton: Princeton University Press, 1989), p. 48.

[75] Plenitude is an extraordinarily demanding assumption, often justified by the roughly equivalent principle of insufficient reason. We do not know why these events should not occur, so they must. More disturbingly, here we have a rule about what should happen eventually, and so it *seems* to actually influence what happens next. But what happens next is taken to be more or less independent of what happened until now.

Both independence and plenitude might be treated not as assumptions but as empirical regularities with some degree of strength. Then many of the issues I pose here would be perhaps less problematic—except that we might ask why we have such hypotheses at all.

[76] Krieger, *Marginalism and Discontinuity,* chapter 1.

[77] J. G. A. Pocock, *The Machiavellian Moment* (Princeton: Princeton University Press, 1975); H. Pitkin, *Fortune Is a Woman* (Berkeley: University of California Press, 1984).

[78] On games, see H. G. Gadamer, *Truth and Method* (New York: Seabury Press, 1975).

[79] To "figure out" should remind us of the shape or figure of an object, and of the notion of a motif or *figura,* as in E. Auerbach's discussion in *Mimesis* (Princeton: Princeton University Press, 1968). For more practical guidance, see R. Neustadt and E. May, *Thinking in Time* (New York: Free Press, 1986).

[80] See, for example, what Robert Caro does in his biography of Robert Moses, *The Power Broker* (New York: Vintage, 1975).

[81] Elster, *Explaining Technical Change,* chapter 5, and pp. 118–119 has the relevant quote from Schumpeter's *Capitalism, Socialism, and Democracy;* A. O. Hirschman, *The Strategy of Economic Development* (New Haven: Yale University Press, 1958), chapters 3, 4.

[82] R. Heilbroner, "Analysis and Vision in the History of Modern Economic Thought," *Journal of Economic Literature* 28 (1990): 1097–1114.

[83] See Pocock, *Machiavellian Moment,* on corruption as a violation of the civic republic (albeit here we have a monarchy of sorts).

[84] Here I am thinking of Oedipus's killing of Laius and of his puzzle-solving skills, the tradition being that of Labdacus.

[85] Fraiberg, "Two Modern Incest Heroes." I am not referring to Socratic irony, at least in the first instance. Rather, as Fraiberg points out, those Oedipal desires are *there* in Oedipus, and he is fulfilling them. For moderns those desires have been lifted out of the given and placed in the stigmatized, and hence we can no longer let ourselves know just what we are doing.

[86] And its further meaning is revealed in *Oedipus at Colonus,* of which more in chapter 5.

[87] Here I am playing on the Greek for such a scapegoat, a *pharmakos*. See Segal, *Tragedy and Civilization;* Girard, *Scapegoat*.

[88] What I am creating here is a theodicy, an accounting for imperfection and sin.

[89] See Sahlins, *Islands of History*. The meaning of innovation and entrepreneurship, the kinds of violations they perform, is open to interpretation. In one context the technology is revolutionary; in another it is more easily assimilated. The problem then is to understand when violations are transformative and catastrophic, and when they are marginal and comfortable.

[90] R. MacMullen, *Christianizing the Roman Empire* (New Haven: Yale University Press, 1984).

[91] This phenomenon of latterly appreciation is a crucial historiographical issue. Clearly, change was in the air in 1925–1926. It is also clear that many of the early innovators in quantum mechanics developed formal methods, wave and matrix mechanics, only later to appreciate the curious interpretation (say Bohr's) that seemed to go along with those formalisms. In any case, most physics students first are taught how to calculate, and only much later might they come to a rather more sophisticated understanding of what they are up to (beyond some litany about uncertainty).

[92] Of course, this abstract story might in some cases be historically inaccurate. A revolution may be understood as a revolution in its meaning and implications, as it is happening. That understanding is often mistaken.

I realize that technologies are often *heralded* as revolutionary. But if that herald were taken seriously, there would be a very serious and crippling reaction to the technology. The violations would be stigmatized even further, modes of social control becoming supervigilant and excommunicating. The heroic story would then be about how the violators, or the technology, triumph nonetheless. But I believe it is more accurate, and in almost all cases true, to find that those heralds are dismissed. The short-term practical consequences of entrepreneurship are what count, what need to be provided if there is to be any initial success that can then lead to a new orthodoxy.

One other note. It could be that the new technology is a random event, and its persistence a matter of increasing returns to scale (as Brian Arthur has argued, for which see note 3). Namely, we may by chance share a set of violations, and in so doing we gain legitimacy among ourselves and so offer an orthodoxy others can find attractive.

[93] Some of the violations go too far, and the consequences are disastrous. Rather than violation leading to a new orthodoxy, the bridge falls down, the society falls apart. Whether or not we fail because we are sinful, here we fail because violations tax our capacities for the restoration of tradition and stability, and sometimes tax them too much or too intensely before we have time for repair. See H. Petroski, *To Engineer Is Human* (New York: St. Martin's, 1985), on eventual failure of structures due to stretching the tolerances as a consequence of rational economic pressure.

[94] P. Rieff, *The Triumph of the Therapeutic* (New York: Harper and Row, 1966).

Chapter 5:

I have employed the Oxford Shakespeare edition of *The Tempest,* edited by S. Orgel (Oxford: Oxford University Press, 1987), including his very useful introduction. As for the Hebrew Bible, I have used the new Jewish Publication Society translation of the Masoretic text, *Tanakh* (Philadelphia, 1988), consulting as well the *New Oxford Annotated Bible* which provides the New Revised Standard Version.

[1] On my use of "perversion," see M. H. Krieger, "Economy, Perversion, and Fetishes," in *Marginalism and Discontinuity* (New York: Russell Sage Foundation, 1989), chapter 5.

[2] G. Steiner, *Antigones* (Oxford: Clarendon Press, 1986), pp. 108–109.

[3] I have implicitly taken the Hebrew Bible to be an epic, but N. Frye (in *Anatomy of Criticism* [Princeton: Princeton University Press, 1957]) suggests it might well be romance.

[4] See C. Segal, *Tragedy and Civilization* (Cambridge: Harvard University Press, 1981), chapter 1, especially on the difference between Greek heroics and modern self-control (as Freud discusses in *Civilization and Its Discontents* [1930; reprint, New York: Norton, 1962]). We are not allowed to "act out" as did the Greeks, for whom the notion of acting out perhaps makes no sense; one just acts. Fourth-century Greece (Socrates) represents the commitment to reason and self-control. As I indicated earlier, Sophocles in

the fifth century is on a cusp between the heroic past and the antiheroic modern age.

[5] Segal, *Tragedy and Civilization,* p. 407.

[6] Here I am thinking of the Russian formalist (Shklovskii's) notion of "defamiliarization."

[7] I have deliberately mixed male and female notions here.

[8] S. Greenblatt ("The Way to Kill Our Literary Inheritance," *Chronicle of Higher Education* [12 June 1991]: 131, 133) is perhaps surer of the connections: "And it is similarly difficult to come to terms with what *The Tempest* has to teach us about forgiveness, wisdom, and social atonement if we do not also come to terms with its relations to colonialism. If we allow ourselves to think about the extent to which our magnificent cultural tradition—like that of every civilization we know of—is intertwined with cruelty, injustice, and pain, do we not, in fact, run the risk of 'deculturation.' Not if our culture includes a regard for truth."

[9] "The entire play [*Colonus*] enacts Oedipus' rite of purification, both literal and figurative. It is a highly complex version of what Arnold van Gennep called 'liminal' rites, rites of entrance, reintegration, and separation. Oedipus performs the lustral rites which purify the holy grove of his intrusion. Simultaneously he purifies himself of his pollution, both in words and in ritual deeds" (Segal, *Tragedy and Civilization,* p. 385).

[10] Here I draw from S. Orgel's discussion in *The Tempest,* ed. S. Orgel, p. 29 (henceforth *Tempest* [Orgel]).

[11] A tragic description does lift the heavy retrospective hand of condemnation of colonialism we might engage in nowadays. I think that such righteousness (even if it is correct) is likely to distance us from those colonists whom we might well be like.

[12] See J. Shklar, "The Liberalism of Fear," in N. Rosenblum, ed., *Liberalism and the Moral Life* (Cambridge: Harvard University Press, 1989), pp. 21–38.

[13] This letting go of the past is particularly hard for tragedy, and in fact is the theme of comedy and romance, namely, marriage. Even marriage need not free one of the past. Ferdinand and Miranda cannot play chess without complicit cheating. See *Tempest* (Orgel), pp. 29–30.

[14] For a different way of putting this synopsis, see chapter 4, "Creative Destruction and Pollution."

[15] See chapter 4, note 7.

[16] *Oedipus at Colonus,* ll. 310–314.

[17] *Oedipus the King,* ll. 1642–1645.

[18] Its disruptions and redemptions are in the end altogether mundane (and it does end with a prospective marriage). S. Orgel, in *Tempest* (Orgel), pp. 4–18 on genre and on readings and interpretations, is my source here and in what follows.

[19] According to S. Orgel in *Tempest* (Orgel), p. 10, Kermode gives to Ariel this role.

[20] Another summary: "The action of the play is Prospero's discovery to his enemies, their discovery of themselves, the lovers's discovery of a world of wonder, Prospero's own discovery of an ethic of forgiveness, and the renunciation of his magical power" (Madeleine Doran, *Endeavors of Art,* quoted in *Tempest* [Orgel], p. 13). Orgel argues that the action of the play is altogether less resolved.

[21] Gonzalo, at the end, reflects this best-of-all-possible-worlds, everything-works-together, philosophy.

> Was Milan thrust from Milan that his issue
> Should become kings of Naples? O rejoice
> Beyond a common joy, and set it down
> With gold on lasting pillars! In one voyage
> Did Claribel her husband find at Tunis,
> And Ferdinand, her brother, found a wife

Where he himself was lost, Prospero his dukedom
In a poor isle, and all of us ourselves
When no man was his own. (5.1.205–213)

[22] F. Kermode, in W. Shakespeare, *The Tempest,* ed. F. Kermode, 6th edition (Cambridge: Harvard University Press, 1958), pp. 133–134, glosses the text as follows: "I am now outside the tale you have just followed; just as I surrendered my powers in that tale, so I now stand before you stripped of imaginary glamour. One might say that the success of my enterprise as an actor is parallel to the happy outcome of my stage-plot. I behaved well in my fictitious character (and I hope, acted well also); my fictitious reward is to return to Italy. To complete the parallel, *you* must release me from the bonds of failure as a performer."

[23] S. Orgel, *Tempest* (Orgel), p. 55.

[24] See R. H. Coase, *The Firm, the Market, and the Law* (Chicago: University of Chicago Press, 1988).

[25] *Tanakh*. I was led to these passages by Rabbi Daniel Landes.

[26] See, for example, R. A. Dye, "Economic Analysis of Bankruptcy Statutes," *Economic Inquiry* 24 (1986): 417–428.

[27] T. Sullivan, E. Warren, and J. Westbrook, *As We Forgive Our Debtors: Bankruptcy and Consumer Credit in America* (New York: Oxford University Press, 1989).

[28] See A. O. Hirschman, *The Strategy of Economic Development* (New Haven: Yale University Press, 1958), chapters 4, 5. But more typically, see F. Modigliani and M. Miller, "The Cost of Capital, Corporate Finance, and the Theory of Investment," *American Economic Review* 48 (1958): 280–281, where they say, "[T]hat there are large and *systematic* imperfections in the market which permanently bias the outcome...is an assumption that economists, at any rate, will instinctively eye with some skepticism." Entrepreneurship in Modigliani and Miller's model would be a comparatively high-risk "stream of investment," uncertainty and market imperfection are not needed in this sort of explanation. Later in the chapter, I employ Modigliani and Miller's ideas to describe entrepreneurship as risky endeavor in a market for risk, where the state is now the firm that is making a debt-equity choice.

[29] J. Elster, *Explaining Technical Change* (Cambridge: Cambridge University Press, 1983), provides the relevant passage from J. Schumpeter's *Capitalism, Socialism, and Democracy* (New York: Harper and Row, 1950), pp. 73-74, and refers to A. O. Hirschman's principle of the hiding hand from *Development Projects Observed* (Washington, DC: Brookings Institution, 1967).

Such markets have been problematic for modern economic thought, since they are resistant to formalization; the unknown factors and misinformation are not so readily epitomized by probabilistic notions of risk (P. Davidson, "Is Probability Theory Relevant for Uncertainty?" *Journal of Economic Perspectives* 5 [1991]: 129–143). In fact, a good deal of modern finance theory and economics of information tries with great ingenuity to more formally and accurately model away these various kinds of uncertainty and disequilibrium.

[30] In effect, real estate was virtuous, real estate development was corrupt. See J. G. A. Pocock, *The Machiavellian Moment* (Princeton: Princeton University Press, 1975), chapter 14, especially pp. 462–467.

[31] M. Weber, *The Protestant Ethic and the Spirit of Capitalism* (1904–1905, 1920), tr. T. Parsons (New York: Scribner's, 1958), p. 271 n. 58.

[32] Weber, *Protestant Ethic,* p. 57.

[33] In the disciplined commercial realm, there is presumably no corruption, and honorable bad fortune might readily make sense. Whether one should ask the debtor to impoverish and indenture his family to pay off such debts has, at least in the Hebrew Bible, a

fixed end point, jubilee. In modern thought, concern about corruption (not only corrupt commerce, but also the corruption of the soul of the debtor if he and his family are let off, and thus the destruction of the fabric of society) made it hard to be so generous.

[34] See B. Weiss, *The Hell of the English: Bankruptcy and the Victorian Novel* (Lewisburg, PA: Bucknell University Press, 1986), chapters 2, 7.

[35] P. J. Coleman, *Debtors and Creditors in America* (Madison: State Historical Society of Wisconsin, 1974), especially pp. 292–293.

[36] As A. D. Chandler shows (in *Scale and Scope* [Cambridge, MA: Belknap Press, 1990]), the very different bankruptcy arrangements in other countries have profound implications for their speculative culture.

[37] See Sullivan, Warren, and Westbrook, *As We Forgive Our Debtors*. Sullivan points out that we have a culture of credit, including corporate limited liability, personal bankruptcy, and compensatory tax deductions, taking "bankruptcy as one of the safety valves that sophisticated capitalism keeps in place to release the pressures of fear and greed that accompany free market incentives" (p. 334).

Such wisdom as Polonius's will not do:

> Neither a borrower, nor a lender be;
> For Loan oft loses both itself and friend,
> And borrowing dulleth edge of husbandry.
> (*Hamlet,* 1.3)

[38] Sullivan, Warren, and Westbrook (*As We Forgive Our Debtors,* chapter 6 on "The Entrepreneurs"), concludes that most business bankruptcies (actually personal liability of entrepreneurs) come from the problems of starting a new business and not from dishonesty.

[39] N. Rosenberg and L. E. Birdzell, Jr., "Science, Technology, and the Western Miracle," *Scientific American* 263 (November 1990): 42–54.

[40] Coleman, *Debtors and Creditors in America*.

[41] C. Warren, *Bankruptcy in United States History* (Cambridge: Harvard University Press, 1935), pp. 13, 20.

[42] See Warren, *Bankruptcy,* p. 159.

[43] Sullivan, Warren, and Westbrook, *As We Forgive Our Debtors*.

[44] P. Tufano, "Business Failure as a Stimulus to Innovation," Working paper 91-039 (Boston: Harvard Business School, 1991).

[45] The perceived riskiness of these endeavors (or is it just their uncertainty?) permits banks to ask for real collateral, the returns seemingly too small for the risks or variance involved. Consequently, many personal bankruptcies are actually entrepreneurial small business bankruptcies.

[46] Here I have assumed that fluctuations grow roughly as $\sqrt{\text{Size}}$, and that we have yet to get to a size that is inefficient and so too large.

[47] L. Daston, *Classical Probability in the Enlightenment* (Princeton: Princeton University Press, 1988); T. Porter, *The Rise of Statistical Thinking* (Princeton: Princeton University Press, 1986).

[48] Hence the political difficulties of windfall-profits taxes.

[49] Readers who choose to skim this technical interlude are encouraged to at least read the quotations from Modigliani and Miller. Much as in the Hebrew Scriptures, highly abstract points are made in terms of man's relationship to domesticated animals, in particular cattle, that are of commercial significance.

[50] The cost of risk is priced out in a market that incorporates a variety of such risks, as in the capital asset pricing model. That the variance does all the required work in measuring that risk is a powerful simplification, a consequence of the equilibrium assumption (P. Samuelson, "The Fundamental Approximation Theorem of Portfolio Analysis in

Terms of Means, Variances, and Higher Moments," *Review of Economic Studies* 37 [1970]: 537–542).

This equilibrium model may be of more limited value if you are an entrepreneur making a "one-time" choice, for which see note 61.

Finally, we might imagine issuing life insurance on firms or enterprises. If we assume that the death rate is explained by the variance (by the random walk or diffusive character), then we have the same model as if we were to issue put options as surrogates for bankruptcy.

[51] If variance or volatility changes, perhaps idiosyncratically—and this makes sense in the entrepreneurial realm—the story is not so simple. Still, there is a story of this sort to be told (F. Black, "How to Use the Holes in Black-Scholes," *Journal of Applied Corporate Finance* 1, no. 4 (1988): 67–73). One might imagine trading in options on an entrepreneurial endeavor, and finding from the Black-Scholes formula that the imputed variance is quite high compared to that of other securities. So a put's price would be high, presumably reflecting formally a high variance but actually reflecting the high likelihood of bankruptcy.

[52] Correspondingly, higher variance means there will be greater exploration (by random walk, in effect by price incentive due to higher rates of return) of new, perhaps more efficient, possibilities, a socially desirable goal it would seem. See D. Capozza and G. Schwann, "The Value of Risk in Real Estate Markets," *Journal of Real Estate Finance and Economics* 3 (1990): 117–140. They point out the importance of a normality (vs. log normality) assumption if a put option is to correspond to actual bankruptcy (p. 135).

[53] I am here concerned with the arbitrage argument or the law-of-one-price argument in interrelated commodity markets (here ordinary and entrepreneurial endeavors), the interplay of various streams of (social) investment, as described in Modigliani and Miller, "Cost of Capital," for a firm. Note that here I am treating *society* as the firm. (Shortly, I will treat an individual entrepreneur as a firm.) Note that I have not yet directly invoked the Modigliani-Miller theorems (I or II). From the point of view of the Modigliani-Miller theorems, in which the debt/equity ratio is shown to be irrelevant (in a particular environment), total growth might be said to depend on changes in the interest rate and people's preference for risk (namely, the environment), not on the debt-equity ratio per se. Total growth depends on the rewards of risk-free investment and people's risk preferences, not on the ordinary-entrepreneurial ratio, so to speak.

[54] Butter's becoming less expensive corresponds to encouraging less risky investments and so perhaps lower growth rates (the price of whole milk).

[55] Modigliani and Miller, "Cost of Capital," p. 280 n. 33.

[56] Modigliani and Miller, "Cost of Capital," p. 280. W. J. Baumol, *Entrepreneurship, Management, and the Structure of Payoffs* (Cambridge: MIT Press, 1993), emphasizes the problem of encouraging entrepreneurship that increases output and is not merely rent-seeking behavior (as in litigation).

[57] Again, we might ask whether disequilibrium invalidates our discussion. From the Modigliani-Miller point of view, entrepreneurial endeavors are just matters of high risk; disequilibrium and uncertainty are sufficiently captured by risk measures (stochasticity), and otherwise play no role. From the Modigliani-Miller point of view, or more generally the view of formal finance theory (that all relevant uncertainty may be seen as risk), their argument *is* consistent. Insofar as one believes entrepreneurship depends on uncertainty and disequilibrium, then the Modigliani-Miller arguments may not apply. Then there is continuing room for arbitrage; there is no law of one price.

Again, what makes the Modigliani-Miller arguments work is the potential for arbitrage between riskless and risky vehicles. The assumption of equilibrium is fundamental to the "arbitrage proof" of "invariance theorems," as these Modigliani-Miller results are interestingly called. Now we might ask if such arbitrage is possible at all (as contrasted to an assumption concerning equilibrium) in the kind of entrepreneurial endeavors we are concerned with. It should be, if we have a large portfolio of such endeavors and a market in which they are priced, and our commitments are flexible enough that we might alter them based on sufficient price changes. But would Moses be so flexible? What might we mean by markets and arbitrage (trade-offs and trades) in Augustine's world, as he acts out his authoritative role as bishop of Hippo or his role as a Christian convert and confessor —finally and forever, never to be converted again (or so we are led to believe)? One can imagine an economic and game-theoretic account of Moses or Augustine; whether that account would be adequate to their entrepreneurial qualities is open to question.

58 S. Grossman and O. D. Hart, "Corporate and Financial Structure and Managerial Incentives," in J. J. McCall, ed., *The Economics of Uncertainty* (Chicago: University of Chicago Press, 1982), pp. 130–131, where they discuss alternative models.

There has been much discussion of whether the Modigliani-Miller model applies when bankruptcy of the firm is a possibility. The crucial issue seems to be the deadweight costs (lawyers, accountants,...). See *The New Palgrave Dictionary of Money and Finance,* ed. P. Newman, M. Milgate, and J. Eatwell (New York: Stockton, 1992), articles on "Bankruptcy and Capital Structure" (vol. 1) and "Modigliani-Miller Theorem" (vol. 2).

59 R. Peiser, "Charting the 1990s: Who Plans America? Planners or Developers?" *American Planning Association Journal* 56 (1990): 500.

60 Here I am thinking of the Onsager regression hypothesis in statistical physics, which says in effect that "all there is" are random fluctuations, and shocks are absorbed through those fluctuations (leading to so-called fluctuation-dissipation theorems, which relate diffusion processes to frictional ones).

Now, in general, it is impossible to know if a single fluctuation is due to noise or to information. What is radical here, and surely untrue in detail, is to take uncertainty and make it into random fluctuation, and then take it that one cannot get "behind" what is going on in any single event. The assumption is untrue because the formal claim that an event is a fluctuation does not prevent historical, documentary, and interview study of what actually occurred—whatever our subsequent interpretation (including that it is random).

61 If you must get a particular (large) return on your endeavor or bet, and less than that is of no value, then you might well make one go-for-broke bet (L. Dubins and L. J. Savage, *Inequalities for Stochastic Processes* [New York: Dover, 1976], p. 2). You'll be nickel-and-dimed to death by "prudently" breaking up your bets (laws of large numbers). Of course, if you can learn stuff along the way, these bets are off, and you can get good advice about such "two-armed-bandit problems." Now, if you are just doing it once (whatever the endeavor), then you want statistical estimators that have small variance. Bias is much less important, and might well be sacrificed here to efficiency. And keep in mind that coincidences are not rare (P. Diaconis and F. Mosteller, "Methods for Studying Coincidences," *Journal of the American Statistical Association* 84 [1989]: 853–861).

62 Carnegie's writing is a paean to creative destruction and capitalism, *and* to stewardship. See "The Problem of the Administration of Wealth," in *The Andrew Carnegie Reader,* ed. J. F. Wall (Pittsburgh: University of Pittsburgh Press, 1992), pp. 130–140.

63 Here I have passed over the arguments that the obligations of the capitalist end with the entrepreneurial work he does, there being no social responsibility beyond that.

64 I have learned what I know of these issues from conversations with and reading the work of Robert Payton.

65 M. Mauss, *The Gift* (New York: Norton, 1967); L. Hyde, *The Gift: Imagination and*

the Erotic Life of Property (New York: Random House, 1983).

[66] I am not unaware of the issues surrounding women (and daughters) being treated as wealth to be exchanged in order to cement society.

[67] Recall that Alonso is on this trip to marry off his daughter Claribel to the king of Tunis, marriage being a process that satisfies that father rather than his daughter.

[68] Steiner, *Antigones,* pp. 17–18, points out that the sororal issues of sister-brother devotion (so Antigone is center stage) have in the twentieth century yielded to the parental issues of an Oedipus complex as a stigmatized relationship.

[69] The limiting act is narcissism. I have here combined the Kant of *Critique of Judgment* (Indianapolis: Hackett, 1987), Hannah Arendt's *Lectures on Kant's Political Philosophy* (Chicago: University of Chicago Press, 1982), and Owen Barfield on participation, in *Saving the Appearances* (1965; reprint, Wesleyan, CT: Wesleyan University Press, 1988). This section is drawn from M. H. Krieger, "Temptations of Design," *Research in Philosophy and Technology* 10 (1990): 217–230.

[70] Émile Durkheim (1912) argues that the source of the sacred is society. The transcendent or the sacralized is literally beyond what any person could have enforced on society. In this sense, we might see the entrepreneur as a collective representation, to use Durkheim's term, or a fetish onto which agency is condensed. See *The Elementary Forms of Religious Life,* tr. K. E. Fields (New York: Free Press, 1995), pp. 225–231 (book 2, chapter 7, part 4), 371–372 (book 3, chapter 3, part 3).

[71] Kant, in *The Critique of Pure Reason,* provides an exhaustive account of the temptation for complete knowledge of the world.

[72] This is the main theme of D. Cuff, *Architecture: The Story of Practice* (Cambridge: MIT Press, 1991).

[73] The Jews could not be pariahs if they follow God's laws by their *own* choice. See A. Momigliano, "A Note on Max Weber's Definition of Judaism as a Pariah Religion," in *Essays on Ancient and Modern Judaism* (Chicago: University of Chicago Press, 1994), pp. 171–177.

Bibliography

Arendt, H. *The Human Condition.* Chicago: University of Chicago Press, 1958.

———. *Lectures on Kant's Political Philosophy.* Chicago: University of Chicago Press, 1982.

———. *The Life of the Mind.* Volume 1. *Thinking.* New York: Harcourt Brace Jovanovich, 1978.

Arthur, W. B. "Competing Technologies, Increasing Returns, and Lock-in by Historical Events." *Economic Journal* 99 (1989): 116–131.

———. "Positive Feedbacks in the Economy." *Scientific American* 262 (February 1990): 92–95.

Atwood, M. "Northrup Frye Remembered." *Michigan Quarterly Review* 30 (Fall 1991): 647–649.

Auden, W. H. "The Sea and the Mirror." In *Selected Poems.* New York: Vintage, 1979, pp. 127–179.

Auerbach, E. *Mimesis.* Princeton: Princeton University Press, 1968.

Augustine. *Confessions*. Tr. H. Chadwick. Oxford: Oxford University Press, 1991.

Bagozzi, R. P. *Principles of Marketing Management.* Chicago: SRA, 1986.

Barfield, O. *Saving the Appearances.* 1965. Reprint. Wesleyan, CT: Wesleyan University Press, 1988.

Barreto, H. *The Entrepreneur in Microeconomic Theory.* London: Routledge, 1989.

Barton, B. *The Man Nobody Knows.* Indianapolis: Bobbs Merrill, 1925.

Baumol, W. J. "Entrepreneurship in Economic Theory." *American Economic Review* 58 (1968): 64–71.

———. *Entrepreneurship, Management, and the Structure of Payoffs.* Cambridge: MIT Press, 1993.

Beker, J. C. *Paul the Apostle: The Triumph of God in Life and Thought.* Philadelphia: Fortress, 1984.

———. *The Triumph of God.* Minneapolis: Fortress, 1990.

Bernal, M. *Black Athena: The Afroasiatic Roots of Ancient Greece.* Volume 1. *The Fabrication of Ancient Greece, 1785–1985.* New Brunswick: Rutgers University Press, 1987.

Boswell, J. *The Kindness of Strangers.* New York: Vintage, 1990.

Brams, S. *Biblical Games: A Strategic Analysis of Stories in the Old Testament.* Cambridge: MIT Press, 1980.

Brown, N. O. *Apocalypse and/or Metamorphosis.* Berkeley: University of California Press, 1991.

Brown, P. *Augustine of Hippo.* Berkeley: University of California Press, 1967.

———. *The Body and Society: Men, Women, and Sexual Renunciation in Early Christianity.* New York: Columbia, 1988.

———. *Power and Persuasion in Late Antiquity: Towards a Christian Empire*. Madison: University of Wisconsin Press, 1992.

———. *Society and the Holy in Late Antiquity.* Berkeley: University of California Press, 1989.

Buchanan, J. "The Constitution of Economic Policy." *Science* 236 (12 June 1987): 1433–1436.

Burke, K. *The Rhetoric of Religion.* Berkeley: University of California Press, 1970.

Burns, J. M. *Leadership.* New York: Harper and Row, 1978.

Buttrick, D. *Homiletic: Moves and Structures.* Philadelphia: Fortress, 1987.

Capozza, D., and G. Schwann. "The Value of Risk in Real Estate Markets." *Journal of Real Estate Finance and Economics* 3 (1990): 117–140.

Carnegie, A. *The Andrew Carnegie Reader.* Ed. J. F. Wall. Pittsburgh: University of Pittsburgh Press, 1992.

Caro, R. *The Power Broker.* New York: Vintage, 1975.

Casson, M. *The Entrepreneur.* New York: Barnes and Noble, 1982.

Cavell, S. "The Avoidance of Love: A Reading of *King Lear.*" In *Disowning Knowledge.* Cambridge: Cambridge University Press, 1987, pp. 39–123.

Chandler, A. D. *Scale and Scope.* Cambridge, MA: Belknap Press, 1990.

Chodorow, N. *The Reproduction of Mothering.* Berkeley: University of California Press, 1978.

Coase, R. H. *The Firm, the Market, and the Law.* Chicago: University of Chicago Press, 1988.

Cole, J., and H. Zuckerman. "Marriage, Motherhood and Research Performance in Science." *Scientific American* 256 (February 1987): 119–125.

Coleman, P. J. *Debtors and Creditors in America: Insolvency, Imprisonment for Debt, and Bankruptcy, 1607–1900.* Madison: State Historical Society of Wisconsin, 1974.

Cuff, D. *Architecture: The Story of Practice.* Cambridge: MIT Press, 1991.

Dales, R. *Medieval Discussions of the Eternity of the World.* Leiden: E. J. Brill, 1990.

Daston, L. *Classical Probability in the Enlightenment.* Princeton: Princeton University Press, 1988.

Davidson, P. "Is Probability Theory Relevant for Uncertainty? A Post-Keynesian Perspective." *Journal of Economic Perspectives* 5 (1991): 129–143.

Davies, W. D. *The Territorial Dimension of Judaism.* Berkeley: University of California Press, 1982.

Diaconis, P., and F. Mosteller. "Methods for Studying Coincidences." *Journal of the American Statistical Association* 84 (1989): 853–861.

Dinnerstein, D. *The Mermaid and the Minotaur.* New York: Harper and Row, 1976.

Drucker, P. *Innovation and Entrepreneurship.* New York: Harper and Row, 1985.

Dubins, L., and L. J. Savage. *Inequalities for Stochastic Processes.* New York: Dover, 1976.

Durkheim, É. *The Elementary Forms of Religious Life.* Tr. K. Fields. New York: Free Press, 1995.

Dye, R. A. "Economic Analysis of Bankruptcy Statutes." *Economic Inquiry* 24 (July 1986): 417–428.

Dyson, F. J. "Time Without End: Physics and Biology in an Open Universe." *Reviews of Modern Physics* 51 (July 1979): 447–460.

Elster, J. *Explaining Technical Change.* Cambridge: Cambridge University Press, 1983.

Finley, M. I. *The Ancient Economy.* Berkeley: University of California Press, 1985.

Fisher, F. M. "Statisticians, Econometricians, and Adversary Proceedings." *Journal of the American Statistical Association* 81 (1986): 277–286.

Fraiberg, S. *Insights from the Blind: Comparative Studies of Blind and Sighted Infants.* New York: Basic Books, 1977.

———. *Selected Writings of Selma Fraiberg.* Ed. L. Fraiberg. Columbus: Ohio State University Press, 1987.

Freccero, J. *Dante: The Poetics of Conversion.* Cambridge: Harvard University Press, 1986.

Freud, S. *Civilization and Its Discontents.* 1930. Reprint. New York: Norton, 1962.

———. *Moses and Monotheism.* 1939. Reprint. New York: Vintage, 1959.

Frye, N. *Anatomy of Criticism.* Princeton: Princeton University Press, 1957.

———. *The Great Code.* New York: Harcourt Brace Jovanovich, 1982.

Gadamer, H. G. *Truth and Method.* New York: Seabury Press, 1975.

Gibson, J. J. *The Senses Considered as Perceptual Systems.* Boston: Houghton Mifflin, 1966.

Ginzberg, L. *Legends of the Bible.* Philadelphia: Jewish Publication Society, 1975.

Girard, R. *The Scapegoat.* Baltimore: Johns Hopkins University Press, 1986.

———. *Violence and the Sacred.* Baltimore: Johns Hopkins University Press, 1977.

Goldhill, S. *Reading Greek Tragedy.* Cambridge: Cambridge University Press, 1990.

Gouldner, A. W. *Enter Plato: Classical Greece and the Origins of Social Theory.* New York: Basic Books, 1965.

Green, R. M. *Religion and Moral Reason.* New York: Oxford University Press, 1988.

Greenblatt, S. "The Way to Kill Our Literary Inheritance." *Chronicle of Higher Education* (12 June 1991): 131, 133.

Greenspan, S. I. *The Development of the Ego: Implications for Personality Theory, Psychopathology, and the Therapeutic Process.* Madison, CT: International Universities Press, 1989.

———. "Reconsidering the Diagnosis and Treatment of Very Young Children with Autistic Spectrum or Pervasive Development Disorders." *Zero to Three* 13 (October-November 1992): 1–9.

Grossman, S., and O. D. Hart. "Corporate and Financial Structure and Managerial Incentives." In J. J. McCall, ed., *The Economics of Uncertainty.* Chicago: University of Chicago Press, 1982, pp. 107–140.

Hacking, I. *The Taming of Chance.* Cambridge: Cambridge University Press, 1990.

Haley, J. *The Power Tactics of Jesus Christ, and Other Essays.* New York: Grossman, 1969.

Halperin, D. *One Hundred Years of Homosexuality.* New York: Routledge, 1990.

Harris, H. S. *Hegel's Development: Toward the Sunlight.* Oxford: Clarendon Press, 1972.

Hearne, V. *Adam's Task.* New York: Vintage, 1987.

Heidegger, M. *Being and Time.* 1926. Tr. J. Macquarrie and E. Robinson. New York: Harper and Row, 1962.

Heilbroner, R. "Analysis and Vision in the History of Modern Economic Thought." *Journal of Economic Literature* 28 (1990): 1097–1114.

Heschel, A. *The Prophets.* New York: Harper and Row, 1969.

Hirschman, A. O. *Development Projects Observed.* Washington, DC: Brookings Institution, 1967.

———. *The Passions and the Interests.* Princeton: Princeton University Press, 1977.

———. *The Strategy of Economic Development.* New Haven: Yale University Press, 1958.

Hodgson, M. *The Venture of Islam.* Chicago: University of Chicago Press, 1974.

Hurston, Z. N. *Moses, Man of the Mountain.* 1939. New York: Harper Perennial, 1991.

Hyde, L. *The Gift: Imagination and the Erotic Life of Property.* New York: Random House, 1983.

Ignatieff, M. *The Needs of Strangers.* New York: Viking, 1985.

Kac, M. *Statistical Independence in Probability, Analysis, and Number Theory.* Providence: Mathematical Association of America, 1959.

Kant, I. *Critique of Judgment.* Tr. W. Pluhar. Indianapolis: Hackett, 1987.

———. *Critique of Pure Reason.* Tr. N. K. Smith. London: Macmillan, 1933.

Keller, E. F. *A Feeling for the Organism.* San Francisco: Freeman, 1983.

Kent, C. A., D. L. Sexton, and K. H. Vesper, eds. *Encyclopedia of Entrepreneurship.* Englewood Cliffs, NJ: Prentice Hall, 1982.

Kierkegaard, S. *Fear and Trembling.* Princeton: Princeton University Press, 1983.

Knox, B. M. W. *The Heroic Temper: Studies in Sophoclean Tragedy.* Berkeley: University of California Press, 1966.

Krieger, M. H. *Advice and Planning.* Philadelphia: Temple University Press, 1981.

———. "Broadening Professional Education." *Liberal Education* 76 (March-April 1990): 6–10.

———. "Contingency in Planning: Statistics, Fortune, and History." *Journal of Planning Education and Research* 10 (1991): 157–161.

———. "Corruption and the Culture of Real Estate Development." *Business and Professional Ethics Journal* 13 (Fall 1994): 19–32.

———. "Could the Probability of Doom Be Zero or One?" *Journal of Philosophy* 92 (1995): 382–387.

———. "Courage and Character in Planning." *Journal of Planning Education and Research* 7 (1988): 191–194.

———. "The Critique of Poor Reason: Using Literature to Teach Analysts." *Policy Analysis* 4 (1979): 505–520.

———. *Doing Physics: How Physicists Take Hold of the World.* Bloomington: Indiana University Press, 1992.

———. *Marginalism and Discontinuity: Tools for the Crafts of Knowledge and Decision.* New York: Russell Sage Foundation, 1989.

———. "Planning and Design as Theological and Religious Activities." *Environment and Planning B: Planning and Design* 14 (1987): 5–13.

———. "The Possibility of Doom." *Technology in Society* 9 (1987): 181-190.

———. "Temptations of Design: A Meditation on Practice." *Research in Philosophy and Technology* 10 (1990): 217–230.

———. "What Does Jerusalem Have to do With Athens: Roles for the Humanities in Planning." *Journal of Planning Education and Research* 14 (1995): 217–221.

———. "Where Do Centers Come From?" *Environment and Planning A* 19 (1987): 1251–1260.

Krieger, S. *Social Science and the Self.* New Brunswick: Rutgers University Press, 1991.

Kruskal, W. "Miracles and Statistics: The Casual Assumption of Independence." *Journal of the American Statistical Association* 83 (1988): 929–940.

Kuhn, T. *Black-Body Theory and the Quantum Discontinuity.* New York: Oxford University Press, 1978.

———. *The Structure of Scientific Revolutions.* Chicago: University of Chicago Press, 1970.

Leach, P. *Children First.* New York: Knopf, 1994.

———. *Your Baby and Child.* New York: Knopf, 1979.

Levi, P., and T. Regge. *Dialogo.* Princeton: Princeton University Press, 1989.

Livesay, H. "Entrepreneurial Dominance in Businesses Large and Small, Past and Present." *Business History Review* 63 (1989): 1–21.

———. "Entrepreneurial History." in Kent, Sexton, and Vesper, *Encyclopedia of Entrepreneurship.* Englewood Cliffs, NJ: Prentice Hall, 1982.

Lovejoy, A. *The Great Chain of Being.* Cambridge: Harvard University Press, 1936.

MacMullen, R. *Christianizing the Roman Empire.* New Haven: Yale University Press, 1984.

March, J. *Decisions and Organizations.* Oxford: Basil Blackwell, 1988.

Markus, R. A. *The End of Ancient Christianity.* Cambridge: Cambridge University Press, 1990.

———. *Saeculum: History and Society in the Theology of St. Augustine.* Cambridge: Cambridge University Press, 1970.

Mauss, M. *The Gift.* New York: Norton, 1967.

Merton, R. K. *The Sociology of Science.* Chicago: University of Chicago Press, 1973.

Modigliani, F., and M. Miller. "The Cost of Capital, Corporate Finance, and the Theory of Investment." *American Economic Review* 48 (1958): 261–297.

Naylor, G. *Linden Hills.* New York: Penguin, 1986.

Neuberg, L. *Conceptual Anomalies in Economics and Statistics: Lessons from the Social Experiment.* New York: Cambridge University Press, 1989.

Neustadt, R., and E. May. *Thinking in Time.* New York: Free Press, 1986.

New Oxford Annotated Bible. Ed. B. M. Metzger and R. E. Murphy. New York: Oxford University Press, 1991.

Newman, P., M. Milgate, and J. Eatwell, eds. *The New Palgrave Dictionary of Money and Finance*. New York: Stockton, 1992.

Nietzsche, F. *Beyond Good and Evil.* New York: Vintage, 1966.

Nussbaum, M. *The Fragility of Goodness: Luck and Ethics in Greek Tragedy and Philosophy.* Cambridge: Cambridge University Press, 1986.

Pagels, E. *Adam, Eve, and the Serpent.* New York: Random House, 1988.

———. *The Gnostic Gospels.* New York: Random House, 1979.

Peiser, R. "Charting the 1990s: Who Plans America? Planners or Developers?" *American Planning Association Journal* 56 (1990): 496–503.

Petroski, H. *To Engineer Is Human.* New York: St. Martin's, 1985.

Pirsig, R. *Zen and the Art of Motorcycle Maintenance.* New York: Morrow, 1974.

Pitkin, H. *Fortune Is a Woman.* Berkeley: University of California Press, 1984.

Plessner, H. *Laughter and Crying.* Evanston, IL: Northwestern University Press, 1970.

Pocock, J. G. A. *The Machiavellian Moment.* Princeton: Princeton University Press, 1975.

Porter, T. *The Rise of Statistical Thinking.* Princeton: Princeton University Press, 1986.

Rapoport, J. *The Boy Who Could Not Stop Washing.* New York: NAL, 1990.

Ribuffo, L. P. "Jesus Christ as Business Statesman: Bruce Barton and the Selling of Corporate Capitalism." *American Quarterly* 33 (1981): 206–231.

Rich, A. *Of Woman Born: Motherhood as Experience and Institution.* New York: Norton, 1986.

Rieff, P. *The Triumph of the Therapeutic.* New York: Harper and Row, 1966.

Rosenberg, N., and L. E. Birdzell, Jr. "Science, Technology, and the Western Miracle." *Scientific American* 263 (November 1990): 42–54.

Rosenblum, N., ed. *Liberalism and the Moral Life.* Cambridge: Harvard University Press, 1989.

Sahlins, M. *Islands of History.* Chicago: University of Chicago Press, 1985.

Said, E. "Walzer's *Exodus and Revolution*: A Canaanite Reading." *Grand Street* 5 (Winter 1986): 86–106.

Samuelson, P. "The Fundamental Approximation Theorem of Portfolio Analysis in Terms of Means, Variances, and Higher Moments." *Review of Economic Studies* 37 (1970): 537–542.

Schabas, M. *A World Ruled by Number: William Stanley Jevons and the Rise of Mathematical Economics.* Princeton: Princeton University Press, 1990.

Scholem, G. *Sabbatai Sevi.* Princeton: Princeton University Press, 1973.

Schumpeter, J. *Capitalism, Socialism, and Democracy.* New York: Harper and Row, 1950.

———. *The Theory of Economic Development.* Cambridge: Harvard University Press, 1934.

Schneider, M., P. Teske, and M. Mintrom. *Public Entrepreneurs: Agents for Change in American Government.* Princeton: Princeton University Press, 1995.

Scodel, R. *Sophocles.* Boston: Twayne, 1984.

Segal, A. *Paul the Convert: The Apostolate and Apostasy of Saul the Pharisee.* New Haven: Yale University Press, 1990.

———. *Rebecca's Children: Judaism and Christianity in the Ancient World.* Cambridge: Harvard University Press, 1986.

Segal, C. *Tragedy and Civilization: An Interpretation of Sophocles.* Cambridge: Harvard University Press, 1981.

Selznick, P. *Leadership in Administration.* New York: Harper and Row, 1957.

Shakespeare, W. *The Tempest.* Ed. F. Kermode. 6th edition. Cambridge: Harvard University Press, 1958.

———. *The Tempest.* Ed. S. Orgel. New York: Oxford University Press, 1987.

Shay, J. *Achilles in Vietnam: Combat Trauma and the Undoing of Character.* New York: Atheneum, 1994.

Shklar, J. "The Liberalism of Fear." In N. Rosenblum, ed., *Liberalism and the Moral Life.* Cambridge: Harvard University Press, 1989, pp. 21–38.

Soloveitchik, J. B. "The Lonely Man of Faith." In L. D. Stitskin, ed., *Studies in Judaica.* New York: Ktav (Yeshiva University Press), 1974, pp. 69–133.

Sophocles. *Oedipus the King.* Tr. S. Berg and D. Clay. New York: Oxford University Press, 1978.

———. *The Three Theban Plays.* Tr. R. Fagles. Intro. B. Knox. New York: Penguin, 1984.

Steiner, G. *Antigones.* Oxford: Clarendon Press, 1986.

Stern, D. *The Interpersonal World of the Infant.* New York: Basic Books, 1985.

Stigler, S. *The History of Statistics.* Cambridge: Harvard University Press, 1986.

Sullivan, T., E. Warren, and J. Westbrook. *As We Forgive Our Debtors: Bankruptcy and Consumer Credit in America.* New York: Oxford University Press, 1989.

Tanakh: The Holy Scriptures. Philadelphia: Jewish Publication Society, 1988.

Timmons, J. *New Venture Creation.* Homewood, IL: Irwin, 1990.

Traweek, S. *Beamtimes and Lifetimes.* Cambridge: Harvard University Press, 1988.

Tufano, P. "Business Failure as a Stimulus to Innovation: An Institutional and Historical Perspective." Working paper 91–039. Boston: Harvard Business School, 1991.

Turner, V. *The Ritual Process.* Chicago: Aldine, 1969.

Tyson, R. L. "The Roots of Psychopathology and Our Theories of Development." *Journal of the American Academy of Child Psychiatry* 25 (1986): 12–22.

van Allsburg, C. *Two Bad Ants.* Boston: Houghton Mifflin, 1988.

van Gennep, A. *Rites of Passage.* London: Routledge and Kegan Paul, 1960.

Walton, D. N. *Courage: A Philosophical Investigation.* Berkeley: University of California Press, 1986.

Walzer, M. *Exodus and Revolution.* New York: Basic Books, 1985.

Walzer, M., and E. Said. "An Exchange." *Grand Street* 8 (Summer 1986): 246–259.

Warren, C. *Bankruptcy in United States History.* Cambridge: Harvard University Press, 1935.

Weber, M. *From Max Weber.* Ed. H. H. Gerth and C. W. Mills. New York: Galaxy, 1958.

———. *The Protestant Ethic and the Spirit of Capitalism.* 1904–1905, 1920. Tr. T. Parsons. New York: Scribner's, 1958.

Weinberg, S. "The Cosmological Constant Problem." *Reviews of Modern Physics* 61 (1989): 1–23.

———. *The First Three Minutes.* New York: Basic Books, 1976.

Weiss, B. *The Hell of the English: Bankruptcy and the Victorian Novel.* Lewisburg, PA: Bucknell University Press, 1986.

Weschler, L. *Seeing Is Forgetting the Name of the Thing One Sees.* Berkeley: University of California Press, 1982.

White, B. *The First Three Years of Life.* Englewood Cliffs, NJ: Prentice Hall, 1975.

Wildavsky, A. *The Nursing Father: Moses as a Political Leader.* University: University of Alabama Press, 1984.

Wilson, J. Q. "Adam Smith and Business Ethics." *California Management Review* 32 (Fall 1989): 59–72.

Winner, L. *Autonomous Technology.* Cambridge: MIT Press, 1977.

Winnicott, D. W. *Babies and Their Mothers.* Reading, MA: Addison-Wesley, 1987.

———. "The Capacity to Be Alone." In *The Maturational Process and the Facilitating Environment.* New York: International Universities Press, 1965, pp. 29–36.

———. *The Child, the Family, and the Outside World.* Baltimore: Penguin, 1964.

———. *Playing and Reality.* 1971. Reprint. London: Routledge, 1989.

Index

T

U

V

W